Stealing Joy

A True Story of
Alzheimer's, Elder Abuse, and Fraud

GLYNNIS WALKER ANDERSON

ISBN: 0692252304
ISBN 13: 9780692252307
Library of Congress Control Number: 2014912369
New Horizon Press, Woodstock IL

Table of Contents

PART THREE

Dedication

To Rosalind Walker, who was a "Joy" to all who loved her.
We will never forget.

Acknowledgements

Everyone has moments in their life when the circumstances are just too extreme to handle alone. I was very fortunate to have the following people help me to get through this. They stuck by me, encouraged me, supported me, and were there on the days when I thought I just couldn't deal with it anymore.

They listened to me; offered their very valuable advice; understood what was almost impossible to understand because such evil is difficult to conceive of; and basically they kept me going. None of us had ever been to a place like this before, but everyone had a mother they loved and so they empathized. I would like to thank, Lauren Wilke, Janet Martinovich, April Harman, Dr. James D. McTague, Bon Hollier, Deputy District Attorney, Paul Greenwood, Former FBI Financial Crimes Chief, Dennis Lormel, Attorneys Mark Handelby and Paddy Guy, Dr. Peter Houghton, Dr. Arthur Prowse and Captain Leo Jean.

I would like also thank Uta, Trish and Bud for being my mother's true friends and for helping me to get justice for her.

A special thanks to my daughters Arabella and Sabrina for all their support, understanding and love, and for being so strong throughout what was, for us, a terrible ordeal.

Foreword

By

Dennis Lormel

(Former Chief of the FBI's Financial Crimes Unit)

I served in law enforcement, as a Special Agent in the Federal Bureau of Investigation (FBI) for 28 years. In December of 2000, I became Chief of the FBI's Financial Crimes Program.

Elder fraud and abuse presents a very serious and compelling challenge for society. Although seemingly an obscure problem, it has the potential to touch each and every one of us. Elder fraud and abuse is a crime problem that is prolific, yet underreported; devastating, yet silent; and repulsive, yet repeatedly perpetrated.

Crimes that target senior citizens come in many forms. They fall into two general categories: fraud committed by strangers, and financial exploitation by relatives and caregivers and "trusted others". The diversity of schemes is vast and occurrences all too frequent. The results can be overwhelming to the victims and the people who truly care about them. When you take the time to look at and comprehend elder fraud and abuse, you realize just how horrific and troubling this crime problem is. Our senior citizens deserve better.

In this book, Glynnis Walker courageously opens herself up and shares her personal experience regarding the fraud and abuses her mother and she endured. The riveting story depicted by Glynnis features a vulnerable elderly woman, her mother, Joyce Walker, who was taken advantage of by three unscrupulous opportunists. As time progressed, their stranglehold on a frail and confused Joyce became tighter and subtlety more bold. Unfortunately, similar stories regarding our seniors unfold all at an increasingly alarming rate.

This is a gripping story that deserves attention, not only for Joyce and Glynnis Walker, but for untold thousands of elderly citizens and their loved ones. By telling her story, Glynnis Walker is putting a spotlight on a crime problem that deserves to be magnified, discussed and addressed. Stories like the one that unfolds in this book, lead to the dialogue that triggers action and the establishment of laws and practices to better safeguard vulnerable seniors.

Our senior citizens merit our respect, love and gratitude for all they have done for us. They deserve to spend their golden years in comfort, being able to trust their caretakers. Thank you Glynnis, your book raises awareness to a truly heinous crime problem that can deprive our seniors of their dignity in a time they need it the most.

Introduction

THE CRIME OF THE 21ˢᵀ CENTURY

*"With good reason, financial elder abuse has been characterized
by some experts as "the crime of the 21ˢᵗ Century."
– J.F. Wasik, Journalist.*

Up until March 2010, I had no idea that I would become involved in the "crime of the 21ˢᵗ Century". I was a single mother and busy investigative journalist, totally immersed in writing a book about the marketing shenanigans and other dark dealings of the baby formula industry. Exposing the dirt in the dark corners of society is what I have always felt compelled to do because injustice offends me, especially when it is perpetrated against those least likely to be able to defend themselves. I suppose it was pure karma that brought me into the murky world of elder fraud, a world where our senior citizens are sitting ducks for scam artists, hucksters, liars, cheats, cons, and, the people next store.

The Older Americans Act of 2006 calls it "exploitation", and defines it as "...the fraudulent or otherwise illegal, unauthorized, or improper act or process of an individual, including a caregiver or fiduciary, that uses the resources of an older individual (generally accepted as anyone over 60) for monetary or personal benefit, profit or gain, or that results in depriving an older individual of rightful access to or use of, benefits resources, belongings or assets".[1] Or to put is more bluntly – stealing from old people. Currently, 58% of crimes against the elderly involve fraud.[2]

In 2011, victims of elder fraud lost over $2.9 billion in the U.S. alone. This was an increase of twelve per cent over 2008.[3] In spite of the frequency of the crime—one in twenty older adults indicate being victims of financial abuse in the recent past—only about one in forty-four cases of elder financial abuse is ever reported for reasons that will be discussed later in this book. [4]

"It is difficult to estimate the prevalence of elder fraud because cases are underreported and the definition of "elderly" varies from state to state. National statistics on elder fraud do not exist."[5]

Few cases of elder fraud are ever successfully prosecuted, not because there was no wronging doing, but because the victims or their legitimate beneficiaries cannot afford to challenge the spurious actions taken against their elderly family member. "The high cost of litigation (upwards of $150,000) has a very strong dissuasive effect for most would be challengers. A court challenge will likely occur only where there are both suspicious circumstances *and* a sizeable amount at issue." [6]

Elder fraud is rampant in all industrialized nations. But the elder is not the only victim of financial abuse. Relatives, spouses, children and grand-children, employers and the community at large are also victims. For the families of the victims, the financial, emotional and psychological devastation sometimes lasts the rest of their lives.

And the losses don't end with the victims and their families. Elderly victims can go from fiscally sound tax payers to being burdens on society, almost overnight. The elderly victims often end up destitute after their assets have been decimated. Taxpayers are forced to foot the bill for billions of dollars a year in health care, social services, investigative, legal and other costs.

What happens to a senior who has been defrauded of their assets? One in ten victims of financial abuse will turn to Medicaid.[7] According to the Congressional Budget Office in 2011, Medicare and Medicaid cost taxpayers roughly $1 trillion. A whopping 64 percent of Medicaid spending goes to seniors and people with disabilities.

According to the Kaiser Family Foundation, 7 out of 10 nursing home residents are on Medicaid. Even middle-class patients often run through their savings while in a nursing home and are forced to turn to Medicaid.[8] This situation is exacerbated when seniors are victims of fraud.

Who pays for the cost for care when the senior becomes insolvent because of fraud? We the tax payers do. The rates for nursing homes rose significantly between 2009 and 2010, to $83,585 a year, or $229 a day. The cost for one adult to stay in an assisted living facility climbed to an average of $39,516 a year or $3,293 a month. Home care aides average $21 per hour and adult day care services average $67 per day[9]

According to the National Funeral Directors Association, the average cost of a simple funeral in 2012 was approximately $7000.[10] Who pays for that when a defrauded senior dies? Sometimes, states have funds to assist the family with funeral expenses. But sometimes, in these cash-strapped times, they do not. Hence the horrendous scene that came to light recently in Chicago where the bodies of the indigent, in blue plastic bags, were stacked up like cord wood in the Cook County morgue, leaking bodily fluids in pools of stench on the floor.[11] The third largest city in the country simply had no funds to bury the poor souls who died indigent after the state cut $13 million from the program designed to assist in the burials of those who died without even the funds for their own burial.

Even more gruesome, the medical examiner's office revealed a plan to donate bodies of those whose families who could not pay for funerals, to science. Stripped of their humanity and their identity, many would end up as skeletons in some anatomy class. The rest were set to be buried in mass pauper's graves, at the cost to the taxpayers of $300 dollars each. Anonymous or unwanted babies were buried several to a coffin. This scene is repeated across the nation.

When someone rips off a senior citizen to the point where they are too impoverished to pay their own bills, we all become victims too, not only because somebody has to pick up the tab for the senior poor, but because as a society we cannot completely bury the guilt we feel in having let down those who fought in past wars to protect us; those who somehow slipped through the cracks and were left literally out in the cold because of the lack of a social safety net; those who committed the unthinkable sin of becoming old and poor in the richest country in world; and those who became victims of the greed of others.

As a society we are now on the precipice of an explosion of elder fraud, simply because our demographics are changing. In 1900, seniors comprised just 4% of the population. "In 2011 the oldest baby boomers -Americans born between 1946 and 1964 - started to turn 65. Today, 40 million people in the United States are ages 65 and older, but this number is projected to more than double to 89 million by 2050. Although the "oldest old"- those ages 85 and older - represent only 15 percent of the population ages 65 and older today, their numbers are projected to rise rapidly over the next 40 years. By 2050, the oldest old will number 19 million. Over one-fifth of the total population will be 65 or older."[12]

This demographic upheaval will have a profound effect on the incidence of elder fraud. Not only are people living longer due to better medical care, but as the Great Generation passes, the Boomers will age into the senior population and they will bring along with them their substantial assets. They will be the richest and oldest population we have ever witnessed. The population aged fifty and up now controls 70% of the nation's net worth.[13] One can see therefore that looming straight ahead, is a significant opportunity for a feeding frenzy of perpetrators driven by greed, lack of regulatory enforcement, and the scent of an easy mark.

The most likely victim of elder fraud is a white woman, living alone - as do 50% of women over 75. She will most likely be aged 80-89. The oldest old – those 85 and over - is the fastest growing elderly population.[14] They will be even more likely to become victims of fraud because they are more likely to be physically and mentally frail. Because women generally live longer than their husbands, they are the ones who inherit the life insurance, the family home, stocks, bonds and other assets. Many of these women are loaded with the assets acquired over a lifetime or grown by inflation.

What makes them even more vulnerable to fraud is not just the presence of available assets. With extreme aging there are frequently changes in mental and physical capacity. In 2012, 5.4 million Americans had Alzheimer's or other forms of dementia. The risk of getting Alzheimer's increases abruptly after the age of 75. Those between 75 to 84 account for 44% of the Alzheimer's population. The population over 85 comprises 46% of the Alzheimer's population.[15]

Ultimately two out of three seniors, most likely women, will become physically or cognitively impaired in their lifetime. They become the perfect victims. They have the assets, but not the faculties to protect them.

Aging Boomers, especially, though not exclusively, women with financial assets, have a bull's eye painted on their backs. They are in line to become the victims of those who attempt to steal, not just their money, but their families, their dignity, their freedom, their remaining precious memories, and in some cases even their lives.

According to the latest Census, forty million people in the US are over 65. Between 1983 and 2007, the median net worth of households headed by White people age 65 and over doubled from about $122,320 to $248,300, three times that of the older black household and the highest it has ever been for that age group. [16] In addition, the wealth gap between seniors and the rest of the population is the widest it has ever been. Envy and desperation take root in ground such as this. Greed is right behind. Ignorance also plays a part as those who deal with the elderly - banks, pharmacies, retail outlets, doctors, the legal system and social services are often ill-informed or ill prepared to cope with elder fraud. They either do not see it happening or they do not want to see it because, once opened, it is a can of worms that will cost them time, effort and resources. The stage then is set for the escalating financial abuse of the elderly in years to come.

The statistics tell the story. An elderly person becomes a victim of financial abuse every five seconds. Women are more than twice as likely to become victims of elder financial abuse. The highest percentage of victims is in the 80 to 89 age group.[17] According to the Census Bureau, by 2030 the population over 65 will triple to over 70 million. It will be like shooting fish a barrel.

In an addition to the burgeoning elderly population with assets, there are also other societal changes that have taken place over the last several decades. Families, who once provided the majority of care for their elderly, have changed substantially in my lifetime. Divorce, the rise of the single lifestyle, women having children later in life, and the eruption of copious stepfamilies have changed the landscape of who cares for whom and where. As of 2007, almost 60% of women, who once would have provided the care for the family's elderly members, are now in the workforce and therefore unavailable to give full time care to senior relatives. As a result of this, only 6% of people over 60 live with a younger relative in the U.S. compared to 70% of seniors in countries such as Japan.[18]

In addition, as families move further from each other, we also have to deal with the obstacle of distance. Currently 3.3 million of us are, like I was for my mother, long distance caregivers. A study by MetLife Mature Market Institute in conjunction with the National Alliance for Caregiving indicated that 23 percent of long-distance caregivers are the sole primary caregiver.[19] That number is expected to double over the next fifteen years.

This has left us with a situation that frequently requires the use of caregivers and assisted living facilities, where the senior is often out of sight of the family for much of the time. Currently, according the Center for Disease Control (CDC), National Center for Health Statistics, over one million seniors live in assisted living facilities and 1.5 million live in nursing homes – places that are often staffed by people making barely above minimum wage.[20]

Seniors who live at a distance from their families are more likely to become potential victims for fraud just because they are more accessible to those who wish to defraud them. Who then is most likely to defraud a senior?

Most people are aware that strangers prey on the elderly because they are easy targets. My mother used to receive several phone calls every evening after my father died – yes scammers do read the obituaries – asking for money for this cause or that. Usually they were bogus, as I had warned her, and after a while she just stopped answering her phone unless it was me calling.

Strangers who prey on the vulnerable elderly go to great lengths to search out their prey. They may watch as the vulnerable senior fumbles with change to pay for her groceries, befriend her when she is walking her dog, or even check out the cars in the church parking lot and run the license plates of models preferred by seniors. There is no end to their chicanery.

But those who are hardest to detect and hardest to anticipate are the "trusted others" - caretakers, neighbors, friends, acquaintances, attorneys, bank employees, financial advisors, ministers and even doctors. It is because they are people that are known to the senior that they are the most dangerous. They use their familiarity as a wedge to inveigle themselves into the lives of their elder victim.

Financial elder abuse comes in three different guises. It can be a crime of occasion – the elder is perceived to have assets; the perpetrator has access to the elder and wants the assets. Nobody is minding the store so to speak. The abuser takes the assets, often starting out with small things like jewelry and cash, then gradually working up to bigger things like bank accounts and property. The small things are often touted as "gifts" that the senior has "given" to the abuser. People who are cognitively impaired can be easily convinced to part with their possessions just for the asking. The experienced abuser knows exactly how to phrase the request.

Elder abuse can also be a crime of desperation – the elder has assets and the perpetrator, out of extreme financial need, wants the assets. This type of perpetrator is more likely to be a male family member between 40 and 60 who lives with the victim. Sons are three times more likely to fit into this category than daughters. There is often a drug, alcohol or gambling problem and the perpetrator is often unemployed and is financially dependent on the elder for survival. A child who lives in their own residence and is gainfully employed is much less likely to commit fraud on their elderly parent than one who is financially strapped.

Lastly, there is the crime of predation. The elder is deliberately targeted because they are vulnerable, living alone and are perceived to have access to assets. The predator or predators work on building a relationship of trust with the elder as a friend, neighbor or trusted advisor (i.e. an attorney or financial advisor). [21] By lies, cunning and manipulation, they gradually take over the elder's life, empty her bank accounts, steal whatever valuables she has, ultimately leaving her penniless, maybe even dead.

PART ONE

Chapter One

PREDATORY PEOPLE

"The world is a dangerous place to live, not because of people who are evil, but because of the people who don't do anything about it." – Albert Einstein.

When our nightmare began, in the spring of 2010, my mother was 86 years old. That was when three women stole her from us, little by little, until she was all gone. I would never in my worst nightmares have imagined anything like this could happen to our family, to any family. Who would be so pointlessly cruel as to destroy a loving family; to torture a little old lady and eventually arrange for her to die a horrible death? But they did, and I wrote this book in the hopes that by knowing what happened to us, it will not happen to you.

My mother's given name was Rosalind Violet Minerva Edwards. Early in her life she came to the realization that the names on her birth certificate were not only too fancy for her taste, they did not represent who she really was. So she called herself Joy. It was short, simple and described her personality perfectly.

Joy was wonderful mother - kind, loving, compassionate, and generous with her time and effort. As our lives moved on and we got older, Joy became my best friend, someone to share a laugh with or offer a shoulder on which to lean. Always caring.

That is what happened to her in the last year of her life and to our family was all the more horrible. We were particularly close. Three generations of women who loved each other, understood each other and cherished each other. We were all we had, a tiny little microcosm of a family. What happened was all the more painful because I lost both my mother and my best friend; my children lost their only grandmother, their connection to the past; and we all lost our faith in a society that allows their fragile elderly to be so easily victimized by greedy people who pretend to be their friends and an indifferent legal system which can't be bothered seeking justice for the inconvenient elderly.

The trio of conspirators who targeted my mother, and later my daughters and me, consisted of the lawyer I had hired to draw up my parents' wills, my mother's next door neighbor, and, a part-time supermarket checker in the sore where she bought her groceries. In time, it became clear that the neighbor had formulated the plan, engaged the help of the lawyer. The two of them then reeled in the help of the supermarket checker with promises of easy cash.

The first two were motivated, in part, by an overwhelming need to control and manipulate others, combined with a truly omnivorous sense of entitlement. They were not just greedy. They were also cruel and vindictive, which is why, when any other fraudster would have moved on and gone looking for their next mark, they kept up their assault on my family for several years after my mother died.

All of three of them were enticed by what they thought, at the time, was the prospect of easy money - an elderly widow living alone, showing signs of cognitive impairment, and far from her family, with a big house (and presumably a big bank account to go with it). It must have seemed like a tantalizing opportunity. More important, it would have looked like a cakewalk. Seniors are the perfect victims, frail, trusting and often cognitively impaired. The one thing they did not count on was me. Even though I had no experience with fraud of any kind and am generally a trusting person, their brazen and peculiar behaviors made me suspicious almost from the beginning. This made me sit up and pay attention.

There are two kinds of elder fraud – "stranger danger" and "trusted others". "Stranger danger" fraud is often easier to spot because it is so well documented. Frequent reports are featured on the nightly news, in newspapers and on the Internet. Fraud committed by so-called "trusted others" on the other hand is another matter entirely.

There is an abundance of information available on the most recent scams committed by strangers, from contractor fraud to the grandchild in trouble scam where a supposed grandchild calls and says they need money to get home from a foreign country, followed by a request for the grandparent to wire them some.

This recently happened to a friend of mine's mother. The "granddaughter" had telephoned and said she was supposedly stuck in Montreal and needed funds to get home. The grandmother was just about to wire the money when her daughter came by to visit. The grandmother, panicked by the thought of her grandchild being in trouble, told her daughter what was happening. The daughter assured her mother that the grandchild in question was safe at home with her and not in Montreal. She even phoned her home and let the granddaughter speak to her grandmother to prove that she was safe. Still, the grandmother would not believe her. This family was lucky because they were there just as the fraud was about to happen and were able to prevent it. Most families are not so fortunate.

Fraud involving strangers as the perpetrators makes up just over half (51%) of reported cases of elder financial abuse. Fraud committed by family, friends, neighbors, and trusted others such as caregivers (34%) is more difficult to spot and to stop. The largest single category of this group includes financial professionals, attorneys and other fiduciary agents.[22] These are the people how much money the senior has and where it is. Basically, the devil you know is harder to fend off than the devil you don't know, because the fraud goes on behind closed doors, out of sight of the general public and family members. Compared to exploitation by trusted others, fraud from the business sector accounted for only 12% of reported cases - a mere drop in the proverbial bucket.[23]

When it comes to the gender of the perpetrator, traditionally men have been more likely to commit almost any kind of elder fraud - 60% - simply because they are the ones most likely to have access to the vulnerable elderly. From the telemarketing hucksters, to the door to door scammers, to the ne'er-do-well nephew who trades on his filial relationship to help himself to a senior relative's assets, they are fully aware of how easy it will be.

According to the June 2010 *Investor Protection Elder Fraud Survey*, 7.3 million older Americans—one out of every five citizens over the age of 65—has already been victimized by a financial swindle. [24] A 2008 Duke University study found that about 35% of the 25 million people over age 71 in the U.S. either have mild cognitive impairment or Alzheimer's disease.[25] The stage is then set for the destruction of millions of lives, not only of the elderly victims themselves, but of their families and of future generations. Elder fraud is a crime that leaves a great deal of collateral damage.

Interestingly, in the workplace, women over 45 in mid-level jobs are more likely to commit fraud or embezzlement than men. Their reasons for committing these crimes include a need for money, revenge against employers they consider unfair, or the thrill of committing a crime and getting away with it.[26] When it comes to elder fraud, women's deeds in the private sector often go unnoticed simply because as caregivers, "friends", and others who deal with the elderly, they are perceived to be doing the unpaid job that society has gladly handed to them. Taking care of the elderly is still largely "women's work". These days, it seems, taking from the elderly is also becoming women's work.

The three women who targeted my mother got as far as they did because they were women who did not fit the standard profile of a female fraudster. Not only were they older than the statistical norm, they were comfortably middle-class, white, were married or in long term relationships, had children, and in one case grand-children. One was highly educated. But they did have something in common that was not obvious to the casual observer. They were predators, plain and simple.

In the world of elder fraud there are two types of predators. Non-institutional perpetrators – they include friends, relatives and titular family – someone who is treated as a family member while not actually being a blood relative. Caregivers often fit into this role. Then there are Institutional perpetrators such as trusted professionals including, lawyers, financial advisors, executors and trustees, minsters and professionals who are in positions of trust. With the former, sons are three times more likely to commit elder fraud than daughters. Neighbors and friends are also more likely to commit elder fraud than daughters. With the trusted professionals, the onus of guilt falls first on financial advisors, followed by attorneys. [27] Of course I did not know all this at the time; otherwise I would have had my guard up.

The coterie of conspirators who took over my mother's life and her money was an unlikely crew. The lawyer, specialized, conveniently, in elder law. When I first met her I was in desperate need of a lawyer who made house calls because my father was dying. Like most people my guard was down because I was distracted by the tragedy that was about to befall our family. I accepted the stereotype – a woman who appeared to be an elder care lawyer who only wanted the best for her clients. Unfortunately, I did not check her out until much later when the invocation of her name promoted groans from both clients and other attorneys alike.

She was a plump, motherly, middle-aged woman who told me that she was married and had a teenage daughter. She once described her husband to me as a househusband, for want of an explanation as to why he did not work. Later on, she told the lawyer I had hired to fight her and her co-conspirators off, that her husband was an independently wealthy businessman and that she practiced law just because she liked to. Neither of those statements was true. These were just part of the myriad of lies and deceptions that defined our association over the next several years. It turned out that she was, among other things, a pathological liar – a symptom of narcissistic personality disorder - something she had in common one of her co-conspirators, the neighbor next door.

For a pathological liar, or mythomaniac, lying is a way of life. They lie even when it would be easier to tell the truth. They lie to get sympathy, to get control, to build a relationship with the abused senior, and for any other occasion when a lie would aid them in getting what they want. Interestingly, mythomaniacs, even though they have a lot of practice with their lying, have a hard time keeping track of their lies. Because they don't remember what lie they told and to whom they told it, they change their story all the time. If the one being lied to isn't keeping track of the lies, the liar's fractured versions of reality become the truth of the moment. Pathological liars put no value on honesty or loyalty. They are also extremely manipulative.

For the lawyer, her work conveniently provided her with endless access to fresh victims. Because I was incautious, I had unwittingly thrown another one into her path – my own mother.

The next door neighbor, whose main connection to my mother had previously consisted of having my mother take her mail in and water her plants when she was off on one of her many vacations. She had never achieved much in her life, except through marriage. She had two grown children and some teenage grandchildren. She was not popular with her other neighbors, who were more than willing to share their negative opinions of her when asked. They found her to be showy. Her red Mercedes convertible was decidedly out of place in an area where blue and beige Subarus and Toyotas are the norm. They also thought of her as manipulative. One lady later told me that whenever she saw her coming, she made sure to go the other way.

The neighbor's second husband spent a great deal of time at the country club, when he was not away on business, which was most of the time. Aside from playing bridge, she spent a lot of time being bored and making silk flower arrangements.

Finally, there was the super market checker. She was a simple, florid faced woman with a minimal education, who lived with her long term boyfriend. She had been a part-time supermarket checker for the past eighteen years at the grocery store where my parents, and later just my mother, shopped. The only outstanding thing about her was that, even though she had never been married, she went by two different last names.

Seventy-five percent female of predators who commit elder fraud are between 30 and 59. With male predators the age range is more dispersed.

Prior to their involvement with my family, the lawyer and the neighbor had never met. Individually, they moved in very different social circles, lived in different parts of the city and had different levels of education. The neighbor, who shopped as the same grocery store as my mother, likely had a nodding acquaintance with the checker, but economically she was way out of her league, so friendship would not have been an option. On the surface, these women had little in common except for their age. But below the surface, they had a great deal in common, as time would soon prove.

One thing that perpetrators of elder financial abuse have in common is that they are very persuasive.[28] They are good at cultivating relationships initially by doing things for or giving things to the selected target. The neighbor, who had been only a vague presence in any of our lives prior to my father's death, suddenly started offering to take my mother to get flowers for her garden or bringing copious amounts of unwanted food over for her.

Then, early in 2009 she suddenly became a larger presence in my life. On one of our visits she offered to lend my daughter, Arabella, her extra laptop so she could work on an assignment she needed for school. When we returned it, she suggested we exchange emails so we could keep in touch. There did not seem to be any harm in that. Then she asked me, matter-of-factly, if my mother had a lawyer in the city – just in case there was some kind of emergency that needed to be dealt with before I could get there. It seemed a reasonable question. I did not realize that we were playing spider and the fly, and that I was the fly, until much later.

Like millions of other caregivers in our increasingly mobile society, distance lent an extra level of concern to my taking care of my mother. So I agreed to share the information. We exchanged phone numbers and emails and I told her where the lawyer's office was downtown. No bells went off. I forgot about it almost immediately. Periodically I would get an email from the neighbor about my mother, or about what she was doing with her grandchildren, sometimes with pictures attached. She loved to take pictures. Looking back I realize that she was trying to build a familiarity with me. Should I have been aware that her cozying up had an ulterior motive? Now, I would be suspicious. But then, I was a still a trusting soul. And I was honestly too busy to plumb the depths of her motives. It was possible she was just a bored housewife and I let it go at that. (Note to self. Be careful of those people who try and create a relationship with you out of thin air.)

These seemingly everyday people were the ones who targeted my family. During their association with my mother they abused her – psychologically, emotionally and financially, isolated her from her family, defrauded her, changed her will, stole her identity, and mine. In the end they arranged for her death.

Chapter Two

A PERFECT STORM OF OPPORTUNITY

*"A brain is only capable of what it could conceive, and it could
not conceive of what it has not experienced"*
– Graham Greene, Brighton Rock

In early 2010, I had been worrying about my mother's wellbeing for several weeks. My daughters and I live in Chicago. My mother lived in Victoria, the capital of British Columbia, about twenty-five hundred miles away. It takes four and a half hours by car, a four hour plane flight and a ninety minute ferry ride to get from door to door – altogether about fifteen hours given wait time. Sometimes it can take much longer if all the connections don't mesh.

Because of the distance, we visited only a few times a year, but every night, I called her to talk on the phone and share the experiences of our days. But, more and more, I realized that I called to make sure she all was all right. She was 86 after all and I sensed that age was taking a toll on her.

Up until the end of 2009, she seemed mostly fine. She knitted scarves for us as Christmas presents and joked and laughed on the phone. She loved to talk about her dog, Babe, and I told her about my dogs and all about what her grandchildren were doing. But, in early January 2010, I started to notice a change in her. It was subtle at first. Some days she seemed forgetful and said things that were peculiar, odd or inappropriate. Some days she said she was depressed. Then the next day she was her normal self again. I began to notice that often she would ask the same question over and over again. I thought maybe she needed a hearing aid so I made an appointment for her to have hearing tested. But I didn't know then that it wasn't her hearing that was the problem.

She would get letters in the mail and become upset because she did not understand them. I would tell her not to worry; I would handle it for her. I had her Power of Attorney since my father died in 2006, and took care of her finances. I had already set up direct debits for most of her bills, so she would not have to worry about paying them. She was not used to writing checks and always paid everything in cash. I worried about that too. I knew she always kept a little stash of cash in her house – about two thousand dollars which she used toward her real state taxes every year. I encouraged her to use her credit card instead, but she stubbornly clung to the habits that had served her for a lifetime.

This hoarding of cash is common among Alzheimer's victims. One lady told me that when she went to clear out her mother's house, the guest bedroom was full of mail that had been opened and then carefully re-sealed. She and her husband were about to throw the mail out when she noticed that one envelope was particularly bulky. She opened it and found a diamond ring. In another she found a gold necklace. She and her husband set about opening all the envelopes. Their finds totaled more jewelry and $10,000 in cash in various envelopes.

Although I wasn't sure my mother was suffering from being lonely and sometimes depressed since my dad had passed, I began to wonder if it could be something more.

According to Raj C. Shah, MD, of the Rush Memory Clinic at Rush University Medical Center, in Chicago, one symptom does not mean a person has dementia or Alzheimer's. Dementia is a chronic loss of cognition, usually affecting memory, and Alzheimer's causes 50% to 80% of dementia cases. [29]

From what I understand now, memory loss and confusion are <u>not</u> a normal part of aging. We all have moments when we walk into a room and forget what we are looking for, or can't remember where we put the car keys. It does not mean we have dementia, merely that we are distracted by the myriad of details that comprise our everyday lives. And too, memory loss associated with Alzheimer's is not consistent from day to day. One day you can remember, a name, a place, an event and the next day you cannot, but then the following day the memory is back. That's why it was so difficult for me to understand what was really going on with my mother. I put her memory issues down to a normal part of aging. I really did not think there was anything seriously wrong with her mind.

On top of my lack of knowledge about dementia, I had little experience with and infrequent contact with the elderly. All four of my grandparents had lived in England. One had died when I was child. Three of them I saw only twice in my life, and my father's mother – the only one I knew well - was still cognitively sound when she died at the age of 93. My mother's father died at 92, also of sound mind. Taking them as my example of what aging meant, I did not consider alternate possibilities. I certainly did not consider Alzheimer's. Not then.

As for my father, looking back with the clarity of hindsight, it is pretty clear that he had acquired some odd behaviors in his later years, but he died of cancer at 83, before any mental decline became noticeable.

In addition to the now-you-see-it- now-you-don't nature of Alzheimer's, my mother had always lived a very regimented life. She did the same things, at the same time every day. Everything was always in the same place. She was organized, and wrote down information such as addresses, PIN numbers and account numbers in the back of her address book.

At the time I thought she was just being her neat and tidy self, but I realize now that as her memory worsened, the neatness, the organization, the strict routine was a coping process that allowed her to maintain the appearance of normalcy and therefore keep her independence, something she valued very highly. That and the fact that I took care of her finances, taxes and household repairs, masked the true state of her cognitive decline for some time.

"The earliest changes in judgment usually involve money. So people who were normally very cautious with their finances will start spending in unusual ways, like giving money to unworthy strangers like telemarketers.[30]

After my father died and we were going through his things, we found that he had been making some unusual purchases on his many credit cards. In one cupboard he had stored away three hundred pairs of identical Calvin Klein socks. In the garage, I found two George Forman grills, that had never been opened, and a wet suit. My father did not grill and he could not swim. I also found cancelled checks to a variety of dubious charities. Telemarketers called the house nightly, so he must have been on somebody's list of easy marks. I put a stop to this after he died and explained to my mother that she should not entertain these people in any way, shape or form.

My father was also extremely paranoid about locking up the house before they went to bed. He went through the same ritual every night. Windows were shut tight. All the doors had multiple locks. The front door alone had a deadbolt, a chain lock and the usual push button lock. The sliding door to the deck had a bar that slipped into the door runner to prevent entrance from the back of the house plus a floor lock that was activated by a button you pressed with your foot. On any given night, the place was locked up tighter than Fort Knox even though their house was in one of the safest areas not only in Canada but in the world. At the time, I just put it down to his being a little eccentric. But now I wonder if his paranoia meant that he too was beginning to show signs of the dreaded disease. People with Alzheimer's disease often exhibit signs of paranoia. They have unrealistic beliefs that someone is seeking to do them harm. [31]

After he died, I was worried about her living on her own, not because of her mental issues – she seemed perfectly fine in 2006 - but because of her physical issues. She had heart problems, though not severe ones. She had three of the indicators for osteoporosis, a tiny frame (she was barely five feet tall, had an early menopause – at 38 – and she had smoked most of her life.) Her hip joints had basically turned to dust. As a result of this she had already undergone two hip replacements in her seventies. So I was worried about her falling. And, like most women her age, she was becoming frail. Because women live longer than men, they are more likely to experience frailty. Research from Johns Hopkins University indicates that frailty is recognized as the concurrent presence of three or more of the following: low strength, low energy, slowed motor performance, low physical activity or unintentional weight loss. [32] Evidence shows that frailty is related to the number of abnormal physiological systems rather than a specific system abnormality. [33] My mother was exhibiting all of these.

Because of all this, I had been encouraging her come and live with us for some time. We had a main floor bedroom that had its own bathroom. But she insisted she could not handle the journey. I told her I would come and get her. She cried and said she did not want to leave her house, because, "that's where Bram (my father) is". She told me that she felt his presence in the house. Sometimes she said she could even hear his voice. I knew how close they were. They had been married for sixty years. Memories of him and the life they lived together were everywhere in the house. I interpreted her statement as meaning that her echoic memory for sounds was allowing her to hear memories of him speaking, like we all hear snippets of songs in our heads that are associated with certain memories. I did not think it meant she was delusional. Not until later.

Like many adult children with aging parents I was facing the same dilemma. I wanted to respect her wishes to maintain her independence, but I knew that she could not live on her own much longer. I could not force her to come and live with me, but neither could I continue to leave her "Home Alone". Also, I knew she would hate living in a nursing home. She was an extremely private person and did not like being around strangers or having other people in her house. She was not the type to socialize with other women. She just wanted to stay in her beloved home with her dog and carry on with her life the way she wanted it. How could I refuse her?

Part of the trouble was, I simply loved my mother too much. This love got in the way of my reasoning. I wanted her to be happy. I did not want to be the one to turn her life upside down by moving her to a nursing home or assisted living facility. She would hate that. And too, somewhere inside me was a small child who did not want her mummy to be angry with her. It was such a difficult situation and I had no siblings to share it with nor any friends who had been through it. So I put it off until I could see how she was on our next visit. Then I knew I would have to confront the inevitable. How, I did not yet know.

At the time, I also had other things to worry about. Like many in my generation, I am a single parent, and in the spring of 2010, my younger daughter Arabella, who was 17, was about to graduate from community college. The two of us were caught up in the extremely stressful dance of finding a university, selecting a major, arranging campus visits, and filling out copious forms for admission and funding. Anyone who has gone through this knows what it's like. I wanted to make a quick trip to visit my mother in the early winter of 2010, but my other family obligations, not to mention my own health problems which were a constant issue, invariably trumped that choice.

Women of the sandwich generation like me are charged with dealing with aging parents and dependent children simultaneously. On top of that, I was not only a single parent. I was an only child. I had no siblings or other relatives to turn to for help when it came to caring for my mother or making decisions about her future. Sometimes this combination of circumstances set my head spinning. How do you choose between the needs of a parent and the needs of a child? Like most mothers, I had not yet figured out how to be in two places at once. But, for the four years since my father had passed, I had still managed to orchestrate the running of two distant households and several lives.

By Mid-March of 2010 however, Arabella's spring break was approaching. We were finally planning a trip to see my mother. Our hectic schedule was about to let up for a bit. It was time to pause for a breath. Or so I thought. But as we booked our flights and arranged for the rental car, I was plagued by the overwhelming feeling that this was the last time we would take our regular spring trip to Victoria. Even though she had been living independently, driving her car, shopping and getting her hair done every week, I knew that the time would soon come when she could no longer manage on her own.

I confided my fears to my daughters. They tried to assure me that everything would be all right. And why not? They had seen me coping with all the vicissitudes of life that could be thrown at a family over the years and I had always managed to keep our boat afloat. In their minds this time would be the same. I was their mother and I would handle it.

I, on the other hand, was not so sure. I had that feeling that something was about to go terribly wrong.

Normally, we were excited to be going to see Mum and visit the lovely island where she and my father had lived for nearly thirty years. Spring was the perfect time to visit Victoria. I had been there during a book tour once and came back enthusing about how beautiful it was. I thought it was the perfect location for my parents to retire. And, in 1985 they did.

Everything was still grey and brown in Chicago, but in Victoria, every plant from the giant pink azalea bushes to the sunshine yellow gorse was trying to outdo each other with their mad splashes of color. The lovely city, on the tip of Vancouver Island, was simply a symphony of spring.

Oddly enough the location played a part in how our story unfolded. How could anything so vile happen in a place so lovely? Canadians are such a happy lot. It's hard to think that behind the façade of Oz lays Dante's' Inferno. So my guard was down – at the beginning.

Arabella adored her grandmother and the city in which so many of her happy childhood memories took place. I always enjoyed seeing my mother and my daughters together, two separate generations of women laughing about shared experiences, stories from the past and hopes for the future. It was something that I treasured and now something I will always miss.

As if to reinforce my fears, the trip to visit my mother went wrong from the start. We got through the eternally long security line at O'Hare, and ran for our gate, only to find out that we had been bumped from our flight from Chicago to Seattle. We had to wait for the next one. Six hours later we got to SeaTac and picked up the rental car, raced north through Seattle to the Peace Arch border crossing – a three hour trip. Still, we missed the five o'clock ferry to Vancouver Island from Tsawwassen to Schwartz Bay by only two minutes.

We had to wait another two hours for the next ferry. We killed the extra time eating Chinese food at the ferry terminal. By the time we got on the ferry it was almost dark. As The Spirit of Vancouver Island wended its way across the Georgia Straight and through the islands toward Victoria, we watched as the last glow of daylight was extinguished behind Mt. Maxwell, the tallest peak on the coastal islands. After that we sailed into darkness. By the time we arrived at Mum's house in Victoria, it was after nine o'clock. A trip that usually took fourteen or fifteen hours had taken much longer. Everyone was exhausted.

We trundled our suitcases up the walkway and rang the bell. In a moment, she opened the door. I knew she had been peaking trough the blinds as she always did, waiting to see our car lights coming up the hill. She had always been tiny – barely five feet tall, just like her mother. But time and age had shrunk her diminutive size even more. Her still auburn hair was only slightly flecked with strands of grey at the temples. Her prefect creamy skin was almost unlined. She looked amazingly young for her 86 years and, in fact, she admitted to being 65 whenever anyone asked. Her eyes, the same bright blue as the dressing gown she always wore, sparkled as usual. "Where have you been?" She scolded, but she was smiling as she ushered us in.

While my friend, Leo, put the bags in the guest bedroom. Mum, Arabella, and I went into the kitchen to make tea. It was a ritual written in a lifetime of family experiences. We were English. Any time anything happened – good or bad - we put the kettle on and got the biscuit tin out of the cupboard. The making of tea was a comforting ritual going back to my earliest recollections of childhood. Tea and biscuits could cure anything, even a long, tiring trip and poor Chinese food. Having tea all together meant that everything with our little family was all right. I had no idea it was going to be one of the last times we would be able to do this.

As always, the house looked the same. Framed photographs adorned every available surface. There was the picture of me that was on my first book cover, one of Mum's favorites. Over by Mother's favorite chair was a photo of my Dad standing in front of the fireplace. Next to that was a picture of Arabella when she was three and crazy into Thomas the Train. On another table was a photo of my older daughter, Sabrina, in her flowing Christening dress. Then there was a photo of me holding baby Arabella, her pink cheeked grin exposing newly acquired tiny front teeth.

Both my Mother and I were dog lovers. Every dog we ever had was a treasured memory in an appropriate frame. As I looked around the room, I saw my family history recorded behind glass. It was good to be back. My job as a radio talk show host and writer had caused us to move frequently over the years, so we had lived in several cities. But comfort was to be found in the fact that at least the house on Amblewood Drive was always there, caught in a time warp, never changing, always home.

We sat in the family room – we never used the formal living room. That was where my father's ashes were placed in their urn beside the window, opposite to where the four little urns sat on the long table against the wall. My mother had each of her dogs cremated and placed in a position of honor next to a picture of each dog.

My mother's current dog was a Yorkie. Her name was Babe. I got this dog for her when my father died so she would have company. Babe was one of several dogs that I had given her over the years. She loved them all but she told me a couple of years earlier that getting Babe was the best thing I had ever done for her.

At the sound of our voices, Babe's corpulent black and tan body waddled out of the master bedroom, her domain of choice. She sniffed our shoes and then satisfied about who had disturbed her slumber, she waddled back down the hall and hauled herself back up on the bed.

"She's not been eating lately," my mother said, passing the biscuits after breaking one in half for herself. "No matter what I feed her, she turns her nose up at it."

"Mum, she's so fat her belly is touching the floor. I think she's fine in the food department. I'm more worried about you. Have you been eating?" I hugged her bony shoulders. She was so thin! I did not know at the time, but losing weight, is one of the signs of Alzheimer's and dementia. Older people often do not feel the hunger pangs that the rest of us do. Victims of cognitive decline often simply forget to eat. They also forget to hydrate, and that increases their mental confusion even more. [34]

Deftly, she changed the subject. "Arabella, darling, how is college?"

"Good Nanny. I'm on my spring break."

I changed the subject back. "How are you feeling Mum?"

"Oh all aches and pains. All part of getting older." She dismissed her symptoms with a wave of her hand. "I get a little short of breath too." I was already worried about her having angina because she had complained of pain across her neck and shoulders and shortness of breath. I had spoken to her doctor, but he said there was nothing to worry about.

"Did you talk to the doctor? I called him and asked him to come and check on you."

She waved her hand dismissively. "All he says is 'Take another Tylenol. Take another Tylenol'." She sipped her tea. "I'm taking eight a day. It doesn't help."

"What did you have for dinner?" I pressed on, trying to find out what she was eating.

"A butter tart. The ones from the grocery store are very good, so I bought some this morning."

"That's all?"

"I'm just not hungry."

Later on, I checked the fridge. Cheese, milk and dog food. There was a half a loaf of bread in the cupboard and a package of butter tarts with one missing. She wasn't eating. I also checked the cupboard where she kept her vitamins. All the bottles were full and out coded. She wasn't taking her vitamins either.

One of the results of eating poorly is a Vitamin B12 deficiency. Data from the Tufts University Framingham Offspring Study suggest that 40 percent of people between the ages of 26 and 83 have plasma B12 levels in the low normal range – a range at which many experience neurological symptoms.[35]

B12 deficiency has been estimated to affect about 40% of people over 60 years of age. It's entirely possible that at least some of the symptoms we attribute to "normal" aging – such as memory loss, cognitive decline, decreased mobility, etc. – are at least in part caused by B12 deficiency.

And yet levels of B12 are not routinely tested by most physicians. And too, the baseline of acceptable B12 levels in the U.S. is too low, well below the level associated with psychological and behavioral manifestations such as cognitive decline, dementia and memory loss. Some experts have speculated that the use of higher normal B12 base levels, as in Japan, explain the low rates of Alzheimer's and dementia in the Japanese population.[36]

Anemia is the final stage of B12 deficiency. Long before anemia sets in, B12 deficiency causes several other problems, including fatigue, lethargy, weakness, memory loss and neurological and psychiatric problems. Vitamin B12 can only be found in animal products. It can, if diagnosed, also be administered through injection on a regular basis. Anemia runs in our family and I knew that my mother had been diagnosed as being anemic many years previously. The doctor did not recommend supplementing her meager diet with B12 shots however, something that could have ameliorated her condition significantly if it had been started years ago. And since she was not eating properly either, she was not getting her B12 from animal products.

I had given her a bottle of B12 supplements a couple of years before after reading an article on how vegetarians lack the vitamin. However what I did not know was that taking over the counter Vitamin B12 supplements is virtually useless after age 60 because, the body has trouble processing the vitamin due to a lack of hydrochloric acid in the stomach. This has been noted as a reason for increased risk of osteoporosis in women over 60 and other problems including brain loss. But most doctors still do not consider B12 levels when doing blood panels on elderly patients, something which would certainly improve their chances of delaying or avoiding the onset of dementia.

I asked my mother about the lack of food in the house. She snapped at me. "Don't keep on. I eat when I'm hungry. The next door neighbor keeps bringing stuff over - yams, soup, some sort of lemon cake." She made a face. "You can have some if you like. But I won't touch it."

"Why not?"

"I just throw it out. It tastes funny. (One change in a dementia patient's is their taste buds. Because they don't experience flavor the way they once did, people with dementia often change their eating habits and adopt entirely new food preferences often focusing on sweets.)[37]

My mother continued on, "I'm not going to eat that muck!" She had never been one to miss speaking her mind, but her words struck me as harsh and, a trifle odd. Apparently that kind of comment is indicative of Alzheimer's. "In mid to late Alzheimer's, a person may begin to lose control of his or her impulses and act out in inappropriate or uncharacteristic ways. They may say tactless things, like 'Gosh, you're fat,' that they would have never said before." [38]

That night, after we went to bed, I lay there thinking about what I should do. It was clear to me now that she had deteriorated since our last visit and that she should not be living on her own.

The next day, I carefully broached the subject of having a caregiver come in during the day to help her and give her some company. But she pooh-poohed the idea. "I'm fine. I like my privacy. I don't want anyone else in my house….. except you." And then she reached up and gave me a peck on the cheek.

That morning, I had gotten up early. It was still dark, but I was on Chicago time. I tried not to wake my mother. These days she slept on the couch in the family room, refusing to sleep in the master bedroom where my father had died. I made tea and went into the den to get started on her taxes. Neat little piles of paper covered the top of the desk. I was encouraged to see that she was still able to handle the task of keeping all her bills and receipts in order, as I had showed her.

I noted that the real estate bill was due to be paid. Thirty-two hundred dollars, but according to her bank statement she had plenty of money to cover it, even after I had the new roof put on the house.

Not long after, my mother appeared at the doorway wearing her blue robe. I told her what a good job she had done keeping track of all her bills and receipts. "I get my brains from my daughter," she said smiling, and went into the kitchen to attempt to feed the dog again. Later on, we stood by the sink waiting for the kettle to boil and looking out at the brightening sky. It promised to be a perfect spring day.

Suddenly my Mother spoke. "Do you know what the worst thing about dying is?"

"Oh Mum, don't talk like that." Since my Father's death, the subject of her dying was always just beneath the surface, as much as we both tried to ignore it.

But she continued. It was as if she felt the need to say this to me now, before she forgot it. "The worst thing about dying is that I won't ever see you again." Suddenly we both had tears in our eyes. I leaned down and hugged her tiny body. Then the kettle whistled, and the moment evaporated with the steam. She was my only parent. We had always been incredibly close. I couldn't bear the thought of her not being there anymore.

When you mix the dangerous cocktail of people intent on committing elder fraud with a population that is not just elderly but made more vulnerable because of cognitive impairment, it is a perfect storm of opportunity.

Chapter Three

"ONE LAWYER TOO MANY"

The trouble with law is lawyers. - Clarence Darrow

alking to their children about the intimate and very personal act of dying is almost as difficult for some parents as talking about that other intimate and personal act - sex. A lot of people just can't handle it so they foist it off onto third parties such as teachers, hence the rise of Sex Ed. But there is no such thing as Death Ed. As such it is not easy being the children of aging parents. You know in your heart of hearts that the time you have left with them is growing short and their place in your life will soon be filled with the grief of their passing. You also have the responsibility of helping them plan for what they want when their time comes to an end. It may be the most difficult discussion you will ever have, but it is the most necessary. Some people recommend including a third party in the discussion, such as a trusted advisor, as a buffer. Most people though tend to just put off the conversation, often until it is too late. Unfortunately, I was in this group. I never knew quite how to bring up the subject of their dying and my parents never volunteered. As they got older, the subject of Death became the proverbial elephant in the room.

My father died in 2006 from pancreatic cancer. This was four years before my mother started showing signs of cognitive impairment. From diagnosis to his passing was a matter of weeks. He was adamant about not wanting to go into a hospital, and so I arranged for the hospice people to come to the house. They were wonderful, both to him and my mother, taking care of her as much as they did him.

My mother told me, after he had died, that he did not speak a word to her after he found out he was dying. He also refused to speak to me. I knew that he was angry about his fate. Once upon a time we had many conversations about the importance of longevity. My father always maintained that the less you did, the longer you would live. We know now that, the truth is exactly the opposite. An active brain and an active body are likely to delay the visit from the Grim Reaper. But the belief that my father had clung to all his life was dashed by a single visit to the doctor; ironically, a visit that my mother had tricked him into going to because was he was losing so much weight.

Although he would not talk to me, not even when in our last moments together I asked him to tell me that he loved me and he just turned and faced the wall, he would let me give him his morphine because he was in a great deal of pain. The morphine came in pre-loaded syringes that my mother placed, incongruously, in a little crystal vase on the table beside the bed - a bouquet of little plastic pain relievers. The only person he would talk to was Leo.

During our visit in September of 2006, when it became apparent that my father was ailing, but before the diagnosis of pancreatic cancer, I tried to have "the talk" with my mother that I should have had with both them years before. I needed to know what my parent's financial position was and what my father's last wishes were. "What would happen to you, if something happened to Dad?" I asked her cautiously one day. "What does he want when the end comes?" I thought that she was the one person who would know, but she just burst into tears and shook her head.

According to Elizabeth Kubler-Ross author of "On Death and Dying," "It is difficult to accept death in this society because it is unfamiliar. In spite of the fact that it happens all the time, we never see it."[39] Unlike my father, who died in his own bed, "80% of Americans die in a hospital or institution. In most cases, they don't die a "natural" death - someone decides to let them go. Every day, 7000 Americans die by decision." [40]

I had never experienced death up close. All of my grandparents died in England. We simply received a phone call. We sent flowers. That was it. I had no idea how the business of dying worked. What needed to be done and by whom? And now here was death staring me right in the face. Once again I was in unfamiliar territory. My mother, like my children, looked to me expecting that I would know what do.

I had no idea. Now I know that it is a kindness to all involved to bring death out of the closet before it sets foot in the door. There is a saying that everyone dies alone. That's not really true. There are always other people involved. Family, spouses, doctors, nurses...the list goes on. In a well-orchestrated death there should be lawyers, financial advisors, insurance agents, minsters etc. consulted in advance. It is important to make a Living Will or an Advanced Directive so that the dying person has a say in their own passing. This also helps those who have to deal with the issues of death afterward. Having a Power of Attorney and a Will is essential to ensure the smooth transition of assets. My father had none of these. Because he refused to confront his own mortality, he set in motion the events that have led me to write this book. So, no matter how difficult or unpleasant it is to talk about end of life decisions, it is essential that it be done both for the sake of the dying and those who live on.

Adding to his refusal to confront his mortality was the fact that my father had always taken care of their finances. He had never shared that information with my mother or with me and I had never asked. My mother, who left school when she was thirteen, had never been al-lowed to make a decision about their affairs. When they moved from England to Canada, my father simply came home with the tickets one day. There was no discussion. That was true for their finances too. My mother had never even paid a bill or written a check. She was more financially naïve than most women, even women of her generation. It was another quality that made her a perfect victim for elder fraud later on.

When we got the diagnosis of pancreatic cancer, I knew that it was time to consider what would happen to her when my father died. But it soon became clear that she knew almost nothing about their finances. All he had said in previous conversations with me was that if something happened to him, my mother would be an extremely wealthy woman. That was it.

In October, we returned to the Island. This time we came without Arabella. I did not want her to see her grandfather in what I knew would be a severely deteriorated condition. When we arrived and I went in to see him, I knew I had made the right decision. He was gaunt. His skin was unnaturally pale and had a yellow tinge. He was curled up in the fetal position wearing a diaper. It was clear he was extremely ill and in a great deal of pain. I called the doctor and asked him for more morphine.

During the long, sad hours as we sat in the family room dinking copious cups of tea, I took my mother aside and asked her where my father kept his private papers. At first she was worried that he would be angry with her for disturbing his papers, but I convinced her that it was time we found out what their financial situation was. There would soon be expenses to be dealt with.

So I started to look for his papers - then and for months to come. It turned out they were all over the house. I found important papers under couch cushions, under the bed, behind the books in the bookcase, piled on tables.

Their financial information was in a state of chaos. After he died, it took me a little over a year to find everything, and much longer to sort it all out. In my initial search, I was hoping to find a will. But, hard as I looked I could find no trace of a will. My search did not turn up any life insurance policies either. What, I wondered, made my father say that my mother would be "an extremely wealthy woman" when he died?

I asked my mother if either one of them had a will or any life insurance and whether or not her name was on the title to the house. She said she didn't think so, but she wasn't sure. Leo was sent into the master bedroom as emissary to ask the pertinent questions, since my father still would not talk to either of us.

A little while later, he returned with the information that there were no wills, but there was plenty of insurance. Once again I looked. What I found was that my father had a small whole life policy and lot of accidental death insurance - the kind of insurance that paid out only in case of an accident, not a terminal disease.

I knew the lack of a will would complicate things for my mother when my father died, especially as I had found the deed to the house and it was only in his name. It was time that I talked to a lawyer.

I went to the local yellow pages, a large phone book decorated with a blaze of red and yellow tulips that sat as always on the kitchen counter. Looking back, I can only think that if I had called any other phone number, all of our lives would have been so different. But fate, as it does, had set the course. The events that played out over the next few years were set in motion by a single phone call.

I got down as far as the C's before I found a lawyer who specialized in elder law and estate planning and who also made house calls. Relieved to find someone so easily, I arranged for her to visit the following day.

That was one of the many mistakes I made. Once she saw the house, the seeds of greed began to germinate.

The next evening she arrived just after seven. She brought along her husband, Douglas. He would witness the document which she had constructed according to my instructions. Since my Dad continued to refuse to talk to me, not even to discuss his final wishes, I had to adlib. I thought he would want my mother to have the house and whatever monies or property he owned. So, that's what I had told the lawyer to put in the will. It was a simple document that, as it turned out, had far reaching consequences. If I had a do-over on this decision, I would certainly take it. In arranging for the estate to be put in my Mother's name only, I had unknowingly made her a victim.

Believing that she was protected financially now the will was in place, I realized that it would be a good idea for her to have a will too and to assign a Power of Attorney so that she would have someone to act for her legally after my father passed. On October 19th, 2006, we attended a meeting at the lawyer's office. My mother signed a straight forward will, passing all her property to me, or if I was deceased, to Arabella. She also signed a Power of Attorney appointing me to act for her. It was an Enduring Power of Attorney which meant that even if she became mentally incapacitated, the document was still in force and I could still act for her. This, as it turned out, was significant.

On October 23rd, 2006, my father passed away, at home in his own bed as he had wished. I wrote his obituary and placed it in the Times-Colonist. As he had requested, years ago when the prospect of death did not loom so large, we had him cremated.

My Dad had been a tall, handsome man. He had always been the life of every party and was known for his sense of humor and wit. When Leo took the lawyer and her husband into the bedroom where my father lay and explained that there was a lawyer here to take care of his will, my father quipped, in spite of his pain, "Well that's one lawyer in the room too many." He would never know how right he was.

After my father passed away, and before the funeral home came to take his body to be cremated, the neighbor came over to visit my mother, ostensibly to give her condolences. I hadn't spent much time with her, but there was always something about her that seemed slightly off. She seemed to have more teeth than anyone I had ever met and constantly smiled hugely, but her eyes were like black holes. It made me uncomfortable to catch her gaze, like she was looking right into my soul.

And apparently, I was not the only one who felt this way. Once, when I was in hospital and my girls were staying with my parents, she took them and her granddaughters, who were about the same age, for an outing. Afterwards, when I spoke to Sabrina to ask how her day out had been, she told me that I needed to promise her that she and her sister would never have to go out with the neighbor again. When I asked why, she explained in her nine-year old way, that she was "creepy". I promised her that I would soon be well enough so that the she and her sister could come back to California and live with me. I told her I would make sure there were no more outings with the neighbor.

At the time, I simply put it down to the fact that my children had been severely traumatized by my life - threatening illness and were uncomfortable with strangers. I did not think about this telephone conversation until many years later.

However, after my father died, something happened that evoked the "creepy" comment Sabrina and had made eight years earlier. My father had been an avid photographer. He loved taking pictures of my mother, the dogs, animals he saw, sunsets etc. and he would send me copies. In turn, I sent copies of the photos that told the story of our lives. He had an old-fashioned, state of the art film camera with lots of dials and buttons and switches, and he always kept it loaded, "just in case".

When we returned to the Island to go with my mother to pick up his ashes from the mortuary, I found his camera by the bed. I noticed there were still twelve exposures left. Over the next few days we took pictures of my Mum and her dog, Mum and Arabella and Mum and I together. When the roll was finished, I took it out of the camera. Mum offered to take it to get it developed, but I said no, I would do it, when I got back to Chicago and then send her copies of the photos.

I don't know what made me do this, but later when I got the photos back, I was really glad I did. Right in the middle of the roll, just before the pictures we had taken, were four photos of my father's corpse! I knew that my mother had not taken them because she did not know how to operate the complicated camera. I also knew that the neighbor had been present right after my father passed. I knew one other thing about her. She too liked to take pictures. In one of the few conversations we had over the years she had mentioned how much she liked to take photos.

She would have assumed that my mother would get my father's last roll of film developed and that she would see the pictures of his dead body. The possibility made me go cold. Why would someone want my mother to see pictures of her dead husband? It took me nearly six years to answer that question.

Chapter Four

A VERY STRANGE DINNER

"The careless shepherd makes an excellent dinner for the wolf."
– Edgar Beggers

As if to confirm the fears that had plagued me about our trip to see Mum in March 2010, my mother complained of chest pains the morning after we had gone to do her taxes. I asked her if she wanted me to call an ambulance and she said yes, so I knew she was really not feeling well. Like most women she usually pooh-poohed her own symptoms and fussed over other people instead.

The ambulance came. They took her vital signs and placed her on the gurney. I had no idea where the hospital was so they told us to follow the ambulance. As Arabella and I hopped into my mother's car to follow the ambulance I noticed the neighbor peeking through her blinds.

On the way, dodging traffic down strange streets, the ambulance blasting out its warning to get out of the way, I got a call from her. Ever the nosey neighbor, she wanted to know what was happening. I told her that my mother was having chest pains and we were going to the hospital. She appeared concerned about the details of my mother's condition. I realized much later that if my mother had died that day, the neighbor's plans for what lay ahead would have been dashed. I cut the conversation short. I was driving and I was frantic about my mother and I told her I had to go. But she seemed to want to keep the conversation going.

"Why don't you come over for a "little bite to eat" this evening?" she smarmed.

I thought it seemed odd even at the time. I was afraid my mother might be dying and she was offering an invitation for dinner! I told her I would have to let her know later. It would depend on what happened at the hospital. I hung up before she could say anything else.

We waited for hours in the crowded and chaotic Emergency Room, standing beside my mother's bed, because there were no chairs. After a while my hip began to hurt – I had been in physical therapy for several weeks because of a recent fall. Arabella went in search of a chair. She found one in the waiting area and brought it back so I could sit down.

Throughout the day the nurses made infrequent visits to our cubicle and were polite but dismissive when I questioned them about what was wrong with my mother. No one seemed to know what was going on. They basically left us to care for my Mum, who by then, was throwing up what looked like coffee grounds. There was no chance to have a consultation with the doctor until late in the afternoon. We were told that my mother would have to stay the night for observation and more tests. That is hospital speak for "We don't have a clue what is going on."

We had no desire to socialize with the neighbor. We were worried about my mother and after spending an exhausting day in the Emergency room, we were tired and just wanted to go home. I called her to say we would not be coming for dinner. But, she would not take "no" for an answer.

"You have to eat," she wheedled.

Reluctantly, I agreed. Also we had left Leo at home with Babe and I was too tired to think up something to get for him to eat. So we went over to her house for dinner. It was, after all, the polite thing to do. (People like these count on us doing the right thing. It makes it easier for them to do the wrong thing.)

The neighbor's house always reminded me of a spider crouched for the pounce. It sits low to the ground, surrounded by shrubbery. Inside it is comprised of several small rooms. Ironically, it also backs onto a cemetery.

Dozens of scented candles burned in each of the small rooms. It reminded me of the set from The Phantom of the Opera – all glitz and glass and chandeliers. The table was set as though it were a formal business dinner party, with a full table setting for each place, multiple crystal glasses at each setting, the "good" silver, linen napkins and several courses, starting with homemade hors'doeuvres. I would have been happy with pizza! It seemed oddly inappropriate, given the circumstances, not to mention completely overdone, but from what I knew of her, she loved to be grandiose and show off her possessions. In fact, she loved possessions so much, she was always up for acquiring more, and in any way she could, as would become apparent.

At one point during the dinner, we told stories about our dogs. Since I got Babe for my mother, I have been rescuing Yorkies. Rescuing animals was a family tradition. My mother used to rescue cats. She once had twenty-seven of them. Between us, we had lots of pets over the years. When I was a child, she was always bringing home some abandoned animal she had found. Of course we kept them all. Our house was a menagerie, and we loved it! My mother had been an unwanted child and had no siblings. It was not surprising that she preferred the company of animals to that of people. She made no apologies for it. Usually, I brought one or two of my Yorkies to play with my mother's dog when we visited. But on this trip I hadn't. It was as though I sensed something was going to happen.

The neighbor had never struck me as a dog person, and indeed she mentioned, at one point during dinner, that she had never owned a pet of any kind before, but she had recently acquired a black spaniel. He was a pretty dog, and reminded me of the black Shitzu I had rescued and given to my mother many years before. My mother had loved her dearly. She named her Sheba, after the Queen. Sheba had died the year before my father passed away. My Mother called me in the middle of the night crying. We were like that. Our animals were not just pets. They were family. We mourned their passing.

The spaniel's name was Hector. When I thought about this later, I understood that getting a dog, particularly one that looked like her precious Sheba, was the neighbor's way of inveigling herself into my mother's company. She would stop by my mother's house and my mother would give him a treat. It would look like two animals lovers sharing precious pet moments, but that's not what it really was. The dog was just a prop; a part of the plan.

Sensing an opportunity to tell a dog story of her own, our hostess launched into a tale about how she had found a poor, starving dog on her visit to Cuba the previous year. She took a lot of exotic trips and spent a month in Palm Springs every winter. She talked about how she had fed the dog every day from her own table at the hotel where she stayed. When she left to come home, she said she had given the taxi driver, who took her to the airport, $150 to keep feeding the dog. It seemed an unlikely story. I could not imagine a poor Cuban taxi driver feeding a stray dog with this unexpected windfall, if indeed she had actually handed over any money. When I asked if she had any photos of the dog, she said she did not. That seemed out character. In any event, I was only half listening. I was thinking about my Mum. What was wrong with her? Would she get better?

I have met people like this woman from time over the years. They tend to be narcissistic and to exaggerate, especially when it comes to describing something they say they have done. In short, they like to make things up, and then brag about them. The Cuban dog story was also a way for her to show that we were on the same wavelength, that we shared a bond, because we both "rescued" dogs. Her story was also a classic case of egotistical one-upmanship. It was also, I suspected, a total lie.

We wanted to leave early, but she kept insisting we stay. I wondered if she was lonely. She had already played the sympathy card, telling us her husband was gone so much of the time she hardly saw him. She told us that the minute he got back from a trip, he'd pick up his golf clubs and be back out the door to go to the country club to which he belonged. I actually found myself feeling sorry for her!

From across the table, Arabella, who had been pushing her homemade banana pudding around the crystal dessert dish for as long as she could, was giving me the "let's get going look". We were tired and had run out of things to say. It was becoming awkward. I insisted we had to leave. We wanted to be at the hospital early the next morning.

Finally, the evening was over. We said our good nights and made it out the front door. As we walked the short distance to my Mother's house, a cold rain began to fall. I kept thinking about the evening. Only two words come to mind to describe it. Endless, and vaguely odd.

The next morning, we went back to the hospital. The mother I knew was gone, replaced by a woman who was delusional and paranoid, with only intermittent moments of clarity. She raved about the dog that she said she had seen running around the ER. Then she whispered to us that all the nurses were talking about her. I assured her there was no dog and that the nurses didn't have time to talk to me never mind talk about her.

During one of these moments she mother cried out, "Keep that blonde-headed bitch away from me!" I tried to calm her down and asked her who she meant. Her reply stunned me. "That lawyer! She's trying to steal my house!"

We did not know it until much later, but my mother had had a series of mini strokes that had exacerbated her cognitive impairment. Arabella and I were scared, seeing my mother in this condition and not knowing what to do. I tried to calm her and assured her that her house was safe. Everything was fine. I had her POA and I would take care of her. She just needed to get better, and then she could go home. At that point, I still thought that that was a possibility. I did not realize until much later, that everything was far from fine; that she would never get better; and that, in fact, her fears about her house were justified. My mother was not raving. She was warning us! The weird dinner party had been held to keep us busy, so the lawyer could go to the hospital and scope out the situation.

After two days in the dark and depressing Emergency Room, my mother's physical condition improved somewhat. They had given her fluids and a transfusion. Two days later, she seemed on the mend and had regained enough of her composure for the hospital to consider her well enough to be discharged. I wanted her to come home because she wanted it so much. When you love someone you want them to be happy. I knew she hated being in the smelly, noisy, crowded ER and I didn't blame her. In hindsight, I can't imagine what the medical staff was thinking. They were supposed to be the experts. Did they not see that dementia was at least a part of her problem? That she should not have been allowed to go home in her condition? It was the first time they had not done due diligence on their patient, but it would not be the last.

At the time, I didn't know much about Alzheimer's. I did not know for instance that those who have it get very good at pretending to be normal, especially when they have a goal in mind, like going home. But someone at the hospital should have seen my mother's condition for what it was, especially since there is such a large population of seniors on the Island, and there is so much documentation about the disease in the medical literature. It's not as if she was suffering from something rare. My guess is that the old, overcrowded hospital simply needed the bed.

A few days after she got home, my mother assured us she was feeling like her old self. She was smiling and bustling around her house, so happy to be home. I believed her, because I wanted to believe her. I wanted everything to be just the way it was before. And too, my other life was calling me back. Leo had to go back to work, Arabella was missing classes, and my other daughter needed me to sort out some trouble she had gotten into. We made the decision to go back to Chicago, at least for a couple of weeks. She seemed so much better now that the doctor had put her on a beta-blocker. But to be honest, I was in denial about my mother's condition because I wanted more than anything for her to be okay. I wanted it so much, it clouded my judgment. I did not let myself see what was really happening to her because I think, inside, I knew what it would mean. I was losing her.

So before we left, I did my own bustling, the way women do when they have to deal with things that they don't want to deal with. It's therapeutic. It takes your mind off of things you are trying not to face. I got her meds from the drug store, picked up the vitamins the doctors recommended, and went grocery shopping for her. Every day, I saw the neighbor walking Hector down the street, even in the pouring rain. She looked over to see if our rental car was still in the driveway, but she did not come to the house.

At the beginning of April, we left to go back to Chicago. When we got home, I started calling around to arrange for my mother to have a caregiver whether she wanted one or not, and to have a Lifeline put in in case she needed to call for help. I was proactive and I felt like I was on top of the situation.

But, on the day the Lifeline installer and the visiting nurse were supposed to come to her house, my mother refused to let them in. They called me and I called her. She started shouting about how no one was going to get into her house. Then she hung up on me. She was obviously not herself.

According to Health.com, "In addition to agitation, rapid and seemingly unprovoked mood swings are another sign of dementia—going from calm to tearful to angry for no apparent reason."[41] I called the police and explained the situation. They told me that there was nothing they could do; that she didn't have to let these people in if she didn't want to. It became a common mantra.

Before I could get back to the Island, my mother was back into the hospital. The improvements in her condition because of the transfusion and the beta-blocker were only transitory. This time, there would be no going home.

The neighbor sent me an email on April 19th telling me that she had met the lawyer at the hospital while she was visiting my mother. She said they had a "very interesting meeting".

Part of the email reads:

I have your Moms(sic) wallet at my house and there is $210.00 in it plus all her credit cards. I thought it would be safer here. I don't think I've forgotten *anything. If you have an objection with anything I am doing for your mother, please communicate with me. I am doing for her what I would for my own Mother, and only care about her best interest and I have taken on the role as her primary caregiver.*

She has told me several times that you are mad at me and I couldn't imagine why! This seems to be on her mind and bothers her. I tell her everything is fine and not to worry. I met Jackie at the hospital today and we had a good talk. It's nice to get the acknowledgement from every one there, that I am doing the right thing for your mother."

Over the years since I received this email I have learned a lot about how people like the neighbor manipulate their victims. One of the ways they do this is to make the victim choose sides. By telling my mother that I was mad at her she was making her choose between the two of us. It was the beginning of the manipulation of my mother's mind and ultimately her loyalties. I do not think this behavior was accidental. I think she knew exactly how to begin her control over my mother.

By telling me about my mother's wallet she was doing two things. She was trying to judge my response to this obviously inappropriate behavior and also letting me know she was gaining control over my mother's life. Both the lawyer and the neighbor exhibited this kind of behavior. It became a pattern of theirs to hint at what they were doing. It was almost like they were gloating about the control they were gaining over my mother and our family.

The comment about her now being my mother's primary caregiver was totally inappropriate. She had no right to say this since she was not even a friend of my mother's, just a neighbor whose presence in my parent's lives had always been marginal at best. I felt a twinge of fear when I read this. Her unilateral assumption of this role in my mother's life was so out of line. I think that is when I understood that she was a threat.

I fired back an email of my own telling her that my mother had a loving family who cared for her and that we had been taking care of her and would continue to do so.

I also suspected she was lying, because previously, when her husband had spent several weeks at the same hospital being treated for kidney cancer, she told me she "wouldn't set foot in the place" because "the hospital was so old and depressing."

She also complained to me about my mother's hospital room. She said that she should at least have a window. Later, when Arabella and I got to the hospital we found that my mother's bed was right next to the window. If she had been visiting her every day as she said she would have known that.

When she went into my mother's house and took Mum's wallet she also went looking for the PIN numbers to her VISA and ATM cards. She told me, in a telephone conversation, that she found the passwords in the back of my mother's telephone book. This was another very inappropriate action and admitting to it was another test to see how I would react.

Seniors often write down important numbers if they have memory issues. It is not a good idea to put them in such an obvious place. I thought her actions extremely unusual and probably borderline illegal. I contemplated calling the police and then decided against it. As long as she put the things back, I decided to let it go. But her actions deepened my suspicions about her true motives. I cancelled the credit card and the ATM card and had new ones issued with my POA on them and new PIN numbers.

It was also during this time that the neighbor asked me if my mother kept any valuables or cash in the house. By then I knew she was up to something. I said that my mother kept no valuables in the house, which was not exactly true, but a warning light had gone off in my brain. This woman was definitely up to no good.

I understand now that her odd behaviors were a form of what the experts call "rationalization". She actually thought she was entitled to take whatever she wanted from my mother. Looking back, I realized she had been taking from her for some time, things from the house, clothes which she would then give to her mother, my father's tools, the power washers etc. It wasn't as if she needed the stuff. She simply wanted it. For her it was all about the taking.

I understand now that what was happening was that the neighbor was beginning to exert undue influence over my mother. People like her start out asking for small things and get the victim used to giving them things. This not only builds a mind set in the victim, it is a test run for when the predator is ready to go for the bigger piece of the pie.

Maybe I should have acted sooner to quell her presence in my mother's life. It all seems so obvious in hindsight. But, to be honest, I was distracted by my concern for my mother's condition. Worrying about her took up all my focus. More than anything, I just wanted her to be alright.

I know now that I should never have allowed these women to visit my mother in the hospital. I should have cut off all communication with them. But since I lived so far away, I thought the company would cheer her up. I was only thinking of making her stay in the hospital easier. They were only thinking of her money.

I had my POA attached to her hospital file so all decisions about her care were supposed to be discussed with me. I was in daily contact with the staff. I did tell them not to divulge any information about my mother's condition to anyone but me. It was family business and they were certainly not family.

At this time, the neighbor's emails got more aggressive. She demanded to know what was going on with my mother. I told her that my mother's condition was none of her business. She told me I was a bad daughter and that I would be sorry for this. People like these two women, as I have learned since, are all about control. They don't like to be thwarted. They are easily frustrated. They will strike back.

As punishment for cutting her out of the information loop at the hospital, she refused to tell me where she had placed my mother's dog. My mother was asking daily about Babe and the neighbor told her she still had the dog in her care. Another lie, designed to make her look like the good guy. Initially, she had told me she thought the dog should be put down, because it was "old and useless". I was afraid she had done just that. Her attitude was in complete contrast to the story about her pretend compassion for the little, starving dog in Cuba that she had told at dinner just three weeks before.

Later, I understood that her comments about my mother's dog were simply foreshadowing. They were an indication of what she had planned for my mother who was also, as far as she was concerned, "old and useless". It took me several weeks to find out what she had done with my mother's beloved dog.

Chapter Five

THE DIRTY LITTLE SECRET ABOUT

DIAGNOSIS

"It ain't what you don't know that gets you into trouble.
It's what you know for sure that just ain't so." – Mark Twain

In 1906 German physician, Dr. Alois Alzheimer, first described "a peculiar disease" that he discovered in an autopsy on of one of his patients. She had suffered from profound memory loss, paranoia about her family, speech difficulties, hallucinations and delusions. During the autopsy of her brain, he noted a dramatic shrinkage of the brain itself and unusual plaque deposits in and around the nerve cells. His assistant dubbed it Alzheimer's disease.[42]

We all have preconceived ideas about what Alzheimer's is and what it is not. For most of us those ideas are only marginally accurate. As I said previously, I always thought memory loss was a natural part of aging. It isn't. I wasn't sure about the differences between dementia and Alzheimer's either. There aren't any. The terms are used interchangeably. Like most people, I thought that Alzheimer's/dementia was an older person's disease. It isn't. Alzheimer's is simply more common in the elderly, but it also occurs in middle-aged and younger populations. In fact the patients that Dr. Alzheimer studied were all middle-aged, albeit the average age at death at the turn of the twentieth century was forty-five.

Alzheimer's disease is quite simply a degenerative neurologic disease that causes cognitive decline. There is no cure, no effective permanent treatment and the only way to be sure that the patient has Alzheimer's is during an autopsy.

The most common cause of Alzheimer's is vascular disease such as what happens after a series of strokes or one massive stroke. My mother had never had a stroke prior to her admission to the hospital in 2010. Indeed the only time I had ever seen her really ill was when she was in early forties and had peritonitis from a burst appendix. Parkinson's disease is another leading cause of dementia, along with head trauma, HIV, syphilis, and hypothyroidism. My mother had none of these. She did have one of the "miscellaneous" causes of dementia however – B12 deficiency, which has already been discussed.

So between my lack of understanding of who gets dementia and how, and my lack of previous experience with any of the main causes of Alzheimer's, I am not surprised that I did not understand what was happening to her. But I still spent over two years beating myself up for not seeing what has now become painfully obvious. I lived my life, afloat in a sea of guilt for what I could have done, should have done or did not do sooner.

And apparently, I am not alone in this.

Even though someone gets Alzheimer's every 67 seconds in the U.S. - according to the Alzheimer's Association - a 2011 Harvard School of Public Health study revealed that 82% of the population surveyed said they did not have experience with the day to day care, finances or decision making for someone with Alzheimer's. However there was a general agreement on symptoms including confusion, wandering, difficulty in remembering things and difficulty in paying bills. Only half the U.S. population understands that symptoms of dementia also include anger, violence, hallucinations and hearing voices.[43]

Multiple studies have shown that a patient can be diagnosed with accuracy about 90% of the time by doctors familiar with the disease. So why are only about half of the patients with Alzheimer's being diagnosed, according to the Alzheimer's Association, even though most of the individuals are already under the treatment by a doctor for other conditions related to aging? This lack of diagnosing contrasts to a recent report from the Centers for Disease Control and Prevention which shows that fully 80% of those with HIV/AIDS are diagnosed.[44]

Now that I understand more about Alzheimer's, I can see that the signs were there from the time my mother was in her mid to late seventies. There was an incident when my older daughter was twelve that should have sent up a red flag. She was sitting in my parent's family room reading the latest Harry Potter book when my mother came in asked her where I was. Sabrina's reply was, "she's in the bedroom." At which point my mother slapped her hard across the face for using the word "she". Sabrina never got over that slap. And though I thought my mother's reaction was totally unlike her normally loving self, I did not see it for what it was - an indicator of the blooming dementia.

And I was not alone. My parent's doctor did not see it either. My mother and father had been seeing the same physician for over twelve years. He had treated my father for high blood pressure and later for pancreatic cancer. He had seen my mother through a variety of minor illnesses, two hip replacements and a bout of shingles. Why had he not seen the cognitive and behavioral changes in either of them?

Even though there is no cure, Alzheimer's patients can benefit from early diagnosis in many ways. Changes in lifestyle, certain medications, changes in diet, can all help. Sharing the diagnosis with family members might insure practical measures were put in place to plan for future protections. I know that that would have been immensely helpful in my case. I would have put my mother's assets into a trust to protect her from potential predators immediately upon learning that she had an incurable, degenerative mental disease for which there was no cure.

And yet neither he, nor any of the many doctors who saw her when she spent weeks in the hospital while they looked for physical reasons to explain her symptoms, ever spoke to me about her having Alzheimer's.

There are reasons for this lack of communication, none of which include them being uncaring doctors. Doctors are people too. They want to find something that is wrong and cure it. A broken leg is one thing. A broken brain is quite different. If doctors see something that is not curable and is also progressive, it makes them feel professionally impotent.

And too:

- The Canadian medical system is essentially available to every person who requests care, but because everyone has the right to medical care, doctors are forced to see more patients. This means that they have less and less time to spend with each one. The little nuances of cognitive changes may not be observable unless specifically brought to the doctor's attention. For families who live at a distance, those changes may not be seen until they are very far along.

- There is no sure fire test for Alzheimer's.

- For the most part the doctors who interacted with my mother were general practitioners, not specialists in geriatric medicine. When my mother was finally seen by a doctor who specialized in aging, he diagnosed her in one visit. By then of course it was a bit too late for me to help her avoid being a target of fraud.

- No one likes to think they can't do their job. That is true for doctors too. Why then open up a can of worms when there is nothing you can do to help the patient? No cure you can aim for. No medicines that will stay the inevitable.

- Alzheimer's is a devastating disease. Some doctors don't want to put the family through dealing with it until it is absolutely necessary.

- People who have Alzheimer's, especially if, like my mother they are uneducated, don't know they have the disease. Not remembering things is not something you remember to tell your doctor. People who have hallucinations don't know they are hallucinating. People who are paranoid are afraid to tell anybody anything.

- Even if she suspected that there was something wrong, my fiercely independent mother would do anything to maintain her independence. Even to the point of feigning normalcy. And while my father was alive it was easier to cope with day to day activities because they covered for each other.

According to James P. Richardson, Chief of Geriatric Medicine, St. Agnes Hospital in Baltimore, "Most of these patients see their primary physicians faithfully for treatment of hypertension, diabetes, hyperlipidemia and other chronic diseases common in older adults. By the time the family has brought the patient to me for an evaluation of memory loss, signs of cognitive decline usually have been present for many months or even years. These signs include poor compliance with prescriptions, inability to perform instrumental activities of daily living, or asking the same question repeatedly. Not only do these patients score poorly on standardized mental status instruments, but they often don't remember their ages, birthdays, former jobs, or how many grandchildren they have. In other words, with few exceptions, the diagnosis of Alzheimer's disease is not difficult to make, especially in patients whose disease has been present long enough to reach the moderate stage."[45] But it is a difficult diagnosis to make emotionally for the doctor, the patient, and the family.

That is why most of us continue to turn a blind eye. Families do not want to see the change in a senior's behavior for what it is because they know what it means. It means someone they care about is going away and will never come back. Doctors don't want to deal with something that cannot be successfully dealt with. And so, cognitively impaired seniors remain targets for those unscrupulous people among us who do see what is going on and who are prepared to take advantage of it.

Chapter Six

SUNDOWNER'S SYNDROME

"Do not go gently into that good night. Rage, rage against the dying of the light." – Dylan Thomas

From Arabella's diary: March 27, 2010

"*A lot has happened in the last couple of days. Yesterday morning my nanny woke up and her heart was pounding. Her heartbeats were irregular and so my Mum called the paramedics. She was pale and weak. They gave her a beta blocker and some shots and that afternoon she looked rosy. They are keeping her for a couple of days. They say she is very anemic and they are going to give her more blood. She is in very good spirits and wants to come home and I don't blame her. The emergency room is so creepy and dark. I couldn't be there very long. Also it brought memories of when I was little and my Mum was sick in the hospital. I cried a little.*"

"*That night Mum fell asleep on the couch. She was so tired. She is sure worried about my Nan and is dealing with a lot of stress but I'm taking very good care or her and Nanny as well.*"

March 28th

"Chaos. Suddenly Nanny has begun to lose her memory and has become para-noid. One minute she is doing well and the next she is ripping out her IV and unwilling to co-operate with the nurses. My Mum is a real hero. I hope I will be as strong as her."

⟨⟩

March 29th

She is out of the hospital! We picked her up this morning. The doctor said the paranoia is normal among elderly patients when they are in the hospital. Now she is back to her normal self."

For seniors of advanced age, just being in a hospital and out of a familiar environment can lead to further mental decline. It is even truer when the patient has Alzheimer's.

"Sundowner's Syndrome is the name given to an ailment that causes symptoms of confusion after "sundown." These symptoms appear in people who suffer from Alzheimer's Disease or other forms of dementia. Not all patients who suffer from dementia or Alzheimer's exhibit Sundowner's symptoms, however. Conversely, some people exhibit symptoms of dementia all day which grow worse in the late afternoon and evening, while others may exhibit no symptoms at all until the sun goes down."[46]

Science is still at a loss to explain why this happens only that it does happen. Theories pin it to late day fatigue, over stimulation, the effects of light on mood – much like Seasonal Affective Disorder, even to the disruption of the shift changes by the staff.

Symptoms include agitation, hallucinations, anger, hiding things, para-noia, and violence – during this time my mother hit one of her doctors

54

with her walker - and wandering. Wandering, especially, is dangerous because the patient often does not know they are wandering.[47] That is why every so often there are stories in the news about patients who have wandered away from nursing homes, sometimes with deadly consequences.

Like many seniors, my mother had become a little profit center for the hospital. While millions of Canadians, who were not hospitalized, are put on long waiting lists for needed medical tests, the hospital lavished a bounty of tests on my mother. In the U.S. medical insurance or Medicare pays for the tests. The more tests the hospital does, the more money they receive in recompense. Whether or not the tests were relevant to improving her condition was beside the point.

Most of the medical expenses incurred in a person's life are incurred in the last three years, as doctors and hospitals spend copious amounts on testing patients who are suffering from something that has no cure - old age. According to the New York Times, older adults in their last year of life consume more than a quarter of Medicare's expenditures, costing more than six times as much as other beneficiaries.[48]

By the end of April 2010, my mother begged me to make them stop doing tests on her. She was always fearful and frequently uncomfortable. Because of her lifelong claustrophobia, tests like the MRI and the CAT scan where agony. Instead of diagnosing her dementia, doctors continued to look for physical reasons for my mother's condition – for six weeks. They tried transfusing her, did X-rays, an EEG, an ECT, a colonoscopy, another transfusion, and endoscopy etc. They did not find anything. Ultimately, they decided she had a kidney infection and gave her anti-biotics. Mentally, she remained confused, befuddled and cognitively impaired.

I spoke to hospital staff and told them that unless the procedures were necessary for improving her condition or keeping her comfortable, that they should stop using her as a guinea pig. Later in the doctor's notes I read that they too had decided that enough testing had been done. Still, at no time did anyone mention Alzheimer's or dementia, although it was clear to our family that, mentally, she had changed abruptly from her old self.

At the beginning of May, we returned to the Island. First thing the next morning, we went to Royal Jubilee Hospital and found my mother in a ward on the fourth floor. There was a young guard on the entrance to the hallway. He was there to make sure that none of the patients wandered away, and also to make sure that the psychiatric patients in the orange jumpsuits, who occupied the rooms at the far end of the hall, did not bother the other patients.

Five people, men and women were crowded into a tiny room that should have accommodated two patients. Fortunately, my mother had the bed next to the window. We were shocked at the conditions, but so happy to see her.

She was sitting up in a chair, wearing a faded green hospital robe torn at the shoulder and a nightie. Her right arm was resting on the window sill. She looked so incredibly tiny, so frail, framed by the window, staring off into the distance. Behind her was the glorious snow-covered majesty of the Olympic mountain range. Usually I marveled at the beauty of it, but today it just made me sad. The mountains would be there for a long time to come, but I was struggling with the knowledge that soon, my Mum would not.

The flowers with the purple butterflies that we had sent for Mother's Day were sitting on the nightstand. We had planned on being there for Mother's Day but the flights were full so we came a couple of days later. I found out later that the neighbor had told my mother that we had deliberately missed being there for this special day to upset her and drive a further wedge between us.

I remember wondering if this would this be the last Mother's Day I would get to send her flowers? I think that was the first time I really understood that I was losing her; that she would never get better; that nothing would ever be the same again. I began to tear up. I knew I had to banish thoughts like this or I would never get through this. And too, I had to think of Arabella. I knew she didn't really understand how serious this was and I wanted to protect her from the truth as long as possible.

I called out to her softly. "Mum?"

At the sound of my voice, she turned from gazing out the window. It took a moment, but then her blue eyes lit up as she realized it was us. We picked our way across the room, avoiding beds, potty chairs, IV hangers and a tangle of cables that snaked across the floor from various machines that monitored the other patients.

Arabella and I leaned down and we both hugged her at the same time. Her tiny frame disappeared into our embrace.

"Where have you been? I want to go home."

"I know Mum, but we have to get you well first." I did not know what else to say to her.

"Hmmmm." She drifted off and went back to staring out the window.

We sat on her bed. To get her attention and cheer her up I thought I would tell her about her dog. "We have Babe. She's back at the house." I had finally got the neighbor to tell me the whereabouts of the dog, right before she left town, the day before we arrived. "Would you like us to bring her to see you?"

Her eyes lit up. So I asked the nurses at the station down the hall if I could take her outside in a wheelchair on our next visit and they agreed. I thought it would be okay to let the dog sit on her lap outside the hospital. So later that afternoon we returned with Babe and my mother held onto her for dear life.

When we went back to her house that evening, Babe trotting along behind us, it almost seemed that things were normal for a moment as we walked through the back door and into the kitchen. The realization that my mother was not there and probably never would be again, hit us both at the same time.

To offset her darkening mood, Arabella went searching for family photographs in my father's den. I sat in my mother's blue chair next to the window in the family room. The dogwood in the back garden was covered with beautiful white blossoms, blooming as it had done every year since my parents had planted it. Why was nature progressing as usual when our world was ending? I sat back in the chair, lost in thought. No one ever imagines how their parents will leave this world. Not for the first time did I wish I had brothers or sisters so I had someone to share the grief.

My gaze wandered to the table next to the chair. Her glasses were there. The book she had been reading was lying face down, open to the last page she had read, as if she had just this minute put it down. But something was different. I sat up.

"Arabella!"

"What?" She stuck her head around the door to the den, holding a picture album.

"Look!" I pointed at the table as she came into the family room.

Where the photograph of my father standing against the fireplace had been, there was a different photograph.

"Where did that come from?" cried Arabella from across the room. She seemed loathe to come any closer. She rubbed her upper arms in the way that people do when they feel a sudden chill.

"Well it wasn't here the last time we were here, and Mum hasn't been back in the house for weeks."

"Too weird." Arabella shook her head, shrugged and went back into the den. "What are you going to do with it?" she called out.

I thought for a moment. It had been my intention to keep my Mum's home just as she had left it. Whenever we were there, we didn't even cook, but bought takeout so we wouldn't make a mess. Even though I was the caretaker of her estate, I did not feel it was my place to interfere with it. Gingerly, I picked up the smiling photograph of the neighbor and her husband and put it face down in the drawer beneath the table. How dare she put a picture of herself among my family photos! I replaced it with a photo of my Mother. This was, after all, still her house.

It was three years later when I was finally able to remove that photo from the frame, which had at some point had been placed back on the table. Behind it was a photo of Arabella and me when she was just born. Why would she want to put a picture of herself over a picture of us? She could easily have bought a different frame. My guess is that in her warped mind she was usurping our bond with my mother. By inserting a picture of herself into the frame she was inserting herself into our lives. We lit a match and watched as the flames crawled across their faces. Then, we threw it in the fireplace.

Every day we went to the hospital. At first, she wasn't allowed to leave the grounds, but there was a lovely garden in the newer part of the hospital and we were allowed to take her there if she was in a wheel chair. Arabella would go down to Tim Horton's, located on the first floor of the hospital, to get coffee or tea for us. We brought Babe, smuggling her into the garden under a blanket or in my shawl. My mother was thrilled to see her "little bundle" and she cuddled the dog as though she would never let go.

She was often confused and repeated herself frequently. Her old memories were still relatively intact though, and we talked a lot about the past. Recent ones proved more difficult, however. She did not remember that my father was dead. One day, she thought I was her mother. Then she asked me who I was. She forgot who Arabella was a couple of times. I was beginning to really understand that she would never return to her old self. It was heartbreaking.

After a few days, we convinced the hospital to let us take her out in the car for a couple of hours. We went to get fish and chips – her favorite dish - down by the harbor and then for a drive around the peninsula. It was a pretty spring day and she held Babe happily on her lap. We had done this drive many times before. I wondered if she remembered.

At a meeting at the hospital a few days later, Arabella and I were told that Mum would need to be placed in a long term care facility.

According to the notes I later obtained from the hospital, *"The problem has not resolved. Patient still confused. Can't send her home. Family agrees that no further investigation is required. It is a good idea that Rosalind stay in Victoria and go into care."*

The consensus among the staff was that she would definitely not be able to return her home. When I asked if she could come and live with us they said we would "not be able to handle her." I did not understand what that meant, at the time. I had no idea that the progression of her dementia would lead her into a very violent place. But, they would have known what was in store for her. They would have seen it many times before. It was not something they wanted to share with us because the truth would be too difficult to take. They kindly reassured us that in any event, and on a practical note, her medical insurance would not transfer to Illinois.

Though it was a sad decision to make, I signed the necessary papers to have her admitted to an assisted living facility, because the doctors and social workers said it would be best for her; that she would be in good hands; that she would be safe. They were wrong. By signing the papers I had put her in harm's way. I cannot forgive myself for that.

During this time I had no contact with the three women who had suddenly become my mother's "new best friends". I thought that since the decision to put her into care had been made and the papers signed, I was done with having to deal with their interference. Again, I was wrong. They were just biding their time.

From Arabella's diary: May 15, 2010

"So my Nanny will be staying in the hospital until she gets placed into a senior home. The place she will be going is really nice and she is excited for it. We brought Babe again and went to the garden to have tea. Mum is doing a great job handling this but she cried when she found out that we could not take nanny to live with us."

My mother was transferred to the long term care facility at the beginning of June. We had been told that we had to accept the first available bed or she would drop to the bottom of the list and have to languish in the over-crowded hospital room until she made it back up to the top of the list. I could not stand to think of her in that crowded, stuffy room for any longer than was absolutely necessary, so we agreed.

Arabella and I Googled the long term care facility that had the first available bed. We were pleasantly surprised. St. Mary's was a beautiful, new building set in lovely grounds with flowers and fountains, right near the harbor in downtown Victoria. It was a far cry from the hospital where she had been. We both felt much better knowing that she was going to be somewhere nice.

I was confused therefore when both Leo and I started getting calls from the lawyer and the neighbor telling us how dirty and disgusting the place was and demanding that we get my mother out of there! It was none of their business for one thing and it didn't make sense either. Unless the pictures on the Internet were a lie, the place looked fabulous, like all the high end condominiums that graced the shores of the inner harbor.

In the beginning, my mother was placed in a double room, though the administrator promised that she would get her own room as soon as possible. My mother's roommate was a lady of about the same age. She was someone's mother or grandmother, but no one had reported her missing. Nobody knew her name either, so, Mum called her Midge, after her best friend when she was in school. "Midge" had been found abandoned in the doorway of a church in downtown Victoria. She had been badly beaten, was covered in bruises, especially on her face and had several broken bones. Twenty-one percent of elder abuse victims suffer physical abuse.[49]

"Midge" moved in and out of consciousness. Periodically, she would scream and cry out, evidently reliving the beating. This unnerved my mother understandably, but a little while later, when a single room became available for Mum, she refused to leave "Midge". She said she wanted to stay put and take care of her.

In spite of her severe cognitive decline, at least part of my mother's personality remained intact. She was just doing what she had always done, taking care of strays.

Chapter Seven

MORAL INSANITY AND AUDACIOUS DEEDS

"Everyone, even the experts, can be taken in, manipulated, conned by them. A good sociopath can play a concerto on anyone's heartstrings. Your best defense is to understand the nature of these human predators." – *Dr. Robert Hare*

From the spring of 2010 onward, the one question that kept plaguing me was; Why? Why were these women so interested in my mother? I never believed for a moment that it was because they were interested in her wellbeing. Their behaviors were too outrageous. But at this point I was not worried about them going after her money. After all I had a valid will; an enduring Power Attorney; and she was in now situated in a very nice assisted living facility with round the clock care. I thought I had done everything possible to protect her. I thought she was safe. Even though her cognitive abilities were declining – a sorrow which I still bore daily, I was determined to make sure the rest of her life was as good as it could be. I would be there for her until to the end. She would die surrounded by her loving family. Of course, it did not turn out that way at all.

These women's continued presence in our lives nagged at me. What did they want? Whenever I can't understand a set of circumstances, I start to research the problem. I needed to know if their behaviors were really as off the grid as I thought they were and if somebody else had seen this kind of thing before. If so, maybe they had an answer as to how to get these women out of our lives.

First, I read Dr. Robert Hare's book, "Without Conscience, the Disturbing World of The Psychopaths Among Us". This led me to Dr. Martha Stout's book; "The Sociopath Next Door" (couldn't get any closer to what was happening to us as I found out.) I knew I was onto something. There on the pages of these books were situations that described those that were unfolding my own life.

Before reading these books, I perceived the lawyer and the neighbor as nothing more than greedy opportunists, hungry to defraud a frail old woman. But, once I read them, I could see that the women I was dealing with operated under a different set of motives and behaviors than most of the rest of us. They were so different in fact that, unless someone had the misfortune to be targeted by women like these, they would be hard pressed to see them for what they were.

I had wasted valuable time questioning myself about what I had done or could have done differently, when I should have been focused on understanding what these women were all about. My new knowledge about what has come to be called "anti-social personality disorder" led me to the conclusion that they would stop at nothing to get what they wanted. And, as it turned out, I was unfortunately right.

This is not to say that everyone who commits elder fraud is a sociopath, but a large number of fraudsters of every kind display sociopathic behaviors – fortunately for the world, not always to this extreme. That's how they have the audacity to do what they do in the first place.

In his article in the Atlantic in March of 2012, author James Silver wrote a piece called, "Is Wall Street Full of Psychopaths?" In it he referenced an article by CFA Magazine writer, Sheeree DeCovney, in which she claimed that 15 percent (at least) of the people in the financial services industry are psychopaths. "Research studies suggest that as much as 15 percent of the general population (that's about 45 million Americans) can be characterized as psychopaths. If Wall Street does, in fact, select for people who display certain characteristics of psychopathy, it is safe to assume that at least 15 percent of people in the financial services industry are psychopaths (and, therefore, more prone to acts of fraud, deceit, and self-serving manipulation)".[50] This is something we as a nation have had a ring side seat to for years as we observed the machinations of Bear Sterns or Goldman Sachs, not to mention the actions of Bernie Madoff.

In the book, "The Wisdom of Psychopaths: What Saints, Spies, and Serial Killers Can Teach Us About Success",[51] author and Oxford psychologist Kevin Dutton notes that "a number of psychopathic attributes are actually more common in business leaders than in so-called disturbed criminals - attributes such as superficial charm, egocentricity, persuasiveness, lack of empathy, independence, and focus." In other words, Ted Bundy was a sociopath/psychopath and a serial killer. He was not a serial killer because he had a personality disorder. It's just the way he applied it. He could easily have worked on Wall Street or run for office with his charm, good looks and ability to manipulate people.

Professions most likely to attract individuals with psychopathic/sociopathic personality traits include:

1. CEO

2. Lawyer

3. Media (Television/Radio)

4. Salesperson

5. Surgeon

6. Journalist

7. Police Officer

8. Clergy person

9. Chef

10. Civil Servant

Jobs which draw people with the lowest rates of psychopathic traits include:

1. Care Aide

2. Nurse

3. Therapist

4. Craftsperson

5. Beautician/Stylist

6. Charity Worker

7. Teacher

8. Creative Artist

9. Doctor

10. Accountant

Note that the lowest ranking professions are ones that require a person to actually care about the needs of others.[52] On the other hand, the second most likely profession to attract an individual with psychopathic personality traits is – lawyer.

First identified in 1835, Prichard's 'moral insanity' was the forerunner of our present-day concept of psychopathic (sociopathic) personality[53] or antisocial personality disorder. About four percent of the population or 7.6 million people are determined to have antisocial personality disorder, according to a landmark study conducted by the National Institute of Health in 2002.[54] From observation, this percentage has increased in the intervening decade as the behaviors exhibited by people like these receive more attention and rewards in our society.

Sociopaths and psychopaths share similar traits, but they are not the same. Sociopaths are people who are affected with a personality disorder marked by antisocial behavior. Psychopaths are people with an antisocial personality disorder, manifested by aggressive, perverted, criminal, or amoral behavior without empathy or remorse.

"David Lykken, a behavioral geneticist at the University of Minnesota, came to an interesting conclusion regarding the differences between sociopaths and psychopaths. Lykken's studies revealed that psychopaths are born with temperamental differences that lead them to be risk seekers, impulsive, fearless as well as not being able to socialize normally. Sociopaths have normal temperaments, and their personality disorder tends to affect their lives regarding parenting, peers, and their intelligence."[55] In either case, with any luck, you will never run into one of these people, but if you do you will recognize them by the following behaviors.

Sociopaths:

- Are glib and charming on the surface but covertly hostile and domineering. Their victim(s) is nothing more than an instrument to be used for their advantage.

- Domination and humiliation of the victim is also indicated. Cruelty is part of that. (What they did to my mother when they got control of her was extremely cruel indeed.)

- Are manipulative and conning with no respect for the rights of others

- Have a grandiose sense of self and their "right" to possess whatever they think should be theirs.

- Are pathological liars who are very convincing to the point where they can even convince themselves their lies are truths. But they find it hard to keep the lies straight.

- Are entirely lacking in guilt or remorse. They do not see others as people only as opportunities that can be used. Even their accomplices can end up as victims.

- Let nothing stand in their way

- Lack empathy. They feel nothing for the pain of their victims

- Live a parasitic lifestyle

- Seek out situations where their tyrannical behavior will be tolerated and want a despotic control over every aspect of their victim's lives.

- Crave the love and gratitude of their victims. In fact one of their ultimate goals is the creation of a willing victim.

- Give the appearance of normalcy so they are very hard to spot. Are remorselessly vindictive if thwarted or exposed. (I can vouch for that from my own experience.)

This all sounded only too familiar to me and would continue to prove more so as time passed. As their behaviors became more extreme and I found out more about what they had been doing and saying, I became more fearful and apprehensive because I knew what the inevitable endpoint would be.

Psychopaths:

- Use superficial charm to lure their victims.

- Are extremely self-centered.

- Must always do something to keep them from boredom.

- Are very deceptive and tend to lie continuously.

- Show no remorse of guilt towards their victims.

- Are very predatory and usually will live off other people.

- Have many sexual partners in their lifetime.

- Are very impulsive with their lifestyle.

- Are always blaming other people for their actions.

- Never have a realistic view of their lives. (king of the world or from another planet)

- Always want psychological gratification in sexual and criminal activities.

- Tend to try suicide, rarely succeeding.[56]

According to Dr. Hare, psychopaths/sociopaths usually don't get along well with one another. "The last thing an egocentric, selfish, demanding, callous person wants is someone just like her. Sometimes, however, sociopaths become temporary partners in crime – a grim symbiosis with unfortunate consequences for other people."[57]

At this time I was still getting phone calls from the neighbor. She was more and more demanding about me changing my mother's living arrangements. I told her it was none of her business and hung up. She called back. This time my daughter Sabrina answered the call and told her to stop upsetting me. She hung up on her. I never talked to her again but that does not mean she did not remain part of my life.

Of all the pleasant neighbors my mother had over the years, she unfortunately ended up with the sociopath next door. As soon as the neighbor told me she had taken my mother's wallet for "safe-keeping" I knew something was going on. Her behaviors were truly audacious. I just wasn't sure what to do about it.

Early on I did not know that the neighbor and the lawyer and formed a bond, so I decided to speak to the lawyer about the neighbor's behavior. I asked her if she thought I should change the PIN numbers on my mother's ATM card and VISA card. She said no. But the little voice inside my head said yes. I began to wonder about if the lawyer's motives were also in question. She did not seem to be representing my best interests as lawyers are supposed to do.

In the odd instances when sociopaths/psychopaths work together, they take on different, but complimentary, roles. According to Dr. Hare's research the neighbor was "The Teller". She developed the plan to take over my mother's life and get control of her estate. Then she went looking for someone equally as greedy and unscrupulous, but with a useful skill set, to help her. That's where the lawyer came in. She was "The Doer". She had the credibility, and the legal knowhow, to make the plan work. In our case, there was a third member of the group. She was the supermarket checker. She was greedy and not very bright. She was also not the sort to ask questions. She just did as she was told by the other two. She became "The Watcher".[58]

Initially, the checker's job was to keep my mother out of the long term care facility until late in the evening, so she could not be evaluated or settle in to her new surroundings. This behavior also served another purpose. It isolated her from her family. Despite frequent telephone calls, it was rare for me to be able to talk to my mother during this time because she was never there. This was the perfect opportunity for the women to work on undermining my relationship with my mother and increased the opportunity for them to gain influence over her. It also worked to set up a reliance on her "new best friends", a psychological bond that helped to turn her away from those who really cared for her. My not being able to communicate with her at this time meant she became more and more reliant on them, especially after they told her I had abandoned her by placing her in care.

It wasn't until later that I discovered that the checker had been added to their little group of conspirators for another reason. Initially she was also there to make sure that we did not get anywhere near my mother. It took almost a year to find out she also had another purpose. She was included in the group so she could cash checks. Lots of checks.

I knew what they were up to because I had frequent calls from St. Mary's asking where my mother was and if these women all knew each other.

They asked me if they were "handing her off" between the three of them. I told them I was twenty-five hundred miles away in Chicago and that it seemed to me that their security regarding their patients was somewhat lax.

I had already decided to put the kibosh on her too frequent outings when I heard about the request for a weekend pass. I called St. Mary's and left a message for the social worker telling her that this was absolutely out of the question. Aside from her cognitive impairment, she also had medical issues that needed daily medication and monitoring. I did not know until three years later when I finally got the last package of hospital notes, that my mother had been put on Seroquel, an anti-psychotic medication, while she was first at RJH in April 2010 because of her violent and aggressive behaviors toward staff. The administration of this medication was never discussed with me – her POA. If it had been I would have refused to let her take it. Seroquel, according to its maker, AstraZeneca, has a black box warning which says it is not to be given to elderly dementia patients because it hastens their risk of death! It also made her high fall risk.

Later a return phone from St. Mary's confirmed the request for an overnight pass.

"Yes I was asked on Friday about overnight passes for your Mum to go home and I said No. It's too soon after admission and besides we would need a doctor's orders so that did not happen and will not happen." (Ginny Pierson)

This was followed by another phone call from the administrator.

"I just wanted to let you know that Debbie took your Mum out of the facility at 11 this morning and I don't know if Debbie and the others are friends or what is going on but I will go and check again to see if she is back yet."(Vicki Thompson)

I found out later that the request for an overnight pass came from the lawyer, not the neighbor, as I had first suspected. Apparently, it mirrored a similar request made in May when my mother was still in RJH.

In any event I was tired of their constant interference in our lives. I sent both of them an email on June 4th, 2010.

Re: My mother

Since Joan has turned off her phone and won't take calls from me I want you both to be advised that my mother is not allowed to leave her care facility overnight, under my direction. This would be detrimental to her health and wellbeing. She has physical health issues as well as mental ones and she is on medication and needs to be under the supervision of a medical professional.

Mrs. Brewer is not a family member and she has no right to take my mother out of a care facility where I have placed her for her wellbeing. If Mrs. Brewer continues to harass my mother or my family in any way I will seek a restraining order against her.

I have advised the facility of my direction and they will not release her into Mrs. Brewer's care.

My email must have alarmed them. I could literally cut them out of my mother's life by using my POA at the facility to make sure they did not have access to my mother. They would have to alter their plans to make sure that did not happen.

They would need to find a way to get mother out of St. Mary's and back into her own home so they could exact complete and utter control over her. As long as she was in St. Mary's there was the possibility that I would show up and complicate their plans. Also while she was in the facility, she would continue to have some kind of protection because of the semi-watchful eyes of the staff. Plus she would have the ongoing medical care that she needed.

At home, alone, it was very likely that something untoward would happen to her. I understood that now, and fought to keep her in the assisted living facility. I knew it was literally a matter of life and death for her.

Chapter Eight

THE PURPLE SHAWL

*"Elderly fraud is a heinous problem that flies
under the radar." – Former Chief of the FBI's
Financial Crimes Section, Dennis Lormel*

O n Friday morning, June 18th, Arabella and I had a meeting
with the administrator of St. Mary's, and the social worker, at
nine a.m. The time is significant because the neighbor later
used it against us in court. She swore that we had only spent a couple of
hours with my mother that day when, in fact, we were there all day – we
just didn't sign in to the visitor's book.

We toured the facility – it was lovely. We signed the admission papers
for my mother and handed over a check for June's payment. I then gave
them a voided check to make sure the monthly payments were deducted
from my mother's bank account. I was trying to make the transition to
her new life as easy as possible for all of us. It was explained to us that
the monthly payment for her stay would be more than covered by her
government pension. This meant she had about fifteen thousand dollars
in her checking account to cover any other bills for a long time – or at
least that was my plan.

There were two things I should have done at this point. Made myself a
co-signer on her bank accounts or moved most of the money into a POA

account in my name only. Unfortunately I did not do either. And this made defrauding her even easier.

But, at that point, I was not thinking about fraud. I thought, errone-ously, that my POA would protect both her person and her assets. I was also trying to deal with guilt of making the very difficult decision to put the mother I loved in a home and turn her life upside down. Most fami-lies wait too long to make the decision to put a parent in a nursing home because by making that decision they are admitting that the end is not far off. According to a study published in the Journal of the American Geriatrics Society, 65% of seniors died within 1 year of nursing home admission.[59]

There are several scales that outline the activities of daily living that can be used to determine whether or not a senior should be moved into an assisted living facility or nursing home. These include:

- Inability to use a telephone

- Unable to shop without assistance or even shop at all

- Needing meals prepared and served or inability to maintain an adequate diet

- Unable to do housekeeping activities

- Needing laundry done by others

- Needing travel assistance or unable to travel at all

- Incapable of dispensing own medication

- Incapable of handling money or making day-to-day purchases[60]

My mother needed help with most of the above.

So, I made the best I could of this life-altering decision and arranged for her to have a little bank account at St. Mary's in case she needed magazines or toiletries; to have a weekly appointment at the in-house hair dressing salon; and to be seen by the resident pedicurist. I was trying to think of everything, so she would be as comfortable as possible in her new home.

Dealing with the details of her new surroundings also meant that I could focus on sorting out the situation instead of sorting out my feelings. Numbness had proved to be an effective emotional band aid for the last several weeks. It covered the wound of losing my mother, slowly, to a disease I knew little about. For moments at a time I could ignore the pain of her loss. It was different to the pain I felt when I lost my father. He was diagnosed and died six weeks later. It was easier to mourn his passing since he was actually gone. My mother on the hand was "gone", her essence removed from our lives. But, she was still there, a living presence, a constant reminder of what we were losing.

When everything was organized, we went to see her. It was a moment I dreaded since seeing her there in situ meant that she really would, in all likelihood, never be coming home again. Seeing her in the hospital was different. Then there was a very dull glimmer of hope that she would get better – at least there was in the back of my mind at that time. Hospitals are usually associated with an element of hope or an element of finality. Generally people get discharged and sent home, or they die and are sent to mortuaries. But nursing homes are like a limbo for the living. Few if any go home again after being in a nursing home. It is difficult to ignore the fact that they are simply holding pens for the inevitable. It now became a question not of if, but when, my mother would be taken from us entirely. Studies show that approximately 70% of people with dementia die in nursing homes.[61]

Each of the living areas or pods in the part of St. Mary's where my mother was to live was named after a tree. Cheerful pictures were painted on the pale yellow walls. Each pod featured a series of bedrooms, a living area with a television, and kitchen where residents could cook for themselves if they did not want to eat the food that came from the main kitchen. My mother's room was in Garry Oak pod. The white oak tree, named after Nicholas Garry, deputy governor of the Hudson's Bay Company, is native to the area. Her room was at the very end of the corridor.

The room was large and had a nice view. My mother was dressed in her own clothes – a beige sweater and pants – people with Alzheimer's often have trouble buttoning things, but Mum usually wore sweaters, so she could dress herself. She was sitting in a chair by the window, gazing vaguely out into the bustling streets of downtown Victoria. Not that she knew that. She did not know much at this point – what city she was in, where her income came from, what her house was worth, or that my father was dead – according to her geriatric psychiatrist, Dr. Prowse. But she did smile when she saw us. We hugged. It was obvious to both of us that there had been a significant deterioration in her mental condition since our last meeting four weeks ago.

We sat down next to her. She reached out and took my hand, squeezing hard and holding on. I told her all about Babe and how we had taken her to live with us in Chicago. We had to wait for her doctor to arrive to discuss her future plans. So I chatted on about the bills I had paid and the state of her house and anything I could think of to pass the time and keep my mind off the fact that the mother I loved had become little more than an empty shell. I knew she was not getting most of what I said. I was so sad.

When I ran out of things to say, Arabella picked up the slack, talking about her college and her jobs and telling her how well she looked.

After a time, I asked her if she was cold because the room was chilly. She nodded. I was wearing a purple shawl and I took it off and draped it around her. She was so tiny she looked lost in the sea of purple, but she cuddled into its softness. Arabella went and got us some tea. The clock ticked. The sun moved across the sky to its apex. High noon. The doctor was late.

I noticed her ankles were very swollen and I told her I was going to take her shoes off so I could see if her feet were swollen too. She was very compliant as I bent down and untied her sneakers. Her feet and ankles were very swollen – edema. Why had somebody not noticed? I knew she needed Lasix to help get rid of the retained water. I had had the same condition before my open heart surgery.

Finally, at 12:30, Dr. Houghton, arrived. He was a tall, handsome man with a very British accent. I had been told that the meeting was to discuss my mother's future living arrangements. Apparently there was nothing to discuss. She was staying put. In her impaired mental state there was no question of her going home. There was no question of improvement either. She would only get worse. There was nothing to be done. Still nobody said anything about Alzheimer's.

It was all over in about five minutes. Any hope that there was would be some light at the end of the tunnel, was dashed.

While this was sinking in, my mother indicated that she wanted to go to the bathroom. I said I would take her. She had trouble getting the adult diaper down and I helped her. She made a joke about there being room for a penis in her diaper. I told her that they were unisex and she thought that was funny. But when she was finally ensconced on the toilet, she looked up at me and said, "Who are you? And what are you doing in here?" She did not know me. It broke my heart.

81

When we got back to the room, I told Dr. Houghton that she did not know who I was. He simply nodded. He had been away in England for a few weeks dealing with his own mother. Perhaps his detachment from our circumstances was part of his dealing with his own numbness.

I asked him about the Lasix for her swollen ankles and he said he would write the prescription. That was it. He left to go back to his office. Our dreams of having my mother return to live out her life in her own home were crushed. I knew that none of our lives would ever be the same again.

Later that afternoon we took her out for lunch and a little drive. She seemed to enjoy it and we tried to make the most of our time together, but it was difficult for both of us to push away the reality of what had just happened. My mother, in her current childlike state, had no idea how much and how permanently, her life had just changed. But I did.

The next day, we came back, spent the morning and took her to lunch again. Then since it was a beautiful sunny we drove down to Dallas Road to the port where the cruise ships come in. She had always liked to go there and watch the massive liners spew their anxious shoppers onto the quaint streets of Victoria. But today no ships were in, so we drove along a little further towards the park on the cliff edge where everyone was walking their dogs.

The sight of all the people walking their dogs seemed to make her happy. I hopped she might have been remembering when she had done the same thing with her own dogs.

Arabella had brought her camera and we took turns taking a picture of each other with my mother against the seawall, with the cerulean sky and the glistening Pacific in the background. In the picture of me and my mother that Arabella took, I am standing behind her with my arms wrapped around her and she is holding tightly onto my hands as if she would never let go.

Then I decided to take a picture of my Mum on her own. It turned out to be a decision fraught with irony. Just before I pushed the button to take the shot, I said, "Wave mum, wave." And she did. But it was not the open-handed wave of someone saying hello. It was the sad, closed fingered wave of someone saying goodbye. It was the last picture I ever took of her.

Later that afternoon she wanted to go back to her house. Naturally, we had tea. The sun was pouring in through the kitchen window, casting scarlet shadows of the Japanese maple in her backyard, all about the room. As we washed the cups up in the sink afterward, she spoke, "I wish it was just the two us, living here." But she did not look up at me when she said it and I wondered if she was just thinking out loud.

"I know, Mum. I know." I think that we both knew that it was a wish that could never be fulfilled. I think I understood better than she did that our life as mother and daughter was coming to an end on this lovely summer afternoon. I could not even begin to imagine how horrible that ending would turn out to be.

She watered her plants and puttered around the house. I asked her if she wanted to take anything back with her back to St. Mary's and she selected two watches that my Dad had given her.

Then about 3:30 she asked us to take her back. She said she didn't want to miss dinner. I was surprised, but I knew that it meant that she was settling into the reality of her new life. It would make it easier for her.

We drove back, accompanying her up to the Garry Oak pod. We went to her room and put her watches in the drawer. The folded purple shawl I had placed around her shoulders was on her chair and she handed it back to me.

"No Mum, you keep it."

"No you take it," she said. And then she unfolded it, reached up and put it around my shoulders. It was a quintessential gesture of motherly love. She was still protecting "her baby".

Almost a year later, the purple shawl took on a new significance for me. It was mentioned in the oddly weird obituary that the neighbor wrote after my mother died. Even though my mother had by then been ravaged by Alzheimer's and abuse, the neighbor's obituary mentioned that my mother liked the color purple – a color which I had never seen her wear. This meant the color had been a connection between us throughout the last horrible year of her life, in spite of the efforts of these women to permanently erase our relationship as mother and daughter.

We were planning on waiting with her through dinner, but she wanted us to leave. I think she understood on some level that Garry Oak was her new life and that she needed to get used to it. In order to do this, she had to put aside her old life and move forward.

"I'm all right. You two go now. You look tired, Glyn. Arabella, look after your mother."

"I will, Nanny."

So she walked us to the door of her pod and raised her face up for a kiss.

"I love you Mum." I was tearing up. I couldn't look at Arabella. I knew that if we locked gazes we would both lose it. "We'll see you soon. We'll be back next month."

She nodded, her blue eyes glittering with tears. She stayed in the doorway for a moment watching us walk down the hall. As the corridor made a right turn toward the elevators, I turned to wave goodbye one more time, but she had already closed the door behind her. We never saw her again. We never got to say goodbye.

PART TWO

Chapter Nine

"KEEP THAT WOMAN AWAY FROM YOUR MOTHER!"

"I am a Physician and Surgeon, duly qualified by the College of Physicians and Surgeons of British Columbia and I am a consultant in geriatric psychiatry. I examined Rosalind Violet Walker on June 22, 2010. Based on my examination and findings, it is my opinion that the patient does not have the capability to attend to her personal, financial or legal affairs and will only get worse." – From the sworn affidavit of Dr. Prowse, August 16, 2010.

It took us two days to get back to Chicago. We had to spend twenty-four hours in the Vancouver airport because the only flight home had only one seat available and I couldn't leave Arabella and she wouldn't leave me, so we decided to wait until the next day.

We kept in touch with Mum by cell phone. When we got home Monday night I called her. She seemed to be settling in at St Mary's and that was a relief. She ended the call by telling us she loved us. It would be the last time she would ever say those words.

Tuesday morning Sabrina, Arabella and I got ready to go to Evanston. Arabella was teaching at the Piven Theatre Workshop at 2 o'clock and the plan was that we would have a girls' lunch afterward.

Just as we pulled into the parking lot of the theatre, my cell phone rang. I was busy looking for a parking spot in the crowded lot and I glanced quickly at the caller ID, figuring I would let it go to voicemail, unless it was urgent. I noted that the call was coming from the lawyer's, so I answered it. Was something wrong with Mum?

But my mother was on the other end of the line. Instinctively, I got that clenching feel in my chest. What was my mother doing in the lawyer's office and how did she get there?

So I asked her.

At first she denied being there. She told me she was not in the lawyer's office at all, but at St. Mary's. I told her I could tell from the phone number where she was calling from and that in any event she could not dial long distance from St. Mary's.

Then in the next few seconds my life changed forever. The mother, who just the previous evening had told me how much she loved us, blurted out her answer.

"You're a thief and a liar. I hate you! I never want to see you again!" And then she hung up.

I was in shock. What had happened? What was going on? I slipped the van into the first available parking spot and told my girls what their grandmother had just said.

Their question was the same as mine. What was going on?

As soon as I turned off the engine, I hit redial and the lawyer picked up.

"What is my mother doing in your office?"

She didn't answer the question, but instead started going about how I couldn't look after my mother because I lived too far away and that she was going to be taking care of her from now on. She smarmed her way through a twenty-five minute conversation, alternately assuring me that it was in my mother's best interests and that I could now attend better to the needs of my own family thanks to her kindly intervention.

I told her, my mother was part of my family. I repeatedly told her that I had been taking care of my mother for four years and that she should stay out of our family business. She continued to answer that I lived too far away.

Eventually the call ended. My heart was racing. I felt sick. I sat in the car wondering what to do, while Arabella went in to teach her class.

The journalist in me took over and I began break the situation down. Why was my mother in the lawyer's office? How could my mother say such awful things that were so obviously untrue? What had the lawyer told her that would cause such a reaction? I would not find out the "why" for another two weeks. As for the lies they had told her to manipulate her reaction - it took years to find out.

Later that afternoon, I called St. Mary's and found out that, according to the log book, the lawyer had taken my mother out of the facility at ten that morning and brought her back at noon which jived with the two hour time difference between Chicago and Victoria. I asked to speak to my mother and was put through instead to the administrator. All she said was "Your mother is very angry with you because of what you have done. If she wishes to call you she will call you at a later time." What had I done?

I was just about to point out that my mother couldn't dial long distance from the facility, when she hung up on me. We never spoke again. The lawyer and the neighbor had made sure I was persona non grata at the nursing home by weaving a web of lies, saying that my daughters and I were guilty of elder abuse thereby effectively making it impossible for me to communicate with my mother. At the same time, I learned later, they were telling my mother that it was my fault she was in a nursing home, that I had "turned the doctors against her," and that I had basically dumped her there.

Days passed. I was still in shock. I spoke to my friends about what had happened. Nobody had any idea what to do, but then at that point nobody knew what had already been done either or what was about to happen.

My mother's birthday on July 1st came and went. She turned 87. I sent flowers as usual. July 4th came and went too. I had already had enough fireworks to do me for some time so I simply sat in the backyard swatting mosquitos until it was time to go to bed. With a series of sharp lies whispered into the right ears, my mother had been excised from my life like a kidney from a donor, except I was not a willing donor. I wanted my mother back!

It was at this time I began to feel fear swelling up inside me. They had deliberately told vicious lies to an old, mentally incompetent woman, ripping her from her family at a time in her life when she was most vulnerable and when she needed our protection. What else had they planned for her? All my instincts told me she was in danger. The only thing she had to offer them was her estate and there was only one way to get that. They were going to get her to give it to them by more deceit and manipulation.

On Wednesday July 7th I got a call from Dr. Houghton. He had just received something in the mail that he thought I should know about. When he told me what it was, I was flabbergasted. Both he and I knew how cognitively compromised my mother was and yet he was now the recipient of a new Power of Attorney and a Representation Agreement, signed by my mother, making the lawyer her new legal representative. So that was why she took my mother to her office. She had told her a pack of lies and manipulated her into signing documents she couldn't understand. Dr. Houghton said he would talk to Dr. Prowse, the local geriatric psychiatrist who had apparently examined my mother for her cognitive condition on June 22, about the situation.

The next morning, Dr. Prowse called me and told me what I already knew, that there was no way that my mother knew what she was signing and that she was too cognitively impaired to make any decisions about her legal or financial situation. He was very comforting and he gave me two pieces of advice.

1) Get a lawyer

2) Keep that woman (the lawyer) away from your mother.

The first one was eminently doable. The second proved to be impossible.

I sent an email to the lawyer about the doctors' assessments of my mother's cognitive impairment. She emailed back that only a lawyer could make a decision as to the competency of a person to sign such documents. I knew that her doctors had already made an assessment of my mother's mental condition. It was clear she had no idea what she was signing.

After the June 23 phone call I had no further response from the lawyer until the following July 7 email:

"Your Mum was, and still is, very angry that you took money from her accounts and charged her visa card. She says you had no right to do that and she had not authorized you to do so."

My mother never said anything of the sort. As her legitimate POA, I had the right and the obligation to protect her and her estate which included paying her bills. I used her VISA card to pay her house insurance which, because the house was now vacant, was just over two thousand dollars.

"She is also very angry that you took money from her wallet, her jewelry and pearls from the house."

As far as I know my mother never had any pearls and the jewelry was costume. Its only value was in memories. The money from her wallet went to pay for her dog's airline ticket. In any event my mother would not have known any of this unless somebody told her.

"She has told me repeatedly over the past few weeks that she does not want you to come to Victoria again and does not want you staying in her home. Last night she gave me the following instructions to pass on to you:

Please do not come to Victoria. You are not to stay in the house or use the car. You are to return all her jewelry, in particular the rings that your father gave her when he was alive."

I should have gone immediately to Victoria, but I didn't. At the time I was still reeling; stung by her words; confused by this sudden turn of events; not sure how best to proceed. Above all I didn't want to make things any worse.

But, over the next few months, I realized that these instructions had not come from my mother. The lawyer was making a paper trail, creating a scenario to suit her own purpose, weaving a web of lies into a perfect blanket of mendacity to cover her own actions and the neighbor's. The email was sent to me, but it was not intended *for* me. It was something she used later to shore up her claim to become my mother's guardian. As a lawyer she would have known that as POA I was entitled to be reimbursed for the expenses incurred on my mother's behalf, mostly plane fare and to pay the house insurance and dog's expenses. My mother's engagement ring, purchased just before my father died, had never been worn. It had been resting safely in my bank deposit box for two years when all this began. I told her I was taking her wedding ring in May for safe keeping since neither ring was insured and there was no one living in the house. By then, I knew that the neighbor and the lawyer had been in and out of her house. I didn't think, as her POA, that it was prudent for Mum to have them at RJH or St. Mary's in case they went missing as her two watches did. Theft is a common complaint from residents in assisted living facilities, nursing homes or hospitals.

"Despite laws mandating protections for residents' personal property, theft and loss continues to be one of the most prevalent (and unreported) problems in California nursing homes. Problems such as missing clothing, rings pulled off residents' fingers, stolen radios, lost dentures, eyeglasses and hearing aids are still too common. Such losses not only undermine the psychological well-being of residents, but in some cases, such as lost dentures, also jeopardize a resident's life.

So few official complaints of theft and loss are filed in relation to the number of actual incidents that it appears theft & loss is an "accepted" consequence of one's stay in a nursing home."[62]

The lawyer continued to maintain throughout the coming years that my mother had the capacity to change her POA, even though her doctors – all of them - and I, knew that was not possible. What the lawyer did not know was that doctors at RJH had first assessed my mother on April 16th when they gave her the MMSE. Her score was 14/30. This meant she was

extremely cognitively impaired. Dr. Houghton had made his determination about my mother's mental state on May 27. Dr. Prowse had administered the Montreal Cognitive Assessment Test (MOCA) on June 22nd. All
came to the same conclusion.

The lawyer did not know what the results of any of these testings
were. She probably thought that she could argue that my mother was
not cognitively impaired when the new POA was signed, even if she
became impaired shortly thereafter. She could not have known that
it was already in her hospital records that she had been found to be
severely impaired at least since April 16th – two and a half months
earlier.

Still, she stuck to the argument that my mother was of sound mind.
Alzheimer's does not generally happen overnight. It is a gradual deterioration for most of its victims. In my mother's case she had a series of ischemic strokes - a blockage in the blood flow to and from the brain, often
caused by atrial fibrillation and more common in women - throughout
the spring of 2010, according to the hospital notes, which exacerbated
her already impaired cognition very quickly. In either case, it is not a
circumstance known to improve with time and had happened months
before she supposedly decided to change her POA.

There are several different tests for cognitive impairment. The MMSE
and the MoCA are two that they used on my mother. When her cognitive abilities were first tested when she was in RJH, my mother's score
was 14/30. A low normal score is 24/30.[63]

Later, when Dr. Prowse administered the MoCA on June 22nd and August
10[th,] my mother achieved a score of 10 out of 30. Any score 26 or above is
considered normal. A score of 10-20 means moderate impairment. Ten
or less means severe in impairment. So there is no doubt that she did

not have the capacity to make any decisions about herself or sign any documents.

In his report on August 16th Dr. Prowse made some notes on my mother's family history. She told him that her father was a metal worker and her mother was a house wife. Neither was true. Her mother owned a restaurant and her father was a civil servant. She told him her parents lived into their mid-sixties. They were 88 and 93 when they died. She did not remember when she and my father came to Canada but suggested sometime in the 40s or 50s. It was 1957. She told the Doctor she was a retired sales clerk, when actually she owned her own business. She also told him that my father was a used car salesman. Actually he managed a nightclub and worked for Cadbury's. The neighbor's husband is a used car salesman.

In any event it would have been prudent to check with me since I know my family history and my mother's medical history and could have attested to the inaccuracy of her answers. But again no one considered it relevant to talk to me. I had been conveniently placed out of the picture.

Dr. Prowse finished his report by saying "In my opinion she does not have the cognitive capacity to manage her own financial affairs or self-care." In his affidavit, Dr. Houghton also noted that in his opinion she was not competent to manage her personal and legal affairs and that her cognitive decline would not improve over time.

That should have been the end of it. But it wasn't. Truth and doctors' opinions notwithstanding, their plan was under way.

What I did not know until three years later was that there had been a whole lot more testing and a certain amount of finagling of her test scores.

In early 2013, on the advice of my lawyer, I retained the services of a well-respected geriatric psychiatrist, Dr. Sandi Culo, to make sense of all this testing and to testify to the true state of my mother's cognition. As an expert witness before the court she was supposed to be non-biased in her determination of what actually happened to my mother and what it meant.

'Mrs. Walker's cognitive testing was indicative of significant disorientation to time, short and long-term memory deficits, erroneous calculations, poor working memory, language abnormalities, visuospatial deficits, difficulty comprehending and following instructions, and poor planning and ability to abstract. Her test scores and day-to-day function suggest she had **moderate to severe dementia** (emphasis as per the report).

The possibility exists that there was some "coaching" or "practice" in preparation for the testing. Copies of these tests are readily available on the Internet. Another concern with the testing is that the Mrs. Walker's scores do not correlate well. It is difficult to understand how the Mrs. Walker could score relatively well on one test (the MMSE) and yet perform so poorly on a similar test done on the same day (3MS)."

In other words my mother was being coached to appear to do better in the cognitive tests when in fact she was getting significantly worse over time.

"The contents of Dr. Jenkins report (another doctor who assessed my mother) strongly imply that Mrs. Walker exhibited grossly impaired recall of her own life events (remote and recent); was very vague with respect to allegations regarding her daughter; had grossly impaired judgment and insight; and lacked appreciation for her current circumstances." [64]

On August 27th Dr. Houghton conducted a follow up MMSE and my mother scored 22/30. Dr. Houghton said "based on my examination and findings and due to the patient's advancing age and cognitive decline, the Patient is not mentally competent to handle both her legal and personal affairs." When my lawyer showed up at Dr. Houghton's office on September 10th to have him sign his affidavit supporting my committeeship application attesting to my mother's cognitive state of decline, the lawyer had been there moments before exhorting him not to sign it.

So in a period of seven months, my mother was tested on eleven different occasions. In normal circumstances, a doctor will not test a patient with dementia more than once every six months because there is an increased potential for "learning" the test which would naturally affect the scores and make them seem to be getting better. It would appear that either the lawyer of the neighbor spent a lot of time and effort in coaching her and practice testing her to make this happen. They also went so far as to lie to the court in their affidavits, saying in effect that her mental state was constantly improving and that therefore she should be allowed to go home.

In her Affidavit of January 6th 2011, the neighbor says of my mother, "though the other patients in St. Mary's need total care, Joyce is fully mobile (not true, she was considered a high fall risk and needed a walker to get around) and able to take care of all of her personal hygiene (my mother could not bathe herself), is able to dress herself and puts on matching clothes and make-up. She enjoys going out for coffee."

In her affidavit of October 2010, the lawyer says that in May 2010 "Joyce was continuously becoming less confused and more lucid every day and she no longer needed hospital care". At the same time Dr. Demott, the doctor who saw her most frequently at RJH, says in his notes of May 14th that he discussed her cognition care needs, based on her MMSE score, with us and that my mother was "still confused, the problem has not resolved. Can't send her home." So while the lawyer and the neighbor insisted she was getting better, all the doctors were saying the opposite.

It seemed the women would do anything to make it appear that she was cognitively sound. They needed that to be true so they could say she had the capacity to change her will and wanted them to be her guardians.

Chapter Ten

UNDUE INFLUENCE

"When it comes to controlling human beings, there is no better instrument than lies." – Michael Ende

While I was busy trying to uncover the truth of what was going on so I could save my mother from the clutches of these women, they were churning out endless streams of lies and falsehoods, contradicting themselves and each other.

They lied about everything to everybody - me, my mother, hospital staff, nursing home staff, government officials, other lawyers, and the courts. It got to the point where I assumed that whatever they said was a total fabrication. Unfortunately, it took three years for anyone else to get on board with that idea.

Initially, I was copious emails from the lawyer attesting to Mum's worsening condition. She insisted my mother didn't have much time left. I knew differently however because I was in touch with the staff at RJH several times a day at this point. Physically at least she was improving a little.

In April of 2010 I got the following email from the lawyer.

Hello Glynnis

I went to the hospital on my way home from work last night. Your Mom was out of bed wandering around. She was very confused and disorientated and wanted me to take her home in my car. She kept asking me to call her Dad....

During this time I went weeks without an email from the neighbor. Then I got this:

"*Yes, your Mom is gradually declining mentally and physically. I visit almost every day, bring her clean socks, magazines and treats. She has a couple friends from the grocery store that have visited.(Debbie Mills)*

Today Allegra (the neighbor's granddaughter) got her hair highlighted and trimmed and we went shopping!! She loves driving our sports car and has some friends here at the university, so it's probably party time tonite (sic). Now I have to worry all over again. I thought I was through with that.

Have a happy Easter and I'll keep you posted."

It was, to say the least, a bizarre email. Like most people with anti-social personality disorder, the neighbor cannot feel real feelings, like remorse or love, so she goes from telling me in one paragraph that my mother is basically dying to telling me that her granddaughter is having highlights put in her hair, as though the two pieces of information are on the same emotional plane. Then even more incongruously, she wishes me a Happy Easter!

But within a couple of months both of them abruptly changed their tune about my mother's condition.

By the beginning of July they were both insisting that my mother should be allowed to return to her own home. The lawyer, who had said previously that I would be shocked at the cost of long term home care, was investigating long term caregivers! This was a ridiculous suggestion since my mother did not have that can kind of money. Twenty-four hours of care in a person's own home can cost between $75,000 and $90,000 a year!

As usual the lies they made up were not for my consumption only. They were uttered to create a parallel truth. Soon they would share them with the court in their multiple affidavits for the guardianship hearing.

In her affidavit of October 2010, the lawyer said that in May "Joyce was continuously becoming less confused and more lucid every day and she no longer needed hospital care". A month previously she had said my mother was confused, disoriented and delusional. Despite this changed in tune, doctors, hospital staff, and my daughters and I all knew that she was getting worse. That's why the staff recommended she go into care.

What boggles my mind to this day is that their lies were accepted so easily as the truth while my truths were dismissed as lies. And too, they had already committed defamation, elder abuse, fraud and were presently pursing undue influence. What was one more crime? In for a penny, in for a pound.

My mother had always wanted to go home. But, according to all the doctors who saw her, she never understood the extent of her incapacities both physical and mental. The simple truth was it would have been dangerous for her to go home with or without a live-in caregiver. Her stay at St. Mary's cost less than $1500 a month and she was under the watchful eye of professional caregivers and medical personnel. In the past, she had already had some serious falls and the potential for her wandering, as Alzheimer's patients do, was very real. St. Mary's was by far and away the safest place for her to be, especially as all the doctors agreed that her condition was degenerative.

But the women wanted my mother back in her own house, not because it would be in her best interests, i.e. she would be happier, but because it would serve their best interests. It meant they could they could exert complete control over her condition, both mental and physical. By removing her from St. Mary's, poisoning her relationship with me, and isolating her from her family, they would effectively remove her from the rest of the world. Then they would be free to exert undue influence over her, far from the prying eyes of family or from the staff at St. Mary's. This would reap them the reward they sought. Her estate.

Undue influence is a term which refers to pressures from others which ultimately negate the free will of the victim. Undue influence may take the form of isolating the victim, promoting dependency, or inducing fear and distrust of others, namely her granddaughters and I, as well as her doctors.[65]

Researchers have found that older persons who are most likely to be financially exploited by care-givers and trusted others through undue influence share one or more of the following characteristics. These include:

- Being physically or mentally disabled and therefore dependent on others for such things a bill paying, transportation and shopping.

- Living alone

- Having few friends or family nearby

- Being depressed

- Losing a loved one on whom they depended

- Being naturally naïve, trusting and open with strangers

- Lacking knowledge about their own finances or experience in handling them.[66]

My mother was a textbook example of an elderly victim waiting to be unduly influenced. She had Alzheimer's, lived alone, had no family nearby by, and no close friends. I knew that the women had psychologically and emotionally abused my mother my telling her lies about her granddaughters and I. It was not until May of 2013 when I finally got the St. Mary's notes that I realized that the neighbor had also stooped to physical abuse. According to the notes in November of 2010, after going out with the neighbor, my mother returned to the facility with a severely injured wrist. For a week the hospital did nothing. Finally, when she was in so much pain that she could not raise her hand to take her medication, they put her in a splint. When they asked her who did this to her she answered, "Joan did this." No incident report was filed.

My mother was no stranger to undue influence. She had spent a lifetime being unduly influenced by first her mother and then my father.

Although, as a young girl, she was very bright in school and wanted to continue on with her education, my grandmother took her out of school so she could work in the restaurant she owned. She lived completely under her mother's thumb. On her wedding day, my mother had to ask my grandmother for a couple of hours off so she and my father could go to the registry office and get married. Then she went back to work. She was used to being controlled. She was not used to making up her own mind.

My father, who was a selfish and controlling man, took over from there. She was never allowed to make a decision of any sort, not even about what she wore or ate. If he did not like what she was wearing, he would tell her to go and change. His parting remark before they went out was always, "Don't forget, you represent me."

When it came to eating, they only ate the food that he liked, a circumstance that led eventually to her escalating frailty since he basically ate only salads and she needed to eat meat to get the necessary B12.

He also always made sure we lived in remote houses, without neighbors. As a result she never learned how to develop any support systems. She was not allowed to learn to drive until she was well into her sixties, after I encouraged her to. He would tell her frequently, in front of me, how stupid and worthless she was. After years of hearing that, she naturally believed it to be true. She was the perfect victim - naïve, easily manipulated and used to doing as she was told.

The two women were the perfect perpetrators. One had an established relationship, though not a close one, as my mother's neighbor. The other was a lawyer who specialized in elder law and knew how to work the system. Both of them were manipulative and cruel. They did not view my mother as a person, despite their frequent protestations to the opposite, merely as an opportunity for gain.

Getting my mother back into her house would require certain maneuvers. First they had to get me out of the way and second they had to have some legal control over her life. So while the neighbor worked on the undue influence side of the situation, the lawyer began her legal machinations by submitting a joint application for the two of them to become co-guardians of my mother – something that would trump my arguably still valid Power of Attorney. So they countered the application I had already made for guardianship.

There was another long care meeting on July 28[th 2010] which I had planned on attending. I wanted to make sure my mother stayed put at St. Mary's because, by then, I had a pretty good idea what they were up to. I discussed my presence at the meeting with my lawyer and his advice was that I should probably not go to the meeting since by then my mother's residency in St. Mary's was obviously for the long term, so what would be the point. He also wrote a letter to the lawyer requesting that she not attend the meeting either, since she had no right to be there.

"We confirm that our client will not be attending the long term care conference at St. Mary's on July 28th. Since your Power of Attorney is in question, we request that your refrain from attending this meeting also."

Like a lot of the advice that this lawyer gave me, it was bad. I didn't go to the meeting. She did. This solidified her presence as my mother's representative, at least in the eyes of St. Mary's staff, and made it all but impossible for me to go there and be allowed to see her in the future.

While she was busy ingratiating herself with the staff at St. Mary's and pretending to legally represent my mother, the neighbor was making sure she upgraded her influence over my Mum by getting her to write a note to me. This would serve a two-fold purpose. It would widen the rift between us because she was reinforcing the lies they had already told her. And, by coercing Mum to put these lies down on paper they then became, in her confused state of mind, the truth. Also, she wanted to see just how much control she could exert over my mother, so she dictated a "Thank you" note just to see how malleable my mother was to her suggestions when it came to writing things down. This would come in handy later when she was getting her to sign checks and later a new will.

There were actually two notes. One was on a page from a kitchen tablet. It had blue flowers on it and, I later found out, belonged to the neighbor.

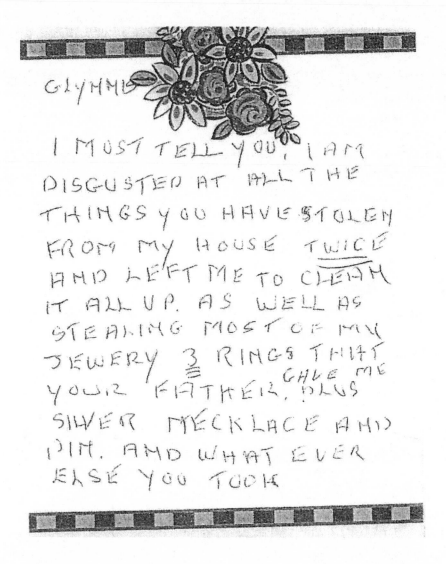

GlYNN∫

I MUST TELL YOU, I AM
DISGUSTED AT ALL THE
THINGS YOU HAVE STOLEN
FROM MY HOUSE TWICE
AND LEFT ME TO CLEAN
IT ALL UP. AS WELL AS
STEALING MOST OF MY
JEWERY 3 RINGS THAT
YOUR FATHER, GAVE ME
PLUS
SILVER NECKLACE AND
PIN. AND WHAT EVER
ELSE YOU TOOK

The other was an actual Thank You card I received. Obviously, my mother was coached because she had to write the note twice. Later they used the same technique when getting her to change her will.

The note I received on July 6th 2010 is written in two different colors of ink, but in my mother's shaky printing. But, all I had to do was read it to know the words were not hers. I have never known my mother to write a thank you note to anyone. It is just not her style. The handwriting is printing and it is wobbly and uneven, not that sort of writing that is done with a purposeful state of mind. I knew, without a doubt, that the neighbor had dictated it and my mother had done, as always, what she was told.

GLYNNIS
THE FLOWERS WERE VERY
NICE. BUT I WOULD HAVE
LIKED MY RINGS BACK
THAT YOU TOOK, DADDY
GAVE ME THOSE, AND YOU
HAD NO RIGHT TO THEM,
OR ANYTHING ELSE IN THE
HOUSE. EMILY RETURN THEM
TO ME   MOTHER

ALSO MY SILVER JEWELRY
I DONT KNOW HOW I CAN
PAY YOUR VISA BILL
MY HOUSE LOOK LIKE A PIG
STY.

Being a communicator by trade I am sensitive to how people use words and what words they use to express themselves. After decades of communicating with my mother, both in person and in writing, I knew what she "sounded" like. That's why I knew she had not written the note of her own volition and that the contents did not represent any facts known to either of us.

To begin with my Mother, as always, spells my name with only one "N" in Glynis. I prefer to use Glynnis with two "n's. The two women only know my name with two "n" s. So I can just envision the neighbor standing over my mother dictating the note and spelling my name as she knew it.

Also, and more telling, is that my mother did not know my address off by heart since I have moved so many times over the years. She always had to look it up in her address book whenever she wanted to send a card or letter to wherever we were. I had had her address book in my possession since May of 2010, weeks before the July note was written. But, the lawyer knew my address because we have communicated by letter over the years on legal matters.

There is no return address on the July note which is not like my mother. She always puts a return address on her mail to me, usually one of the little stickers you get from charities who want donations to their cause.

In the note my mother also referred to my taking her "silver jewelry". My mother had a silver necklace and matching earrings that my Dad gave her when I was about ten and which I had last seen on her dresser in June of 2010. It was still there when I went into the house in June 2013. In the lawyer's email she refers to the pearls. I had neither, but obviously they didn't compare stories before getting into the letter writing business. They just wanted my mother to think I was stealing from her.

Also in the note she writes "I don't know how I can pay your VISA bill". The VISA bill, as previously discussed, was the $2012 for the vacancy insurance on her house which I paid with her VISA card on June 19th, 2010. This is obviously not "my VISA bill" and for to her think so means someone had to tell her that.

The last sentence is very interesting. "My house look (sic) like a pig sty." My mother was a very tidy housekeeper and when we left it on June 20th the house was pristine as always. We did not even eat there while we were in Victoria so we would not make a mess and we made the beds before we left. We even washed the two mugs we used for tea and put them away. However while we were there in June 2010 we bought a set of green glasses at Walmart since she only had a couple of plastic tumblers. In the neighbor's affidavit she mentions that when she visited the house with my mother there was broken green glass all over the floor. Somebody had to break those glasses and make the house into a "pig sty" and it wasn't us. Therefore they must have taken her there to see what we had supposedly done. Three years later when I took possession of the house half the green glasses were missing from the cupboard.

When I read the note I knew that my mother had been a victim of undue influence. They were basically controlling her with their lies and her poor weak mind, trained by decades of control by first her mother and then my father, absorbed and obeyed.

And, the note had a twofold purpose. Not only did it solidify the things they had told her so that she now believed they were true, it was also a way to hurt me and keep me at bay. But it didn't work. It just confirmed to me that my mother was a victim of undue influence and made me more determined than ever to fight for her.

Without my knowing it, Arabella wrote to the lawyer at the end of July. She knew how upset I was and she was worried about her Nan.

"I'm Rosalind's granddaughter, Arabella. We have met before. I am really distraught and confused about what is going on with my grandmother and her needs and care. I haven't been able to talk to my grandmother either even though I call her. Is there anything I can do to be reconnected with her and to try and solve

this messy situation? Again, I'm still confused about what is happening, and all I want is for my only grandmother to be fine and taken care of, as well as being apart (sic) of her life."

The return email was quite shocking, considering that the lawyer was a professional adult who was supposedly keen on "protecting" my mother's interests. She comes across more like a cruel and vindictive woman – showing her true colors.

"I have sent emails and a letter to your mother and she has not, to date, responded. I have instructions from your grandmother not to divulge any information about her to your mother, and I presume that also extends to you. (Why would she presume that?)

Given that your mother has retained a lawyer in Victoria I suggest you discuss this matter with her. (My lawyer was man.) *I can tell you, and please pass this on to your mother, that if there is any hope of reconciliation with your grandmother her jewellery (sic) must be returned ASAP.*

The note and the email had the opposite effect to what the women had intended. Instead of driving a further wedge between my mother and me, it provided further proof to me that they had created a situation of undue influence over my mother by lying to her. It was also proof to me that they did not have her best interests at heart at all. Who would deliberately separate a loving grandmother from a seventeen year old grandchild whom she had always loved dearly? They were being deliberately cruel; using the influence they had gained over her to their own advantage. I knew for certain now that mum was in danger; that their pretense of caring from an elderly lady who was supposedly the victim of abuse was just that – a pretense. I knew that I had to do everything I could to try and save her from them.

Chapter Eleven

WHERE THERE'S A WILL, THERE'S A WAY?

"We have to do whatever we can to get rid of Glynnis"
the neighbor to the lawyer, 2010

When I was made aware of the above comment two plus years later, a chill ran through me. I was glad that the once inconvenient international border that had divided my mother from the rest of our family was there, because I was by now under no illusions as to what these women were capable. I was, literally, afraid of them.

My persistence was obviously ruining the cake walk that they had planned on for stealing my mother and then her estate. I was supposed to have folded my tent and gone home by now. They had made sure that my mother hated me and that I knew she hated me. They had made it impossible for any of us to contact her or find out how she was, they had defamed me as a daughter, made Arabella cry with their cruel email, cost me a lot of money in legal fees, and basically rendered my family asunder. Still, I was unrelenting.

I wrote to the attorney general. I called the premier of British Columbia. I wrote to the Law Society and made a formal complaint about the lawyer. Every now and again I called or emailed the Public Guardian, though to no avail. I called the Victoria Police Department. I contacted every elder abuse group on the Island. I wrote to Herb Kohl, senior senator from Wisconsin and head of the senate committee on aging. I wrote to Dick Durbin, the senior senator from Illinois, who I had interviewed on my radio show. The only ones I heard back from were Durbin and Kohl who sympathized but said they could do nothing since it was a Canadian matter.

Still, I was not about to stop fighting to protect my mother, even if it was impossible to repair our relationship. I felt it was my duty, a duty that no one else would perform.

While I was trying everything I could think of to get some kind of leverage in the situation and get these women out of our lives, they were making sure that all that undue influence they had been practicing on my mother did not go to waste.

In the long hours at night when I could not sleep, I pondered their actions. What was their ultimate goal? Where was this all heading? Although they had convinced everybody else that they were motivated by concern for an old woman whose family had abandoned her (so untrue, since I spent most of my time trying to thwart them and save her from them), I knew instinctively that they had another motive entirely. Money! But there was also the niggling feeling that it was about more than just that. They wanted her money to be sure, but more importantly, they wanted her granddaughters and me not to have her money or her house. That's why they wasted away her banks accounts, around $20,000, and ran up bills on her credit card, until there was only $50.00 left in the bank and $3000 outstanding on the Sears card. That's when I realized that my poor mother was just a pawn in their game. The real targets were my daughters and I. But, how could they go about making sure that they completely disinherited us? There was only one way. They would have to change her will.

In 2006, when my father died, I thought that my mother should have a will because it would make things much simpler later on. I had no idea how complicated the situation was going to become, but having her make a will while still in her right mind, turned out to be an excellent idea and I highly recommend it.

A will is a legal declaration that is signed by a person to indicate his or her wishes about the distribution of their property upon their death. It can also dictate how the person wishes to be treated after death. My mother wanted to be cremated and that "a simple and dignified memorial service be held for me." I was only able to fulfill the first half of her request because by the time she died, she only had $50.00 left in her bank account and all my savings had gone to support legal actions against those who had reduced her to penury. `

In order to sign a will, a person must be over eighteen and be of sound mind or have "testamentary capacity" (see below). A will also appoints an executor to handle the distribution of the assets mentioned in the will. To be legal, a will must also be witnessed by two impartial people – i.e. people who do not benefit from the will.

> *"Forgery - The making of a false document knowing it to be false with intent that it should be used or acted on as genuine to the prejudice of another."*[67]

My mother signed three wills in her lifetime. One in October, 2006, before she got Alzheimer's, and two in September 2010, after she had been declared cognitively impaired – a multitude of times. The first of these wills was executed in Jackie Horton's office following all legal requirements. The other two were written in the neighbor's house, the first in her own handwriting. The first of the September wills was written on the same blue flowered kitchen notepaper that she had used to rehearse my mother to write the Thank You note back in the beginning of July. The September 15th will was typed. My mother never learned how to type.

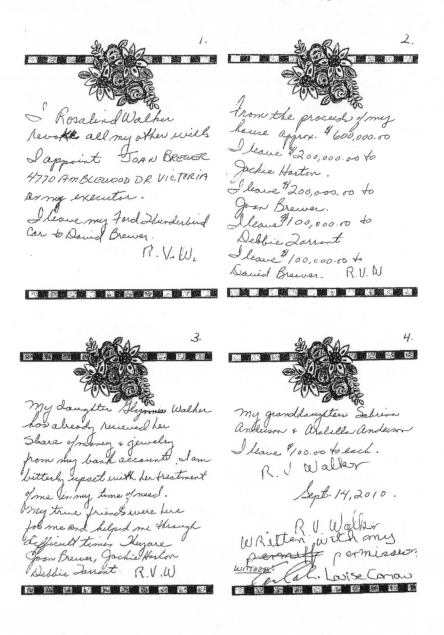

Rosalind Violet Walker, Victoria, B.C.

My Last will and testament

I Revoke all my other wills.

I appoint Joan Louise Brewer, Victoria,B.C. as my executor.

I appoint Jacqueline Horton as my alternate executor.

To my daughter Glynnis Joyce Walker, you have already received your share of money and jewelry taken from my bank account and house. I am bitterly upset with your treatment of me in my time of need.

My true friends were here for me and helped me through difficult times and I bequest to them:

Jacqueline Horton, Victoria,B.C. $ 200,000.00

Joan Brewer, Victoria,B.C. $200,000.00

Debbie Tarrant, Victoria, B.C. $100,000.00

David Brewer, Victoria, B.C. $100,000.00

Sabrina and Arabella Anderson, Chicago,Il. $100.00 each, for reasons they know.

R. V. Walker

Rosalind Walker

September 15, 2010

K.T. MacLean.

Victoria B.C

Margot J. Moore - Victoria

The wording in the second September will is more legal sounding than in the hand written will. It is likely that she showed the handwritten will to the lawyer and was told that the handwritten would simply not fly, so she amped it up a bit with some legalese, probably gleaned from the lawyer, and typed it to make it more official looking.

It is interesting to note that in these wills it specifically says that the monies to be shared out shall be taken from "the sale of my house". The sum mentioned for this sale is $600,000. The house was then worth about $750,000. Though the neighbor would have had an idea on the value of the house since she lived next door but what made my mother's house worth more than hers was that it was larger and on a double lot. But the neighbor, though greedy and cruel, was not terribly bright, so she just ball-parked the sum and came up with a nice round number - $600,000 - making sure that each of the beneficiaries, including her husband and the supermarket checker were taken care of.

Then there is the matter of the contents of the house, the classic Thunderbird, and the money in the Guernsey account that I had frozen were not mentioned in either one of the bogus wills, which it decidedly odd. Why not divide up the whole ball of wax? Why just the house?

In the Sept. 14 will, written in the neighbor's handwriting, my mother's Ford Thunderbird is left to her husband, who just happens to be a used car salesman in Alberta. By the time she typed up the Sept. 15th will, all mention of the car is gone. Someone (the lawyer?) must have pointed out that it must have seemed just too much detail to include the car. Or perhaps she felt it might have seemed that her greed was showing.

The only thing my mother knew about her car at this point was that it was white, not what model it was. I remember when we visited her at RJH in May of 2010; you could see the hospital's back parking lot from her window. She always asked me to point out her car. I knew she loved her car and the freedom it had given her over the years, so I would point out a white car for her. Any white car would do. I did not tell her that we always parked in the front of the hospital in the visitor's parking and that the parking lot she could see was for staff. It made her happy to see "her" car.

And too, my mother rarely saw the neighbor's husband – in June she had not remembered who Arabella and I were – so it is highly unlikely that she would think to put him in her will or even know who he was several months later when her cognitive impairment had declined even further. He spent his weeks in Edmonton and his weekends on the golf course. Yet, in both wills she supposedly decided to leave him $100,000 while she leaves her formerly beloved grandchildren $100 each! It boggles the mind.

In the wills she wrote, the neighbor implies my mother's grandchildren were out of favor. Indeed she told my mother's neighbors that both of her granddaughters had had abortions and that my mother had been forced to pay for them. Neither statement was true. Both girls got $100 "for reasons they know". I suppose that she could not legitimately come up with a reason for leaving the grandchildren out of my mother's will since she knew very little about our family, so she made this obtuse comment.

My current lawyer believes that the lesser bequests were put in to make the wills seem more legitimate. She couldn't just make herself the sole beneficiary. It would look too suspicious. But she also had to make sure she got the largest share of the pie. (At one point in 2012 she made me an offer that she would not try and probate her bogus will if I would agree to give her alone $300,000. Needless to say it was an offer I refused.)

The September 15 will appoints her as my mother's executor and the lawyer as her alternate executor. These are not terms my mother would have been familiar with even in her right mind, never mind after she became cognitively impaired. The lawyer still insists that she knew nothing about this will. I find that hard to accept if for no other reason that I cannot believe the greedy neighbor would willingly hand over $200,000 – albeit of someone else's money – to anyone, even her partner in crime, without that partner knowing about it. She could have just taken it all or given more to her husband and the checker.

Under section 366 of The Canadian Criminal Code, *"Making a false document includes (a) altering a genuine document in any material part; (b) making a material addition to a genuine document or adding to it a false date, attestation, seal or other thing that is material; or (c) making a material alteration in a genuine document by erasure, obliteration, removal or in any other way. (3) Forgery is complete as soon as a document is made... (4) Forgery is complete notwithstandin it should be used or acted on as genuine to the preju g that the false document is incomplete.*

I believe that both women are guilty of brazenly making false documents. The lawyer created the POA and Representation Agreement she had my cognitively impaired mother sign in June of 2010. The neighbor created the two September wills.

Legally speaking the most recent will generally prevails. If the person wants to make changes to a previous will, but still keep it intact, they can add a codicil, detailing the additional information. A handwritten will is also acceptable.

That being said, my mother, in her impaired state of mind, would have had no idea what making a will entailed or what she was signing. On the other hand, in her right mind, she would certainly have been aghast at doling out huge sums of money she didn't know she had to people she barely knew.

In my entire adult life she had never offered me a penny, and I had never asked. Except for my first year of undergraduate school, which my parents paid for, I paid for my own education, working two jobs and taking classes at the same time. Gifts to her grandchildren were restricted to $100 at Christmas and birthdays. Period. It wasn't that she didn't love them. It was just that she had grown up in the Depression and World War Two, when government rationing meant one egg a week and a small quantity of sugar and tea. I remember once, after the War, when England still had rationing, my father's mother had asked to borrow a small quantity of tea until the new ration coupons arrive. My mother told her in no uncertain terms that she would not give it to her – and she liked my grandmother very much. It was just that generosity was not part of my mother's life experience. So this gifting of hundreds of thousands of dollars to people she barely knew was totally against her normal behavior.

The three wills my mother executed were the most common type of will - an attested will. That means that it is a document that is witnessed. The general legal requirements for an attested will are that it must be in writing, signed by the person whose will it is, and must be witnessed by two witnesses in the presence of the testator.

Even though at the bottom of the Sept. 14th will my mother has tried to write shakily "written with my permission" twice, she spelled "permission" with two ff's and had to rewrite it. One of the witnesses' signatures is illegible and the other was a woman who has never come forward to comment on the circumstances surrounding the signing of this will. These are not the same people who witnessed the Sept. 15th will. The neighbor must have thought it unwise to get the same people to witness two different wills on two consecutive days. It might look a little fishy.

The other general requirements for a will to be legally valid are that the person preparing the will must have testamentary capacity and testamentary intent.

Testamentary capacity means that the person whose will it is must understand that the document they are creating is a will. They must only have this testamentary capacity at the time the will is actually created, so if someone is heavily medicated or mentally disabled, but created their will in a period of lucidity, they may be found to have had testamentary capacity even though they may have lacked such capacity on a general day-to-day basis. My mother did not have testamentary capacity. She had not been lucid for months according to the hospital notes. Not only was she severely cognitively impaired, but she had been on daily doses of Seroquel since April 2010. The neighbor actually complained about the fact that whenever she took her out of St. Mary's, my mother slept almost the entire time. She asked them to stop giving her the drug and after that they would give her the pills to take with her. It is noted in the hospital records that some days my mother was not receiving her medication.

Then there is the fact that the date of the supposed signing of the September 14th will, my mother was at St. Mary's being served by the court with papers detailing my guardianship application. The lawyer was there. My mother became extremely agitated and upset, so the chances of her having the capacity to sign a will on that day in particular are extremely remote, if not impossible. Later, out of the eyes of St. Mary's staff, she would have signed whatever the neighbor put in front of her, including the two notes, lots of checks and the two wills.

The circumstances of the signing of the second will are extremely unclear since the witnesses, friends of the neighbor's, refused to talk to my lawyer because they "didn't want to get Joan into trouble".

There are four specific requirements regarding what constitutes testamentary capacity:

- The person must understand that they are making a document detailing what should happen to their property when they die. As the social worker at RJH had told my lawyer back in the summer of 2011, when he remembered her from her stay at RJH in spring 2010, "anyone could have gotten her to sign anything".

Besides, my mother did not make the document. The neighbor did, and it was she who determined the contents of both wills. It is interesting that my mother knew the checker by a different last name – the one she used at work - and that is how she introduced her to Arabella and me on one of our visits to the grocery store. And yet, in both the wills that the neighbor wrote, the checker is referred to by the last name of Torrance.

- The person making the will must have an understanding of what property they own and are including in the will. In the 2010 wills, the bank accounts, which still had money in them at that point, and the contents of her house are not included, only the house. She had no idea of the value of her real property – she thought the house was worth $100,000 - or even what it was, as Dr. Prowse's report proved.

- They must be able to understand that their heirs would generally be their spouse, their children, etc. While they do not necessarily have to leave these potential heirs any property in the will, they must understand that these people *would* have been potential heirs but for the fact that they are being excluded from the will. In British Columbia there is something called the Wills Variation Act. "It provides that where, in the court's opinion, a will does not make adequate provision for the proper maintenance and support of the Deceased's spouse or children, then the court has discretion to vary the will to make the provision that it believes to be adequate just and equitable in the circumstances."[68]

- Even though my mother had been trained to hate me, she did not have any reason to hate her grandchildren. It is difficult to imagine the neighbor's husband and the checker from the local supermarket superseding her beloved grandchildren in a will that my mother had created of her own free will.

- Lastly, the testator must be able to keep all of this information and understanding in their mind long enough to make a reasoned decision regarding how they want their property to be distributed. Obviously my mother did not have the capacity make a "reasoned" decision. If she had been able to keep anything in her mind for any length of time she would have remembered signing a will on September 14th and another slightly different will on September 15th. The fact that she did not question signing two wills a day apart indicates a lack of testamentary capacity.

I believe that the neighbor, in consultation with the lawyer, would have known that the September wills would look a little suspicious which is why they kept them secret until after they were sure my mother was dying.

"Section 368 of the Canadian Criminal Code deals with Uttering a False Document. *(1) Every one who, knowing that a document is forged, (a) uses, deals with or acts on it, or (b) causes or attempts to cause any person to use, deal with or act on it, as if the document were genuine, (c) ... liable to imprisonment for a term not exceeding ten years; or (d) is guilty of an offence punishable on summary conviction.*"

In the summer of 2011, my lawyer at the time sent two emails regarding the three wills, one to the lawyer who handled the guardianship hearing for me and one to me.

In the first he questions why the September wills were not revealed in court. This left the judge with the impression that my valid will was the only will and that therefore the lawyer and the neighbor were not in it for the money. *"I am not coming up with an elegant reason to raise this with the Justice, who I think would be most annoyed if he new about this so much so that his order might be changed,"* my lawyer wrote.

Later in July he wrote me this email.

"I got a call from Horton late yesterday. She told me that she had the original 2006 will (my will) but no longer does so, that she had given it to someone else she would not identify for me, that it is protected...... *Horton told me that she wants nothing more to do with this, that she did not received a dime's compensation for the hundreds of hours spent looking after your Mum, nor does she want any."*

This as it turns out was a total fabrication. I believe that there is no way she could not have known about the bogus wills which left her with $200,000. It was just one more lie in an unending string of lies.

It is a requirement of Canadian law that a will be delivered either to the Court or to the Executrix – me – after the death of a person. The lawyer did neither. Why was she anxious to obfuscate the whereabouts of the legitimate will?

Under section 341 of the Canadian Criminal Code, *"Every one who, for a fraudulent purpose, takes, obtains, removes or conceals anything is guilty of an indictable offence and liable to imprisonment for a term not exceeding two years."* The lawyer concealed the whereabouts of the 2006 will and the neighbor concealed the 2010 wills from the court during the guardianship hearing. There is no question about their motives.

For some months I had suspected they had made another will. It fit the profile of their actions. But, I had no proof. It was a matter of pure luck that I found out about the September 15th will. I think their plan was to quickly probate the September 15th will without my ever knowing about it.

The last requirement for a will to be valid is that the person whose will it is must have testamentary intent. This means that they intend for the document to be their will. My mother had already seen what a real will looked like in 2006 and how it was produced, though doubtless she did not remember. But, for anyone to think that someone else's handwriting on a piece of kitchen notepaper with blue flowers on it is a real will, stretches the imagination. The two women may have been able to convince my mother, but did they really think their bogus wills would convince a judge?

Some things continue to remain a mystery to me. Four different people witnessed two different wills supposedly on two consecutive days. Where were these wills witnessed? They are supposed to be witnessed in the presence of the testator – my mother - but my guess is that that was not the case since the witnesses to the September 15 will –friends of the neighbor - would have to have been aware of my mother's deteriorated state of mind if they were with her even for a few moments. It was so obvious. These two witnesses were subpoenaed to explain the circumstances surrounding the witnessing of the will. (However when the process server came to their home, they were gone and a realtor's lock was on the door. Their condo was for sale and their household possessions were sold at a garage sale in October 2012 by non-other than the neighbor who advertised the sale in the local paper.)

I do not think for one moment that all four witnesses trooped into St. Mary's, pens in hand, to witness the wills in front of my mother and all of the staff. Likely, the neighbor had my mother sign both wills in the privacy of her house and then the wills witnessed at a later date.

Perhaps the biggest mystery of all is, if, as the lawyer claims, my mother kept insisting that she wanted to change her will, why then did they not take her to a legitimate lawyer and execute a proper legal will? It's not like they were afraid of spending her money. I believe the answer to this question is that another lawyer, outside of their little conspiracy, would have refused to create a will for a woman who was so obviously cognitively impaired for fear of losing his/her license to practice law.

Chapter Twelve

CRIMES AND CHRISTMAS

"You can taint the evidence but you can't destroy the memories."
- unknown

*F*all 2010 was a busy time for the neighbor and the lawyer. While one was busy writing wills, the other was busy writing letters to banks.

First she contacted my mother's bank in London, closed the account and transferred the funds to an account that she had opened up in the TD Trust a bank in Victoria. I know, from talking with the bank manager, that she brought my mother into the branch on a Saturday morning at the end of September. Approaching a teller whom she knew, the account was opened in my mother's name with $20.00. A few days later on October 1st approximately $5000 was wired into that account from my mother's account in London.

I don't know whether the lawyer pretended to be me in order to conduct this transaction since I had already sent them my POA years ago –in which case this would be identity theft - or whether she used her phony POA to transfer the funds and close the account. In any event, I got a letter dated September 28th from the bank saying as per <u>my</u> instructions the account had been closed. I had been POA on Mum's accounts since 2007 which was why the letter came to me. But, I did not, would not have closed that bank account, because I knew that that is the account where her British Pension went. Once it was closed, the Pension Service had nowhere to send the money to and so they stopped sending it as I found out many months later when they contacted me. The lawyer would not have known this little detail. To her it was just another pile of money free for the taking - like my mother's account at the Royal Bank in Victoria.

That accomplished, the lawyer went after the big fish - my mother's larger account in Guernsey, about $80,000.

Her letter to the bank read in part:

> *"Further to our telephone conversation today, I sent you a letter on October 6th advising that Glynnis Walker's Power of Attorney has been revoked.*
>
> *I am Mrs. Walker's solicitor and Power of Attorney since it was discovered that funds were missing from her bank account in Victoria. I have advised the Public Guardian of this matter and there may an adult guardianship hearing in the next while.*
>
> *Please let me know what steps need to be taken in order to close the Guernsey account and deposit the funds in her Canadian account.*

Everyone is usually of the opinion that lawyers, because of their occupation, must be of more than passing intelligence, but this is not always the case. I knew that the laws in Guernsey are an odd combination or French and British law. It was not possible to have the funds transferred simply by making a request. A lawyer from the island has to be hired to go to court and register a Power of Attorney before it can be used to transfer funds. These women did not do their homework. They just assumed, like the request to the bank in London, that all they had to do was ask for the funds to be transferred and it would be done.

The lawyer always insisted that she never invoked her POA, another obvious lie, since in this letter she describes herself as my mother's POA. And, technically speaking, she was not mother's solicitor either but mine. As such she owed a fiduciary responsibility to me. Representing my mother was therefore a conflict of interest. I was the one who hired her in the beginning and the one who kept in contact with her over the intervening years since my father's death. In fact, her phone number does not even appear in my mother's telephone book and neither does that of the supermarket checker. And since my mother had to write down everybody's number as her memory became faulty, how much contact could they have had?

What these women did not know was that in an effort to stay one step ahead of them, I was also writing letters. In an attempt to thwart their continued pillaging of my mother's accounts, I sent the following email to the bank in Guernsey on October 26th 2010.

"Thank you for forwarding my mother's bank statement for her money market account. I think you should be aware that even though my mother is in St. Mary's Hospital and is suffering from Alzheimer's and cannot understand or take care of her own affairs that two women copied the key to her house, went inside and found some of the old bank statements from Lloyds going back to 1986. I understand that a woman calling herself my mother's lawyer has requested the transfer of those funds to Canada. I have engaged a lawyer and made a formal complaint to the Law Society of British Columbia about her behavior. I have also previously sent records to you from my mother's doctors as proof of my mother's mental incapacitation which I hope you have received. Both of these women have gained influence over my mother by nefarious means and I am concerned about her wellbeing and her estate. I am requesting that you do not transfer any funds of my mother's to anyone. What these two women are doing is fraudulent and I am proceeding along every legal channel to stop them. This is apparently going to take some time. In the meantime please put a hold on all funds that belong to my mother.

If you have any questions about this please call or email me."

The bank obligingly froze the account, as I requested. It remained frozen for several years in spite of their efforts. Like their failure to possess my mother's two rings, this must have infuriated them no end. That $80,000 dollars would have been a delightful little extra wallop on top of the value of her house - a little something to divide between them, with perhaps a sop to the checker who ended up getting the funds that remained in the TD Trust bank account – about $2600 – in the spring of 2011 according to records provided by the bank manager.

Meanwhile, The Law Society investigated Horton's behavior and said it didn't find anything awry. Basically as I found out later, the Law Society does very little if anything to sanction lawyers. Still I was beginning to think that I was losing my mind. No matter to I whom turned, either I was offered sympathy but no support, or those I contacted for help, were of the opinion that nothing untoward was going on. Meanwhile my American lawyer, who continued to advise me, assured me that what they were doing was very, very wrong and most certainly illegal.

Christmas was horrible. The two women had put an end to our calling my mother months ago, but my daughters and I decided that with a skeleton staff at St. Mary's on Christmas Day, we might be able to get a call through.

Surprisingly, we got a nurse's aide to bring Mum to the phone. Her first words broke my heart. "Why haven't you been looking for me? "She cried!

I don't think she knew it was me. I started to cry and handed the phone to Arabella. She also tried to talk to her Nan but had no luck getting through to her. She had no clue who we were. When the call was over, I was emotionally devastated. It was the last time we ever spoke to her.

In one of her affidavits, the neighbor tells a different story about Christmas Day. Apparently when/if she saw my mother that day, I supposedly told my mother "you've won Mum, you've won." Won what?

This comment joined the jumble of lies and fictions that peppered her relentless affidavits and yet nobody questioned her veracity. This was just more of her "word salad" statements. She frequently came out with nonsensical comments and reported on details of other people's conversations at which she had not been present. It was easy to do. She just made it up. What surprised me throughout this is nobody thought to call her on her lies.

A great deal of the evidence presented at the guardianship hearing was indeed hearsay. It was just lies heaped onto top of lies, suppositions heaped on top of suppositions. They contradicted each other and themselves, and what they did not know, they made up out of whole cloth.

Hearsay evidence is something that is generally said outside of the courtroom and therefore not sworn under oath. A judge must weigh the admissibility of this as evidence if it used in a court case.

In R. v Abbey 1982 2 SCR 24, the Supreme Court of Canada justified the rule against hearsay as follows:

"The main concern of the hearsay rule is the veracity of the statements made. The principal justification for the exclusion of hearsay evidence is the abhorrence of the common law to prove that which is unsworn and has not been subjected to the trial by fire of cross-examination. Testimony under oath, and cross-examination, has been considered to be the best assurances of the truth of the statements of facts presented."

As I have said before, they wrote copious affidavits to support their claim for guardianship of my mother. An affidavit is a document sworn under oath to be true "to the best of his (or her) knowledge". Anyone who swears that the contents of an affidavit are true, knowing that any part is untrue, is guilty of perjury. Perjury, quite simply, is an intentional lie given while under oath or in a sworn affidavit. It is a very serious crime.

So, while I was busy gathering evidence and backing up my sources refuting the ever-mounting pile of fiction they were swearing to, the women were having a gay old time fabricating contents for their affidavits.

The neighbor was particularly adept at this. She swore to things in her affidavits that she had no way of proving, such as the long and enduring friendship she had with my mother – which I knew was untrue; the sexual harassment my mother was experiencing at St. Mary's – hence a good reason for her to leave the place - also untrue; the fact that my mother had no other family - untrue; the fact that we never came to see my mother – untrue, etc. None of these statements was true, but it made it into her sworn affidavits anyway and her lies were never questioned.

I gathered a small ton of photos of all of us together over the years to show how close we had always been, in despite of the geographic distance, along with a list of our family members from all over the globe, and sent them to my lawyer.

What did I have to do so that the powers that be would see the reality of what these women were trying to do?

As the end of 2010 drew near, frustrated beyond belief at the Canadian's system's lack of concern for the protection of their senior population from predators like these, and the fact that no matter what proof I offered to the contrary, their lies prevailed. I sank into a deep depression.

Chapter Thirteen

LIES AND COERCION

"If you tell a big enough lie and tell it frequently enough,
it will be believed."

*I*n order for their plan to work to get complete control of my mother, she had to say that she wanted them to be her guardians in case the judge actually thought a blood relative (i.e. me) would be a better choice. So they arranged for a new doctor, Dr. Jenkins, to assess my mother again and ask her who she wanted to take care of her.

There are six qualified geriatricians on the Island. These women did not choose any of them. Instead they stepped down the ladder and chose a gerontologist instead. "The primary difference between the two professions is that geriatricians are fully-trained physicians, and provide direct treatment for age-related disorders. Gerontologists play a more supportive and educational role, though applied gerontologists might build long-term relationships with their clients that include coordinating diet, exercise and cognitive therapies."[69]

I believe that the women chose this particular gerontologist because one of them knew her and that they chose her to make the assessment because she had a background in geriatric cancer and palliative care, not cognitive impairment. Many years ago she had written an abstract on the MMSE but, according to her CV, which still lists her Edmonton address, even though she has been living in Victoria since 2003, she has no expertise in dealing with patients with Alzheimer's. In fact, the closest she had come to dealing with anyone like my mother was when she had done a term of geriatric grand rounds at the University of Edmonton 1994 in Non-Alzheimer's degenerative dementias. She does not have a private practice, according to the Vancouver Island Health Authority, but works out of RJH. But perhaps her lack of expertise in the area of evaluating Alzheimer's patients was why they chose her to evaluate my mother. It would be easier to pull the wool over her inexperienced eyes.

Unfortunately, in spite of her lack of background in this area, the court gave considerable weight to her report on my mother's condition because the women were about to play another card, one that I would not know about for some months.

The gerontologist's report would add weight to their application for guardianship, not by showing improved tests scores, that was virtually impossible at this point, but in a different way. They would get my mother herself to tell the doctor that she would prefer them to be her decision makers and that she wanted nothing more to do with me. Then, when they became a permanent legal presence in her life, as per her request, they could move her back into the house, out of sight and under their complete control.

The gerontologist's testing was done on October 23, oddly enough the anniversary of my father's death, and revealed similar scores as the tests done back in May, June and August by the other doctors. The gerontologist's opinion was that my mother was at the "level of moderate dementia" and that "I agree with Dr. Houghton and Dr. Prowse that Mrs. Walker is not competent to direct her own care and will require guidance with both her personal and financial decisions."

However, she too was manipulated by the neighbor, who was present at the testing supposedly to divert some of the stress from my mother who had literally been made afraid of doctors at this point by her two caring friends. The neighbor's actual purpose however was to provide disinformation to the doctor and prompt my mother with answers when she did not know how to respond to the questions that were asked.

"Mrs. Walker was anxious and fearful about the interview" wrote Dr. Jenkins. "For these reasons I modified the interview cutting short some of the formal cognitive testing. I allowed her friend in for much of the interview once I had established that Mrs. Walker trusted her. This was a clinical decision to protect Mrs. Walker from additional distress." [70]

According to the Merck Manual for Health Care Professionals article, Evaluation of the Elderly Patient, "unless mental status is impaired (my mother was, but they claimed all the way to the end but she could make her own decisions about care and finances), a patient should be interviewed alone to encourage the discussion of personal matters. The clinician should ask the patient's permission before inviting a relative or caregiver to be present and should explain that such interviews are routine."[71]

The gerontologist does not indicate in her report that she asked my mother's permission. Her decision was unilateral. "If indicated, clinicians should consider the possibility of drug abuse and patient abuse by the caregiver. "[72](ibid) Obviously this was not something the doctor considered either. She violated both protocols.

Other issues arose from how this interview was conducted. Anyone familiar with elder abuse knows that an effort should be made to detect if the victim may have been coached about details. One of the classic signs of abuse is that during interviews, the abuser, if present, often speaks for the victim. If the neighbor had not been present at the interview, who knows what my mother might have said about either of them. We will never know because she made sure my mother never had the opportunity to answer freely without being prompted.

Dr. Read, a clinical professor in the department of psychiatry and bio behavioral sciences at UCLA who also maintains a private practice in geriatric and forensic psychiatry, wrote in an article on elder abuse for Psychiatric Times that "the victim will not give credence to the abuser's ulterior motives." [73]

As with my mother, the abuser may convince the victim that they really care about the victim and are the only ones preventing the victim from going into a home – or in my mother's case getting out of a home. This relationship between victim and abuser is often likened to the Stockholm Syndrome. For this reason, Dr. Read recommends that a clinician maintain an attitude of "healthy suspicion".[74]

Deputy District Attorney Paul Greenwood, who heads the fraud and elder abuse task force in the DA's office in San Diego, has years of experience in dealing with elder fraud. When I approached him for his opinion in November 2012 on how the interview with my mother was conducted, his response was that "it is standard practice for investigators to separate victims from any possible suspect during an interview. Suggestibility and coercion are always concerns. So what you have described would not be appropriate here."

Allowing the neighbor to stay with my mother through the interview was inappropriate. Someone who has years of experience as a gerontologist should have realized that an abused senior will say whatever they have been taught to say to whoever asks.

Jenkins however writes in her report, "In my opinion her friend's presence did not affect the interview." [75] But it did. Later in the report she confirms that the neighbor prompted my mother when she was asked about the lawyer. My mother could not remember her name, only that she was a lawyer, so the neighbor supplied the name. (This is a woman to whom the previous month my mother had bequeathed $200,000!) As for the neighbor, my mother could only remember she had known her for a long time, but not the circumstances under which they were acquainted, until prompted by the woman that they were neighbors. In spite of this lack of memory of the relationship with the two of them, my mother told Jenkins that these two women were the ones she would trust to make decisions for her. This statement would later have disastrous consequences.

While in the gerontologist's office, and in the neighbor's presence, my mother suddenly spoke "spontaneously" of her relationship with me. This word jumped off the page when I read the report. My mother was not "spontaneous". She had spent a lifetime keeping her opinions to herself to the point where she would not even share her concerns about her own health with Dr. Houghton and had me do it.

According to the report however, my mother volunteered that she felt that I had betrayed her trust and she no longer wanted me in her life. Victims of Stockholm Syndrome often take on the opinions of their abusers, especially if they are present, to make sure that the relationship with the abuser remains intact, or because they are afraid of them.

The main concerns my mother, who I believed was rigorously rehearsed because her short-term memory was so damaged she could not hold onto recent information, expressed about me were:

I had taken her jewelry, used her credit cards, and taken her dog. Though I did not yet know it, by this point they had taken thousands from her bank accounts and used her Sears card frequently. Unlike me, they hadn't been paying her bills with the money they took, but were frivolously squandering it away.

She also says that I took the money because I needed money, an impression planted by these two women. I did not need the money. The subject of the rings still fascinates me. They made such a huge deal about them, partly I know to make me look like a thief, but also because I think by keeping the rings in my care, I had cheated them out of what they thought was rightfully theirs. The rings were not valuable. I had them valued by three different jewelers. I had even offered to send them back to the PG if he would pay to have them insured. He never got back to me.

My mother also recalled going to visit her house with the neighbor and there being broken glass all over the floor. My guess is that the neighbor did that deliberately or because she was in a rage that I had dared place something in what she no doubt now considered to be "her" house.

My mother also told the doctor I had only come to visit her once in St. Mary's, and then only for a few hours. This lie also appears in one of the neighbor's many affidavits so I know where it originated. She had taught it to my mother. She got the information from the log book. She had no way of knowing that I didn't sign in and out because I didn't know there was a log book.

My mother also had no memory of her stays at RJH, the most recent of which had been in August 2010 – only two months before, or why she was in St. Mary's, but she supposedly "remembered" that I had only stayed for a few hours and didn't mention Arabella being there at all. But then the women didn't know Arabella had been there with me, so they could not have rehearsed my mother about that. In fact, both Arabella and I had spent days with my mother during that visit.

My mother told Dr. Jenkins I had not been around when she was dealing with my father's death. It's true that I had had to return to Chicago shortly before he died, but I came back the next week and made all the arrangements, went with her to pick up his ashes, settled his insurance and arranged for a new roof for the house. I had the leaks in the ceiling fixed and took care of pruning the trees.

The women had apparently told her I was responsible for taking her dog. How low can you get? My mother loved the dog with a passion only a pet lover can understand. For me to take her precious Babe would have made me look very bad indeed in her eyes. The shysters also lied on their affidavits by saying they had bought the dog for her! I had the papers to prove I had brought her from Illinois. But still the lies prevailed.

The two women had also told my mother that I was responsible for her being in St. Mary's. They told her that I had succeeded in turning the doctors against her, while they were doing everything they could to get her back into her house. It wasn't true of course, but that was what they had told her and that is what she volunteered to the doctor.

Having only the two women as sources for information, the doctor, having little experience with Alzheimer's patients, was easily manipulated into accepting their story about my mother and her distrust of me and her preference for having them represent her. She certainly did not maintain an attitude of "healthy suspicion".

The content of my mother's spontaneous recollections is seriously tainted. Any good doctor should have been able to see this. My mother could not remember signing documents (either POA), her stays in RJH, why she was in St. Mary's or any details about her "trusted friends", but she did remember, glass on the kitchen floor and the loss of her dog and that she wanted nothing more to do with me.

An abuser frequently convinces a victim "that family members, friends and other previously trusted persons are trying to put the victim in an institution and take their assets".[76]

Even though she had detailed memories of why she hated me, the details of her relationship with the two women were sketchy at best. She said that the neighbor had always been there for her and gave an as an example that she had taken her clothes to the dry cleaners. The gerontologist did make a note that my mother thought that by having them as her decision makers she would be allowed to go and live in her own home. That was evidently the carrot that the two women had continued to dangle cruelly in front of her. But the doctor did not see that that was undue influence.

Dr. Jenkins does mention that talking about me was a source of distress for my mother and that she became tearful. I believe that even though they constantly tortured her with their lies, and rehearsed her until she could spout those lies verbatim, some part of her still knew the truth and that the conflict between these two opposing realities was more than she could bear.

Fortunately, the gerontologist did maintain an inkling of "healthy suspicion" for her next point was "I cannot be absolutely certain whether Mrs. Walker had direct memory of these events or merely remembered what she had been told about these events".[77]

The doctor also notes, probably because the women had told her this, that Dr. Demott had to override my decision to not make basic investigations and treatments for my mother while she was in RJH. This was not the case. In his notes at the family conference on May 14th, Dr. Demott says "outlined the various specialists who had seen patient and the tests she had had", which I knew about. Then he says "family agrees that no further investigation is required." They had been testing her for weeks and come up with no conclusion. It wasn't my decision to go no further. It was the staff. I simply asked him, because my mother begged me to stop all the tests, to do no "unnecessary" tests on her because they made her uncomfortable and frightened.

But the women painted a very different picture. They continually made it sound like I did not want her to receive any treatment and that is what they said in their affidavits. Dr. Demott was never asked to give an affidavit.

Throughout this ordeal, it never ceases to amaze me that otherwise reasonably intelligent people – doctors, lawyers, judges, police – so easily accept lies over truth.

Of course they do not see them as lies, merely acceptable possibilities. Did the gerontologist ever question the "realities" that my mother put forward for hating me and wanting the two women to be her caregivers or why she could so clearly remember my supposed transgressions and hardly anything about the women she was about to entrust her life to? Was the neighbor's taking clothing to the dry cleaner a rational reason for casting her only child and her grandchildren out of her life? Was wanting them to be responsible for her life, a rational choice, especially since she could not remember when and where they had become acquainted or even one of their names? No

My mother had an excuse for her erroneous beliefs because she had Alzheimer's and had been psychologically and emotionally abused, but the gerontologist suffered under no such burden. She was a rational person who specialized in geriatric issues and yet she accepted the lies they had taught my mother to believe over the truth that she had read in my affidavits, and over pure common sense. She knew that putting my mother into care was not the wrong decision and that I did not have the power to "turn the doctors against" my mother. Any thinking person would have understood that I did not "take" the dog or break the glass and leave it for my mother to see or "steal" the rings. Why would I? But she seems more concerned with not causing my mother any undue stress than she is in getting to the bottom of things. Did she not think that making a vulnerable old lady believe lies about the daughter she had loved so much and isolating her from her grandchildren was stressful for her?

Of course it was. We had been an unusually close family. I had looked after her after my father died and she relied on me to protect her. These women isolated her from us at a time she most needed our help and told her horrible lies that created a lot of anguish for her. They basically ripped the emotional rug out from under her. This type of emotional or psychological abuse - inflicting mental pain, anguish, or distress on an elder person through verbal or nonverbal acts, can prove devastating. Psychological abuse accounts for 36% of all cases of elder abuse. [78]

This psychological abuse would naturally have been very stressful for her. The body's answer to stress is to release more cortisol, a hormone produced by the adrenal glands. It is the "fight or flight reaction" that saved our ancestors from dangerous situations. But constant stress, especially in elderly people with Alzheimer's, meant that my poor mother's cortisol levels went higher and higher, damaging her brain cells even more and hastening her descent deeper into the disease. "If we are chronically stressed and experience chronic "dis-stress" as a result, then we are constantly releasing cortisol. Chronically high cortisol levels have been shown to cause brain cell dysfunction, to kill brain cells, and to cause atrophy of the brain. Cortisol levels go up, but they stay up longer and go down slower. We become more prone to the psychological effects of stress if we are dis-stressed, and the effects last longer. More brain cells may dysfunction and more may be killed. [79]

At this point I had to ask myself why perfectly sane people prefer lies to the truth.

There are several reasons:

- People believe people who are like them – educationally, racially, and economically. In my mother's case a lawyer and a middle-class neighbor, both of whom are middle-aged women like the gerontologist, who appear to be comfortably off and therefore would seem to have no ulterior motive, seem eminently believable. More so than a daughter who lives far away and who can be lied about with impunity because she is not there to defend herself and who has already been accused of elderly abuse by them.

- People believe people who are paying them for the service they provide over those who are not paying them.

- People believe those who lie first since that information is now set up in their minds and taints all future information about a given situation because it has already been accepted as the truth.

- People are uncomfortable holding two sets of conflicting beliefs - cognitive dissonance – so they choose the one that makes them most comfortable.

- People believe possible truths over plausible truths because we all like to give others the benefit of the doubt, unless the lies are really outrageous or impossible.

- There is a lot of misinformation about elderly financial abuse. Most people, even those who work in the area, don't know the statistics on who is most likely to commit what, and so their opinions about it are skewed by ignorance.

- And lastly, accepting the lie is easier. You don't have to go digging or think too much, you just accept a possible scenario as believable and move on to the next patient.

I did not know this was all going on until months later when I obtained all the relevant documents. At the end of 2010, I was bereft about losing my mother, listening to my lawyer of the moment, who told me my application for guardianship would only take six weeks, even though it had already been six months, and wondering what I was supposed to do about all this. I was obsessed with fixing the situation, with putting things back the way they were, the way they should have been. I had not yet come to the realization that that would never happen.

None of the people I had turned to for help were interested in the truth. They were just happy to have an explanation that fitted the stereotypes. They also had no vested interest in finding out the truth. The gerontologist got paid regardless. My lawyer got paid regardless. Public officials either ignored me, passed the buck, or suggested options which were not useful. Groups who were involved with senior issues, including fraud, believed me and sympathized. They suggested I get a lawyer. Back to square one.

Chapter Fourteen

YOU CAN BANK ON IT

Perseverance is not a long race; it is many short races
one after another. – Walter Elliott

January 2011 dawned cold and grey as it always does in Chicago. The bleakness of the skies was in tandem with my mood. As usual we had sent my mother her favorite flowers for Christmas. I wondered if she had received them. I wondered if I would get another rehearsed note about some other fictional transgressions I had supposedly made, just to grind salt into our already stinging emotional wounds. But the mailbox remained empty. I thought of the long year that lay ahead and shivered, not from the cold but from the dread of what would happen next. What were they up to now?

By the beginning of 2011, I had come to terms with five things:

- No matter what I did, it was a very real possibility that I would never be able to put everything back the way it should have been. My mother had Alzheimer's and would never be her old self. She would live the rest of her life believing the awful lies they had told her about me. This was a difficult realization, but one I had to come to in order to get up every morning and face the day. According to my therapist, Dr. McTeague, I was now suffering from Post-Traumatic Stress Disorder.

- Was I angry? Yes. It was difficult enough losing her to Alzheimer's, but losing her to these three women was unbearable. Was I angry with her? Yes. The daughter in me still questioned how she could so easily believe their lies. I loved her so much and I know she had loved me. Was I angry with myself? Definitely. Although, looking back, I realized that once these women had our family in their sights, nothing would have dissuaded them, I still felt somehow responsible for what was happening.

- I understood they had total control over her and would never let go.

- No matter how much they tried to play the part of doting friends, their true intentions were becoming clearer by the day. They would never stop until they had taken everything she had. And there was only one way to accomplish that. I was increasingly afraid for her life.

- It had started out to be all about her money. They wanted it, and given their complimentary personality disorders, they felt were entitled to it. But now they had moved their assault to a new level. I knew that they wanted to hurt my daughters and me in any way they could because we had gotten in the way of their plans by fighting back.

- I also understood that I would probably never see my mother again. This was very difficult to come to terms with.

For the first week of the year I wallowed in my depression. Should I just accept the inevitable and stop fighting? Most people in my position do give up. The stress takes a huge toll both personally and financially. All of this was hurting my family. The girls refused to talk about what was happening with their grandmother. Any mention of her sent everyone into a spiral of desultory silence. I was all alone with this. I deliberated about what I should do. The guardianship hearing that was supposed to have taken six weeks back in July was not moving ahead. My lawyer of the moment had stopped answering my emails. My guess was that since he had been paid up front, his enthusiasm and involvement in the case had waned to the point of utter disinterest. On top of that I was being blitzed with a tsunami of affidavits from their lawyer, who also was an officemate of Horton's. Each of them was pages and pages long. Each point had to be answered by me, in detail. It was time consuming and very difficult to read the ridiculous, hurtful lies that they had sworn about me, my daughters and our family. I had spent my life telling the truth either on air or in print. Reading their fabrications actually hurt my brain.

My friends rallied behind me. Every week we got together for tea, invariable we talked about "the case". Sometimes we even laughed at the ridiculous things that they were saying because they were so far from reality. My friends had been with me throughout this craziness and knew the truth of the situation.

Lauren, one of my friends quipped, "When does the lawyer have the time to practice law, she is so busy writing affidavits?"

I had the feeling that the women were keeping me busy, answering their increasingly outrageous accusations against me in order to keep me occupied and off balance. In a way too they were torturing me.

Once, when we lived in California, I saw a pack of coyotes trying to bring down a large Rottweiler. They kept tag-teaming him, first one, then the other, nipping at him from different directions, until the dog was confused and worn out. Then they struck. The dog had no fight left in him. They savaged him until he was dead. I knew I was the dog in this scenario. No wonder I felt physically ill because of the stress. But as I lay awake in the middle of so many long wintery nights, I knew in my heart that I could not give up; could not leave my mother to be their victim until they found a way to take everything she had including her life. What kind of daughter would that make me? What kind of role model would I be for my own daughters? If I did not fight on, it was tantamount to telling them that I was okay with what they were doing.

And so on the second Tuesday in January, I woke up feeling differently, probably because I had, for the first time in a long time, a decent night's sleep. Sometime during that peaceful slumber, my brain had been working on my next move. I had gone to be bed wondering again if I should just call it quits. I had woken up knowing that I would do whatever I could to nail the women were trying to destroy my family.

I made a cup of coffee, picked up a pen, a yellow legal pad and copies of all their affidavits. Though salted with lies, they were also a veritable mine of information. In the attached exhibits they had included information I could use against them! I grabbed my day timer and my cell phone, and sat down at the dining room table. I knew what I had to do. I might lose, but I had to fight on. I had to do this for myself, for my girls and for my mother. She would never know it, but I would know that I was going to do everything I could. I started making phone calls.

I had copies of all my mother's bills because I had been making sure they were paid after my father died. Because of this I had all the account numbers associated with them.

I started with the telephone bill. I dialed my mother's home number even though I knew she was in St. Mary's. Part of me wondered what I would do if somebody picked up. The phone rang and rang. I could imagine the sound echoing through the silent rooms of my mother's house. No body picked up. That was a relief of sorts. I had an idea that the checker may have been spending time in my mother's house since it was so close to where she worked.

But the number was still connected. So I looked on the phone bill for the toll free number for Telus, and dialed. I got through to customer service and explained, briefly, the situation. They were very willing to help since I had put my name on the account as well my mother's when my father died. I don't know why I did this, but I had done it for every one of her bills. I recommend doing this, since with all the twitter about privacy these days, sometimes you can't access information about another person's – senior, teen etc. - account otherwise.

I listened to the canned music for a minute or so, and then the customer service agent came back on the line. She told me that the number was still in service – which I already knew because I just called it – but the phone bill had not been paid since September 2010. This I didn't know. I thanked her and hung up.

If the lawyer was really playing POA, she was supposed to make sure the bills were being paid. Obviously, she was not paying attention to that required task. Next, I called Shaw cable. The account was being paid every month and in fact was paid every month until my mother went into hospital in May 2011.

What did this mean? They had not paid the telephone bill since September because they knew no one would call. The cable bill was another matter. The only reason to keep paying the cable in an uninhabited house was because somebody was watching TV!

I continued with my phone calls. Next was the hydro. BC Hydro had been paid at the end of December 2010. By then her bank account had gone from $15543.78 on May 31, 2010 to $865.00 by Christmas Eve. What had they done with the money?

Perhaps the most alarming payment and one which gave me a sick sinking feeling was the payment for her BC health insurance premium at the beginning of January 2011. It covered the six months until the end of June 2011. Six months. Did that mean that she wasn't going to need her health insurance after June 2011? Not only was her bank account running out of money, my instincts told me that my mother was running out of time.

I called her bank, where I also have an account, and spoke to one of the customer service people – someone I had met before and spoken to over the last few years.

I explained to her that I was afraid my mother had been a victim of fraud. Rather than being helpful she was unexpectedly aggressive. "We do everything we can to protect our client's interests!" she practically screamed over the phone and then she hung up on me.

I ruminated on her attitude for a few minutes. Obviously they had not done everything they could to protect my mother's interests. She was living in an assisted living facility at least a thirty minute drive away. She was not accessing her account, so, who was, and how?

Getting braver by the minute, I called the fraud division of the bank. I had to find out what was going on with her account and where her money had gone. Surprisingly, I got through to the head of the fraud division who, even more surprisingly, was willing to help. He put me on hold. I doodled on my yellow pad, listening to more canned music until he came back.

He told me that he could only see the checks on the account going back for the last two months. That was disappointing. The rest of the checks were kept at the branch. I knew where that was going leave me. I pressed him for more information. What was her current balance? Was there any unusual activity on her account? He consulted his screen. He told me what checks had come through since November – including the one to BC Health. It seemed normal enough. I didn't feel I was getting anywhere.

There was a moment of silence while I tried to think of another leading question that might reveal suspicious activity. Before I would speak again, he asked me a question. "Do you know who Debbie Mills is?"

The floor dropped out from beneath my feet. Did 1! She was the supermarket checker who was part of this little triumvirate of cheaters.

"Well, he continued, there have been a lot of checks written to her over the last two months and it looks like she cashed them in the branch." I asked him for the amounts of the checks. He read them off, including the check numbers. The largest amount was $640! Why would my mother be signing checks to the supermarket checker?

I quickly scribbled down the information on my pad as he continued to list off the checks for me. Mostly they were consecutive. Inside my head a little voice was whispering "I knew it! I knew it!"

I thanked him profusely and told him how much I appreciated his giving me the information. It confirmed all my suspicions. The women who were playing concerned friends and good neighbor were stealing from my mother. As I thanked him one more time, he volunteered something else. "Just one more thing."

What now? What other nugget of priceless information was he about to offer up?

"It's about the logos on the checks. Some of the checks have the old logo, the one we haven't used in years. I hope that helps you."

I told him it did, thanked him again, and rang off. Checks written to Debbie Mills! With a logo the bank hadn't used in years! His voice was replaying in my head. What did it mean? Suddenly, the light bulb when on. Debbie Mills and the other two were using my mother's house! That's where they found the old check book. That's why the cable was still on and the utilities were being paid, but the phone bill was not! Pieces of the puzzle began to fall into place. They would take my mother out of St. Mary's and get her to sign checks out of the way of prying eyes.

This was later confirmed by Mills' affidavit of January 14th 2010. She says that in October of 2010, the neighbor suggested that Mills become a companion for my mother at a rate of $20.00 an hour. Mills then says that she would take my mother to her house and that the two women would "help" my mother write checks to her. (It should be noted that Mills had no professional experience in dealing with an elderly Alzheimer's patient and that in removing her from St. Mary's, they were actually putting her in jeopardy since she was considered a high elopement risk and a high fall risk. Also the highest rate of payment for a professional, experienced caregiver in Canada is $18.00 an hour, but they didn't care what they paid Mills. It wasn't their money after all.) My mother did not need to pay for a companion. She lived in a nursing home! I suspected that Mills was there in case we showed up.

It took me another year to get copies of all the checks written off my mother's account in the last year of her life. I had to submit a freedom of information request (see below) to the estate division of the bank, but eventually I prevailed.

What I found out was eye-opening. Starting in October 2010, Debbie Mills received a total of $3445.94 from my mother's account. And in the spring of 2011 she got a further $2600 from another account at TD Canada Trust. A friend of the neighbor's who ran a concierge service got $442.50 - probably for taking in the dry cleaning. The women also retained a lawyer for my mother with a $2000 retainer, also paid for from my mother's account. Why did my mother need a lawyer? The gardener I had hired in May received $436.00 for gardening duties in May through September of 2010 on October 21. On October 22, the neighbor wrote the consecutively numbered check to pay her own gardener, also for the months of August and September - $201.10. So she was paying her gardener out of my mother's account.

When I got the package of checks from the estate division of the bank I was also able to see that in 2010 both women had written checks from both the old checkbook and the newer one, though the neighbor had written most of them. For both women to have access to both checkbooks in the same period of time meant that the check books were kept in my mother's house and not the neighbor's house or the lawyer's office.

After the beginning of 2011, only Horton wrote checks off of my mother's account. Prior to that, both women had been dipping their beaks too frequently into the account without keeping track of each other's actions. I think that the lawyer must have realized they were treading on thin ice. She might have been able to play the POA card if questioned, but the neighbor had no legal presence in my mother's life at all at that point. She was just the woman who lived next door.

In February of 2011, the lawyer wrote a check to Mills for $550.00. It bounced. Also in February, the gardener's check bounced. The direct debit I had set up for St. Mary's was also NSF.

They must have realized by then that they had reached the bottom of the well of free money. Now what? The only way they could keep their boat afloat as they awaited the guardianship hearing in March was with an infusion of cash. On February 2 the infusion arrived in the form of a transfer from the TD Canada Trust – the bank where the lawyer had set up an account with my mother's money taken from her bank in London.

By May 12, 2011, my mother had $50.00 in the bank. In less than ten months they had defrauded her of over almost $20,000.

One of the last calls I made that morning was to Sears. My mother used her Sears card infrequently to say the least and then usually only for large purchases like the new washer and dryer and the new fridge and stove. The reason for this was that not only was she a frugal woman, but to get to Sears from her house meant driving through traffic. As she got older she felt nervous about doing this. She was also the kind of person who liked to shop in person, so for her to use the card at all was a rarity.

I spoke to the store and once again I told my story. They referred me to the head office in Ottawa which then referred me to the fraud division of Chase Bank which handles Sears credit cards in Canada. The last time I had paid her bill was on June 17th, 2010. for $200. At that time, the outstanding balance was about $1900. Six months later in January 2011 it was $2900. This was information I found in one of the neighbor's affidavits.

Sears was very co-operative and promised me a full run down of all the activity on my mother's account for the last four years. They then asked me if I wanted to cancel the card. I thought about it for a moment and decided not to. By the end of the second week in January I had the feeling that the women knew I was looking into their hijinks. I felt that keeping the card active would be baiting the trap. So, I left it alone.

Oddly enough, another affidavit arrived later that week, from the neighbor. In it she rants on about me cancelling my mother's Sears card and how, as a result, this poor little old lady could not buy underwear. More lies. More slander. More disassociation from reality. More perjury?

From July 2010 to April 2011 there were 31 different purchases on my mother's Sears card. In the previous several years there had been only four.

The first purchase was for two sweaters. Reasonable enough, except that whoever made the purchase used two coupons. The coupons come in

154

the newspaper. My mother did not have access to a newspaper and I never knew her to read the newspaper or to use coupons. Then there were two pairs of pants. Then more sweaters and shoes. More pants, for a total of seven pairs. Oddly enough a lot of these purchases were in black or grey. My mother never wore black or grey. She liked light, happy, pastel colors for sweaters and tan pants. The neighbor, on the other hand, almost universally was wearing black or grey whenever I saw her. Years later when I finally cleared out my mother's closet to donate her clothes to charity there was nothing grey or black among the clothes and nothing purple either.

This went on for a couple of months. My mother at this point was almost 88. She had closets stuffed with a lifetime clothes, shoes, purses etc. Whenever we would go shopping together in the years after my father died she would browse, but never buy. She would always say "I've got enough stuff." And she did. But, suddenly, she was shopping like the Sultan of Brunei.

On October 28th, 2010 she bought two winter coats in the same color, at the same register, but in different sizes. The transactions were made fifteen minutes apart. In December, she brought jewelry. Then more pants, more sweaters, more purses etc. Her signature on the receipts now was shaky and she spelled her last name incorrectly. By February, her signature had deteriorated even more. Just before Valentine's Day, she bought three greeting cards and four boxes of chocolates - one card for each of her good friends? And a box of chocolates for each too? And, one for my mother too, of course, since they were being generous with her account. My mother was not in the habit of sending Valentine's Day cards to anyone, not even to her grandchildren or me. When she was growing up in England during the Depression, Valentine's Day was not a holiday that was celebrated.

To coerce her into buying cards for the three women who had taken over her life on a day made for celebrating loved ones, is more than vaguely creepy. It does fit nicely in with the obituary Brewer later wrote for my mother, however, in which she writes "Thank you to Joan, Jackie and Debbie for each playing a huge part in making the last year of her life meaningful and happy."

Throughout all of this, it appears that the neighbor craves acknowledgement for her actions toward my mother. That's what the cards and the photographs and the obituary were all about. They were all about her. My mother was just a tool to feed her ego and validate her actions. It was a classic indicator of her social affective disorder.

Next, two bras were bought – not her size – in caramel and cassis. Mum only ever wore white bras, when she wore a bra. She had had a breast reduction in her sixties – of course they would not know that - and was very happy that she did not need to wear a bra any more. The bras were not present when I donated her clothes.

By March her signature was illegible. She bought more greeting cards and notepaper at the end of March. Who was she writing to? This time she printed her name. Finally at the end of April, her last purchase was a striped scarf. She never wore a scarf in the six decades I knew her and did not like stripes.

Obviously, one of the women would take her on these little shopping trips because she had no other way of getting to the store. That was if indeed she was always present during the use of her card. By this time she had to use a walker to get around and was deeply sedated most the time, and a high fall risk, so I have my doubts about who was using the card. Sears/Chase fraud department doubted it too. They forgave all these purchases because they understood that she was not able to foment the intention to make them or even be present for most of them.

Over ninety countries around the world have some form of freedom of information legislation including Canada and the U.S.. In Canada access to information laws distinguishes between access to public records and access to records that contain personal information. Generally, individuals or their representatives (in this case me) have a right to access records that contain their own personal information under the Privacy Act. The general public does not have a right to access records that contain personal information about others under the Access to Information Act. In other words, I was able to get the information about my mother's banking and Sears accounts because I was representing her interests, but a random person would not have access to this information.

Like most places, British Columbia has forms which can be used to access personal information. They can be found online and mailed to wherever a person is requesting information from. I made four such requests – to my mother's bank, to Sears, to the hospital where she died, and to St. Mary's assisted living facility. Only, St. Mary's refused my request, although they did give some of my mother's hospital notes to the neighbor. I know this because they turned up in one of her affidavits. I could have appealed this denial, but I already had the information I needed, courtesy of the neighbor herself.

I felt now that I was not only getting a handle on what exactly was going twenty-five hundred miles away, but that I was no longer a co-victim. By being proactive I was gaining a sense of control over what was happening. It felt good.

Chapter Fifteen

WHY ELDER FRAUD OFTEN

GOES UNPUNISHED

The power to investigate is a great public trust.
– Emanuel Celler

According to Paul Greenwood Deputy District Attorney of San Diego, elder abuse of all kinds, is a crime that is going unpunished, is predictable and is escalating. In terms of prosecutability however, it is where child abuse was thirty years ago, a dirty little secret that has been continually swept under the rug by a society that does not want to recognize it exists or, if does, does not have a clue how to deal with it.

It wasn't until 1977, when pediatrician, Henry Kemp, an expert on child sex abuse gave a speech in which he described the sexual abuse of children as a "hidden pediatric problem and neglected area," that people began to examine the issue in earnest.[80] Two years later, several ground breaking studies, including one by David Finkelhor author of Sexually Abused Children, focused national attention on what had heretofore been a problem that was not part of the cultural dialogue. More studies in the early eighties and the rise of the feminist movement shone light on the previously hidden problem of sexually abused children.

In 1985, The Chicago Tribune noted that "the topic of child sexual abuse has only recently come under widespread public discussion." [81] The next year Oprah revealed her own experience with sexual abuse as a child, thereby putting the subject literally front and center on the public stage.

Slowly, laws began to change to reflect a new awareness of an age old problem. By the end of the eighties courts dropped the requirement of corroborating witnesses when children testified. In1990, the Supreme Court allowed victims to testify through one-way closed circuit video so they would not have to face their abusers. Twenty years later, the scientific community is debating whether or not children need to testify at all, since there is evidence of psychological and emotional repercussions to the victim.

The dawning awareness that was once applied to sexually abused children now needs to be applied to those at the other end of the age spectrum – seniors.

Currently, according to the NCEA (National Center on Elder Abuse) prosecution of perpetrators is rare. Only 1 in 25 cases is ever reported and only one in 100 ever successfully prosecuted. Victims of elder abuse often fear retaliation or a disruption of the dependent relationship they have developed with the offender. My mother's case was further complicated by a lack of capacity to describe the crimes that had been committed against her, or even understand she was a victim of a crime. Other seniors are deceased by the time the crimes come to light and therefore are not available to be questioned or to testify in court.

"Elder abuse can be hard to prosecute, according to Douglas County District Attorney, Charles Branson. "Often the victim depends on the perpetrator of the abuse. (the women worked diligently at making my mother dependent on them by eliminating her real family and making promises to her that they knew they would never keep – i.e. having her move back into her own home.) Cases can involve victims who might not remember they were taken advantage of or don't realize they were victimized." [82]

There are other reasons why police don't investigate elder abuse, as I came to find out. Police agencies don't like dealing with the elderly. They are stereotyped as forgetful, grumpy, senile, too talkative, or too fragile. The prevailing attitude is that the elderly – like the children of the past - make terrible witnesses.

My mother had been so indoctrinated by these women that she would never have testified against them, if indeed anybody had asked her to. She did not have the capacity to understand the questions. These women knew that though they might have been able to put words in her mouth in a doctor's office, as Dr. Jenkins' report shows, prompting would not have been allowed in a courtroom. By eroding her relationship with us and constantly feeding her lies, she had become their own Get Out of Jail Free Card. They could do what they liked, and she would never tell on them.

In many cases, including my mother's, police feel that if money or possessions are given "voluntarily" then no crime has been committed. In my mother's case, the women would just say that my mother wanted the locks changed on her house; to write a new will; to buy the goods at Sears; to sign the checks for Debbie Mills etc. and that was that. And that's exactly what they did say and the police accepted it. The question of undue influence never came up.

After she died from the operation they arranged for her to have, it was even more difficult for me to proceed with proving that crimes had been committed against her. They knew that too. Police frequently hold the belief that if a victim is deceased they cannot prosecute because the victim cannot testify, which as Mr. Greenwood points out, is like saying that just because a person is murdered and cannot testify about it, does not mean they are not dead.

Mr. Greenwood also believes, that in cases like my mother's where death is suspicious, medical examiners or coroners should establish a protocol for reviewing these deaths - an Elder Death Review board consisting of people who examine the circumstances of the death of the person and investigate to see who, if anyone, benefits. In my mother's case, the consent for a surgery that several doctors said was likely to result in her demise and then benefit the two women who signed that consent, would certainly have looked suspicious.

Thirty years ago, police were reluctant to prosecute an abuser on the word of a child. The belief set was based in the idea that children are always making things up. And so the adult offender generally got the benefit of the doubt. A secondary part of that belief set was that children, as long as they are not permanently injured, will forget the abuse in time. Though heinous, the effects of the abuse were thought to be temporary. The memories of the crime would evaporate if left alone long enough and the child would be as if it had never happened. As with a deceased senior, the child victim may not remember the abuse and if they do, the statute of limitations laws, which vary considerably from state to state, may have run out. Even if the crime may be acknowledged, the ability to prosecute is lost. We now know of course that the emotional and psychological scars of child abuse last a lifetime. We know too that the fallout, psychological, emotional and financial for all the victims of elder fraud – including the families - can be devastating and permanent.

The prevailing belief set about elder abuse and one which I believe is instrumental in why the police often fail to prosecute elder abuse cases, is that they sub-consciously think that old people are going to die soon anyway, so why spend valuable time and resources on investigating crimes against them, especially if they are unwilling or unable to participate in the investigation? But the collateral victims are still around. The damage inflicted on the family is real and ongoing.

For myself, I knew I had two choices. One was to turn my back on what these criminals had done to my mother and my family; to slink away with my tail between my legs like a whipped dog and feel, for the rest of my life, like a victim. The other was to fight on and bring their crimes to light, both for my own sanity and to help others who were or would be in the same boat. I also wanted to teach my daughters that, no matter what hand fate gives you, it's the way you play it that counts.

There is also the unspoken perception in our society that both children and the elderly are perceived as less important in the social hierarchy than adults or their interests (i.e. a religion or a university football team, for instance), which is why both groups continue to be easy targets for abuse. They are more vulnerable to abuse and the abuse is easier to cover up with threats or intimidation. If anything, the essential vulnerability of these two groups means we should take even more interest in their wellbeing. *Your* child or *my* mother are not disposable, and are never replaceable. They both deserve the same shot at justice as the rest of us.

As with child sexual abuse, there has been a gradual awakening in society to the problem of elder abuse of all kinds. In 1988, the National Committee for the Prevention of Elder Abuse (NCPEA), the first non-profit group to identify, prevent and respond to abuse, neglect and exploitation of seniors, was established. In 2010, a new law establishing an Office for Protection for Older Americans in the new Consumer Agency, dedicated to tackling the growing threat of elder financial exploitation, was passed. In March 2011, at the hearing of the Senate Special Committee on Aging, Senator Herb Kohl introduced the Elder Abuse Victims Act, S.462, which remains in committee. Unfortunately like most bills, it has about a 2% chance of being enacted (only 3% of the bills reviewed by the previous Congress made it into law).

On March 23, 2011 the Elder Justice Act did make it into law. It established, among other things $777 million to fund a federal response to combating elder abuse including support for Elder Abuse, Neglect and Exploitation Forensic Centers.

While on the national front, laws are slowly being introduced, and more local police agencies are squeezing resources for an elder financial abuse unit out of their ever tightening budgets, here in the trenches families and seniors are falling victim to financial abuse in ever greater numbers as unscrupulous deceivers of all sorts continue to prey on them.

In January 2011, I was not aware of any of this. I still believed if I proved what these women were doing, I would prevail and at least save her from their clutches, even if I never got the chance to repair our relationship. It was partly this naivete that kept me going at this point. I still believed that right would prevail and that justice system actually worked.

When I was a little girl, my mother always told me that if I got into trouble of any kind I should find the nearest policeman. So initially, taking the British Columbia Attorney General's advice, in September 2010, I had done just that. But, I had gotten a very chilly reception. I was confused as to why there was so little interest in the story I told the Victoria PD. It seemed a pretty cut and dried case of elder fraud to me, my American lawyer, Senator Kohl's office and Senator Dick Durbin's office, and everyone else I shared it with agreed.

Little did I know that a year earlier, in August of 2009, The Victoria Police Department instituted the *"You are not alone"* campaign aimed at building trusting relationships between police and seniors. *You are not alone* was supposed to encourage the reporting of elder abuse. But the message that they put out to the public and to their staff focused on the commonly held misconception that financial elder abuse is most often committed by adult children who care for or live with the victim.

Once again the specter of the abuser was a "perpetrator often suffering from mental health, drug, or alcohol-related issues". While not completely untrue, the campaign focused only on one type of abuser, perpetuating an old stereotype. Telemarketers, salesmen, service providers, nursing homes, caregivers, financial advisors, insurance brokers, attorneys, neighbors, acquaintances, religious officials and just plain strangers were not part of the picture, though they should have been. The message that was put out there implied that it would be wise for seniors to be cautious of their adult children, but everybody else was ok - a total reversal of the reality of the situation. It was akin to telling Little Red Riding Hood to watch out for the wolf, but not worry about the lions, tigers and bears. And, because this message came straight from the horse's mouth, i.e. the police department, it carried additional weight and no doubt brought a lot of local seniors into the sights of those wishing to target them. A potential abuser could always point to the police campaign and say, "See I'm not your adult son or daughter. You 're safe with me."

And that's what these women did to my mother. Their script throughout the last year of her life was that they were saving her from me, when in fact they were the ones abusing her and stealing from her. It was a clever ruse designed to refocus everyone's attention away from them and onto me – the stereotype. That's why I had no credibility with the police department in 2010. They did not return my calls, leaving me feeling both more frustrated and desperate. Much as police personnel used to tell frantic parents that their missing children were just runaways to explain their sudden disappearance, so the Victoria police department was using an old stereotype to explain what had happened to my mother. The lawyer especially had jumped on this bandwagon right at the beginning by telling the PG that I was abusing my mother. The neighbor turned the same screw over at St. Mary's and later that summer at the hospital, telling everyone that my children and I were responsible for my abusing my mother. Their lies had turned me into the walking stereotype of the financially abusive child.

CARP is a Canadian, non-partisan, non-profit organization committed to promoting and protecting the interests, rights and quality of life for aging Canadians. They provide the following, more accurate, information about financial elder abuse in their 2011 Financial Fraud Report.

Following are the key findings of the report:

- Close to one quarter of members have had financial fraud attempts made against them, and, in the majority of cases, these succeeded.

- The perpetrator of fraud is most likely a stranger, but can also be a family member or person in authority such as an insurance broker or financial advisor or lawyer.

- Only about one half of fraud cases are reported to the authorities, and fewer than half of these are resolved satisfactorily.

This report provides a more realistic and accurate picture of financial elder abuse and those who are the perpetrators. Unfortunately, none of the people I dealt with had read it.

By the end of January, 2011, I knew for sure what the women were up to, thanks to my phone calls. I also knew that they had to be stopped. So this time, taking Paul Greenwood's advice that persistence pays off, I wrote a long letter to the Victoria police department detailing everything that had happened. Somehow, it landed on the desk of Det. Rick Anthony, one of the two detectives who handle the overwhelming number of cases of elder fraud in Victoria.

The B.C. Centre for Elder Advocacy and Support, which was very sympathetic when I called them, takes about 200 calls a month on its toll-free line, with 70 per cent of them relating to elder financial abuse. But they did not offer up any information I had not already come up with by myself.

On February 7, 2011, I was in the supermarket with Arabella when my cell phone rang. I checked the caller ID. Restricted. My heart jumped into my mouth, the neighbor's number was restricted. Fortunately I answered anyway. Detective Anthony was on the other end of the line.

We spoke for twenty minutes and he agreed to look at the information I had gathered. He was very sympathetic, probably because his mother had Alzheimer's too. He told me that he just had a case come across his desk where an old man was literally taken off the street and into his bank and convinced to withdraw a large sum of cash and give it to a total stranger!

Finally, I thought I had found someone who understood what was going on. I sent him the time line I had constructed and all the documents and letters I had on a flash drive, and he promised to look at it. I believe that he did, because he opened a police file which is standard procedure for beginning the investigation of a case.

On March 2, 2011, Det. Anthony also swore an affidavit in favor of my guardianship of my mother. In the affidavit he noted:

"Based on my training and experience, some of the indicators or financial elder abuse are as follows:

    a. Significant withdrawals from the elders accounts. (By February 2011 my mother had no money left in her bank account and checks were bouncing like ping pong balls at a table tennis tournament.)

    b. Sudden changes in the elder's financial condition (two of her bank accounts were empty)

c. Items or cash missing from the senior's house. (Jewelry and money had been taken from her house and not by me.)

d. Suspicious changes in the senior's wills, power of attorney, titles or policies. (A new POA had been created and I suspected a new will, even though she was too cognitively impaired to understand what she was signing.)

e. Addition of names to senior's signature card.

f. Unpaid bills or lack of medical care although the senior has money to pay for them. (They had not paid her phone bill since September or her Sears bill since December. I was now paying for B.C. Hydro.)

g. Financial activity the senior could not have done such as use of an ATM when the senior is bedridden (There are many withdrawals using my mother's ATM card from the branch near the neighbor's house a half an hour's drive from St. Mary's.)

h. Unnecessary services, goods or subscriptions (My mother didn't need a concierge service, another lawyer to represent her, a paid companion, or all the purchases made on her Sears card.)

"With at least four of the above indicators in place, according to preliminary investigations we made, we have started an investigation and opened a file."

When I read this I was overjoyed. Finally somebody was going to do something!

But then he finished his affidavit by saying that because there was a civil motion underway with respect to guardianship of my mother, the investigation would be suspended pending the outcome. My brief moment of elation was over. Even though he believed that fraud was occurring, because the case currently involved a civil action, he was putting his investigation on hold. And it stayed that way. He told me later that his superior had told him to "back off" because this was a civil case. He too stopped answering my calls.

According to Paul Greenwood, police will often say that elder fraud is a civil crime and that's why they do not prosecute. I think that is just an excuse for not getting involved. The difference between a civil case and a criminal one is that a Criminal action is when the Police prosecute a person who has been charged with a criminal offence – a crime against society. A Civil action is when a lawyer initiates a legal action for causing harm to a person or their property.

But in the Criminal Code of Canada, fraud is defined as a crime because it intentionally deprives a person of their property. Under section 380 it says "A person commits fraud who dishonestly by a) deceit; b) unfair nondisclosure; c) unfair exploitation induces any person or the public to part with any property or to suffer a financial loss". Isn't that what happened to my mother? Hadn't these women intentionally caused her to suffer a financial loss?

Unfair non-disclosure is defined as:

a) a special relationship entitling the victim to rely on the accused or (they had created a dependency on them)

b) conduct by the accused creating a false impression in the victim's mind (they had lied to her about her granddaughter and me in order to get control of her)

c) Circumstances where non-disclosure would create a false impression in the mind of a reasonable person (they had lied to the hospital and at St. Mary's about us.)

Unfair exploitation means exploitation:

a) of another's mental deficiency (My mother was very definitely mentally deficient)

b) of another's mistake intentionally or recklessly induced by the accused or

c) Another's mistake induced by the unlawful conduct of a third party acting with the accused. (These women acted together to defraud my mother of her money by getting her to write checks that were of benefit to them or others that they knew).

There are a lot of statutes in the Canadian Criminal Code of which they were guilty. One of them was perjury. Later on when I spoke to a local police sergeant about the case, he once again gave me the "this is a civil case" line. I asked him if lying to the court or in a sworn affidavit was not perjury.

(131. (1) Perjury. Everyone commits perjury who with intent to mislead makes before a person who is authorized by law to permit it to be made before him a false statement under oath or solemn affirmation by affidavit, or deposition or orally, knowing that the statement is false).

He agreed that it was. And, I asked him if lying about the existence of the September wills was not perjury He admitted it was. Well then...... But he never did anything about it.

I contacted the RCMP, BC Prosecutor, Robert Prior and the Chief Constable of Victoria Police Department. Neither of them replied. None of them did anything to protect my mother.

On November 27, 2011 The Times Colonist, the local newspaper, ran an article written by Andrew Duffy. It was entitled:

"Seniors Vulnerable to Financial Abuse"

In the article he quoted Det. Rick Anthony.

"According to Det. Rick Anthony, fraud investigator with the Victoria Police Department, because it victimizes the most vulnerable and often comes from so-called loved ones, elder financial abuse has to be considered heinous.

"It really is the most reprehensible of all the financial crimes," he said. "Fraud is just as violent in its effect on people's psyche and ability to sustain themselves as robbery – with robbery it's fast, while fraud tends to be more thought out and pre-planned and by the time you know you've been taken, it's gone.

"It is every bit as violating as robbery or assault – if you get punched in the nose the nose will heal, but lose $100,000 and you'll never get that back. It may not seem as violent, but it is every bit as life-altering." (aduffy@timescolonist.com Victoria Times Colonist November 27th 2011)

His quote perpetuates the stereotype of elder fraud "often coming from loved-ones" even though when we spoke he only told me about cases he was working on that involved strangers. He was right about one thing though. It is certainly heinous, reprehensible and life-altering. He avoided calling it a crime.

Chapter Sixteen

WHAT THE JUDGE ATE FOR BREAKFAST

"Justice will not be served until those who are unaffected are as outraged as those who are."
– Benjamin Franklin

The guardianship hearing was set for March of 2011. We had bought our plane tickets and were set to go when, at the last moment, my lawyer sent an email not to come because the hearing at been cancelled. There was no available judge to adjudicate it. A couple of days later however they found one and the hearing went ahead. We were not there of course because we did not get enough advanced notice. If anyone had any doubts about my abandoning my mother in her hour of need the fact that I did not show up for the hearing would have confirmed their belief that I was a bad and uncaring daughter. The fact that I lived fifteen hours away and couldn't get a seat on a plane going anywhere near Vancouver Island at short such notice seemed to have skipped everyone's notice.

Benjamin Franklin, one of America's greatest thinkers, made a lot of accurate observations that far outlived his time on this earth. The above quote is one that rang particularly true for me and anyone who has ever brushed up against the justice system, however briefly.

From the undeserved parking ticket to the murderer who goes free on a technicality, the justice system we continue to endure serves itself far more than it does those who are not lucky enough to avoid it. This is especially true as it is applied to women whether they are convicted of a crime or are innocent petitioners trying to get justice for a wrong. This is because there is still significant gender bias in the justice system.

According to the American Bar Association, as of 2010 there were 1,225,452 practicing lawyers in the U.S:

o   73% were male

o   56% were between 40 and 64

o   88.1% were white

o   Only 30% of active United States district (or trial) court judges are women. [83]

According to the National Women's Law Center (www.nwlc.org), "When women are fairly represented on the federal bench, women, and men, may have more confidence that the court understands the real-world implications of its rulings. For both, the increased presence of women on the bench improves the quality of justice: women judges can bring an understanding of the impact of the law on the lives of women and girls to the bench, and enrich courts' understanding of how best to realize the intended purpose and effect of the law that the courts are charged with applying."[84] This is especially important because victims of elder fraud are more likely to be women and the judges who decide their fate are than likely to be men.

The gender bias in the justice system simply reflects a societal system that still does not yet take the problem of elder abuse of all kinds seriously.

Consider the following:

- The Senate Special Committee on Aging estimates that less than 2 per cent of federal "abuse prevention" funds go toward elder abuse even though elders comprise 12 per cent of the population.

- Adult Protective Services, the front line responder for elder abuse, does not even have a federal office or federal standards. It lacks oversight, training, data collection and reliable funding.

- The National Institute on Aging spent only 1/1000th of its budget on elder abuse research in 2008.

- The Center for Disease and Control and Prevention spent only .00062 per cent of its 8.8 billion dollar budget on elder abuse issues.

- The Administration on Aging spends just .5 percent of its 1.4 billion budget on elder abuse.

- The Office of Violence Against Women at the DOJ (Department of Justice) spends just 1 per cent of its funds on elders even though women comprise 20 per cent of the population it serves.

- The Office of Justice Programs, part of the DOJ spent less than .5 per cent of its 2.3 billion dollar budget in 2008 on elder justice.

- There is no Office of Elder Justice, only an informal Elder Justice Initiative with a one million dollar annual budget. In comparison, the OVW (Office of Violence Against Women) has a budget of $400 million and the Office of Juvenile Justice and Delinquency Prevention has a budget of $383 million.

- A report released by the Congressional Research Service in 2009 revealed that of the total federal dollars spent on abuse and neglect, 91 percent is spent on child abuse, 7 per on domestic abuse, and only 2 per cent is spent on elder abuse.[85]

The elderly, and elderly women in particular, are invisible to both the government and the courts. The Secretary General of the United Nations acknowledged the role of both ageism and sexism as contributing factors in elder abuse and cast such abuse within the broader landscape of poverty, structural inequalities and human right violations that disproportionately affect women worldwide. [86]

During the fight to get my mother back and later to save her from these women before they exacted the ultimate price, I hired – consecutively – six lawyers. Four were men, and two were women. The judge who ruled on the case for guardianship was also a man. I believe that the over- representation of men in this case is what caused it to go on for so long and for the judge to make the ruling he did. The men simply did not get it. Or, if they came close to understanding what was going on, they lost interest in the case because, according to the first female lawyer I retained who was the one who took the guardianship case to the court, mine was "the messiest case I've ever seen". She told me this several months after my mother died when she called me to find out why my case for proving the will had not yet resolved and when the rest of her bill would be paid.

When it comes to the law, or anything else, men like things that are cut and dried; things that make sense; they like games with rules which they can use to define their appropriate behavior. This case had none of this. With my first lawyer, a man who told me that the guardianship hearing would only take six weeks, my case file was soon pushed to the top of his desk and subsequently other files landed on top of it until it was suffocated by the heap of other legal wranglings that were equally messy and therefore unappealing to deal with.

In 1982 psychologist Carol Gilligan, wrote a book, "*In a Different Voice*. She claimed that female moral reasoning is fundamentally different. Men, the theory goes, prefer their law with rigid rules, clear lines, and neutral principles; women, meanwhile, want to look at the totality of the circumstances and apply broad discretion, preferring what Gilligan calls an "ethic of care" to an "ethic of rights." [87] I sincerely wished my guardianship case had been heard by a female judge.

In her book, Gilligan also notes that women are raised to be selfless and that men tend to think of all women that way because they have mothers, wives and secretaries who put their own lives on the back burner to benefit the males in their lives. Men, inside or outside of the law, have this perception about women. Women invariably are expected to live up to this perception and so they do. Therefore when the judge perceived the lawyer and the neighbor in the courtroom, he saw two middle class older women, well dressed, smiling (the neighbor smiles constantly to the point where it is creepy), pretending to be concerned about a little old lady who he believed had been abandoned by her family. They were fulfilling his expectations as to the appropriate role for women of their kind to play. Self-sacrificing. He even noted that these concerned women were asking for nothing, had asked for nothing in return for their administrations to my mother. They had even hired a companion for her! On her dime of course. But hey, it was the thought that counted. He did not see that Debbie Mills was being paid to deal with my mother because they did not want to be bothered with her. For a judge, he was not very people savvy. His reasoning was beyond naïve.

My daughters and I, on the other hand were not even present in court. Our absence from the hearing would have been seen as the proof in the pudding. I was a perceived as a selfish and uncaring daughter that did not even "bother" to attend the court hearing. The women on the other hand were fulfilling their expected roles of caring, self-sacrificing friends. Naturally, they got guardianship of my mother, who had no idea what was going on.

The judge even admonished me, in absentia, for daring to question the motives of these two obviously caring women. He said I had no right to be suspicious of their motives, no right to go to the police, go to the Attorney General or contact The Law Society and ask them to investigate the lawyer's behavior. He also said that I should never have transferred my mother's house into a trust as advised by my American lawyer to save it from being stolen by these women. He ordered it to be transferred back into her name, an act that insured she would continue to be victimized by the two women who wanted her estate. Apparently being a victim in our justice system removes more of your rights than being a felon.

One study examined the effects of cognitive biases on judicial decision making using data from 167 federal magistrate judges.[88] The results of this study showed that judges are just as susceptible to certain cognitive errors (including hindsight bias and egocentric bias) as were jurors.

Another study published by PNAS.org (Proceedings of the National Academy of Sciences) showed that when male judges make repeated rulings in a given court session, they show an increased tendency to rule in favor of the status quo. This tendency can be overcome by taking a break to eat a meal, consistent with previous research demonstrating the effects of a short rest, positive mood, and glucose on mental resource replenishment. Indeed, the saying that justice is what the judge ate for breakfast might be more than just sarcasm.[89]

On the other hand, plaintiffs were significantly more likely to win when a female judge was on the bench.

Men approach moral issues by looking at individual rights and considering what is just, fair and easy. Women approach them with caring and compassion and constantly consider the effects of their decisions on relationships. A female judge would likely have considered that separating a woman from her family was, in all likelihood, not ultimately in her best interests.

It is still amazing to me that a judge in the Supreme Court of BC could be so blind to what was really going on.

- Did he not see that for two women, who barely knew my mother, to suddenly take over her care was not about being kind? It likely had a mercenary motive.

- Did he not see that they hired a companion and depleted her bank accounts just because they didn't want to actually have to deal with caring for her?

- Did he not think it cruel that these "kind, caring" women deliberately lied to a cognitively impaired old woman, turning her away from a family that loved her?

- Did he really think that it was better for my mother to be put into the hands of a woman she didn't remember meeting and a woman who "took in her dry cleaning"?

- Did he not see that in spite of the distance, I had been a dutiful and caring daughter, doing everything I could for her and always having her best interests at heart FOR THE PAST FOUR YEARS?

- Did it ever occur to him that, if I was the demon daughter they described in their affidavits, why did I just not make myself the beneficiary of father's will in 2006? I could have done that. Nobody would have known about it or questioned it if they did.

- Did he not understand that I could have taken the money from England any time after my father's death? But did I? No.

- Did he ever wonder why I had put my life on hold trying to save my mother from their clutches for the last eighteen months? In typical manthink he assumed I was after her money, money I could easily have taken long ago. He never stopped to think that my motives were based on the fact that she was my mother. I loved her and over the preceding months I had been increasingly fearful of the plans they had for her.

Instead of considering these questions in making his decision he blithely turned my mother over to the care of the two women most likely to benefit from her death!

Not only was I afraid for what they had planned for her, apparently, I was also very sick because of the stress. I had begun experiencing odd little fainting spells. At first they were once a week, but as winter turned into spring they were happening several times a day. I would put my head between my legs for a minute or two and then get back to dealing with the case and working on this book. I did not have the time to be sick, so I pushed my symptoms away and carried on.

At the beginning of May, I had been to a meeting with my friends Lauren and Janet. They told me I was looking a little grey. I was definitely not feeling well. That evening I had trouble driving home. I wondered if I should pull over. I kept feeling like I was going to pass out.

On Monday, I called Lauren and told her that I was feeling decidedly unwell. She offered to drive me to the hospital, but on that morning my little Pomeranian, Carmen, had died in my arms. We had loved her for twelve years and I was too upset to go to the ER. Lauren told me that she was coming to get me first thing Tuesday morning to take me to the hospital. No discussion allowed.

Good to her word she showed up at 9 a.m. and drove me to the ER. Typically, I had researched the local hospitals to see who had the best cardiologists on staff. I knew that my symptoms were heart related since I had had two open heart surgeries and a valve replacement years before.

We spent the morning in the ER, and then they admitted me to the cardio ward. My funny little "spells" were my heart stopping. I had bradycardia, a very slow heart rate. They told me that it had been brought on by stress. No kidding!

I spent two weeks in the cardio ward while doctors decided what to do. I used the time to work on this book and look for yet another lawyer.

At the end of two weeks, I went home, new pacemaker in place, feeling not bad, but not great. But, I was ready to see if maybe the new lawyer would actually do what the others had failed so miserably at.

He worked with his wife, who was a QC. She totally got my case, asked me all the right questions. She did not ask me how I could prove that my mother loved me as two of my previous lawyers had done. She told me that my mother loved me because she had actually seen the file of pictures I had send to the first lawyer. She mentioned one particular picture, taken on the last day we were together down by the seawall. "Look at how she is holding onto you," she said. "She obviously loved you very much".

Since I have spent much more time dealing with the legal system that I ever wanted to, I have discovered that victims often end up being victimized not only by those who turned them into victims in the first place, but those who are supposed to provide them with relief because they are representatives of the law. The judge who handed my mother over to the two women didn't care about her. He made a bad decision. It was a decision that ended up costing her her life. He will never be found accountable for his decision and neither will the lawyers who mishandled my case. This total lack of accountability in the legal system is something that needs to be addressed so that more seniors and others who strive for justice on their behalf will not end up like my mother and my family.

Aside from a complete lack of accountability, we have unfortunately also developed a legal system that is accessible only to those who can afford to pay for it. Lawyers cost money. Court time costs money. Faxing, couriers, copying documents, all cost money. This puts access to the legal system and eventually justice for the victim out of reach for a lot of people. Seniors who have been defrauded have no money to spend on pursuing justice, even if they understand what has happened to them. There are lawyers of course who work pro bono (for the good), but once again you only get what you pay for. At the end of the day, we need to redesign our justice system to be accessible to everyone who needs it, not just those who can afford it.

Chapter Seventeen

YOU CAN DIE WITH A LITTLE HELP

FROM YOUR FRIENDS

"There are no good-byes, where ever you'll be, you'll be in my heart." – Grande

My mother died on Friday, June 17th, 2011 at 10:30 in the morning. The hospital did not call to say her death was imminent. They did not call to say she had passed away. They did not call at all because the women had told the staff that her granddaughters and I were guilty of elder abuse. They never called to check on that either.

I had already had year to deal with the reality that, to all intents and purposes, the person I knew as my mother had died the previous June when she closed the door behind us at the Garry Oak pod. The poor creature who gasped her last breath at RJH was someone I had not met.

Arabella, who got the email from the lawyer, came into my room to be comforted. She was crying, her slim shoulders shaking as she sobbed. I put my arms around her and said soothing things. But my eyes were dry. I had already shed all my tears months ago. Later that afternoon, I booked tickets for Victoria for the following day. There were arrangements to be attended to. It was my job to attend to them.

On the flight, I started thinking about what needed to be done and what I had to do next. I knew I needed to know how and why she died.

When I returned from Victoria, I requested the doctor's and nurse's notes from the hospital. I had already established a relationship with the young lady who doled out the documents when I had asked for the notes from my mother's first stay at RJH the previous year. She and the lady who handled estate fraud at Chase were the only ones who were forthcoming with the information I requested. With everyone else I had to fight to get the information I wanted. But in the end I did get it.

The fat package from the hospital detailing my mother last days arrived about three weeks later and sat on the dining room table for a few days. I eyed it frequently, wondering what it held, wondering if I could handle knowing what my mother's last weeks were like. Did she die peacefully or in agony? Who was with her? Was there any kindness shown her in her last moments? I was so emotionally raw by this point; I had to work up my courage before I could open the package.

Finally, one morning when the house was quiet and everyone was out, I sat down, opened the envelope and pulled out the contents. Fifty-six pages, in many different hand writings, using hospital terminology and shorthand, all wrapped in a thick elastic band. Fortunately, I could understand the hospital-speak from reading my own copious hospital notes. It was not easy reading, but it was necessary for me to know how she died and what role the three played in her death.

The clock ticked in the quiet house. My yellow highlighter squeaked across the pages. When I finished reading them, I put the notes back in the envelope and the envelope into my desk. I now knew exactly what had happened to her, what they had done, and why. I was infused with a cold anger. It was clear that she was physically failing, but the fact that they wanted her dead, and as soon as possible, was also all too clear.

This is what I learned from the notes.

On May 26th, 2011, the day after my birthday, I was just about to go into a meeting, when my cell phone rang. I checked the caller ID. It had a 250 area code which meant it was coming from Victoria. Even though I didn't recognize the number, a little tingle of dread started to run down my spine. I sensed before I answered that it would be bad news. But I answered it because I had to.

The call came from the office at St Mary's. The woman on the other end told me that my mother had been taken to hospital. I was surprised that they had called me since I had been persona non grata at the nursing home as well as the hospital for the past year thanks to the lies that had told about my children and me. I asked the woman on the other end of the call if it was an emergency. She said she didn't know the details, but she thought it was. I thanked her for calling and hung up.

I knew instinctively what the call meant. My mother was going to die. As usual when I cannot deal with feelings, I went into robot mode and simply did the logical thing. I called the hospital where I knew she would have been taken and asked for an update on my mother's condition.

They told me that there was no one by her name on the patient registry.

I knew of course that she was at RJH because that was the hospital she had been treated at the last two times she had been admitted to hospital. There are only two hospitals in the city and the other one – Victoria General Hospital – was a long way from St. Mary's. I thought for a minute and then called back. I told the woman who answered the phone that I knew my mother was there, that the person who called me from St. Mary's had told me she had been taken there. I told her I was very worried about her and wanted to know what her condition was. This time she told me that the staff had been instructed not to give out any information to me about my mother or her condition by her court appointed guardians. The two women had stuck again!

I then got both of my daughter's to call the hospital. I reasoned that even though they had blackened my name with their lies, my mother's grandchildren would certainly be allowed to find out how she was. But they got the same story. Drunk with the power of guardianship, these women were leaving no loose ends. They "owned" my mother and they were letting me know that. They could be as deliberately cruel as they wanted to be because the Supreme Court of British Columbia was backing them up by making them guardians of person the previous month. The fact that the judge, in his court decision suggested that they keep me in the informational loop about my mother was a small detail that they had decided to ignore.

In his order the judge, "suggested that the committees of person keep you in the loop regarding your mother's decisions". (He still didn't get it. My mother was way past the time where she could make informed decisions about herself.) He also said that they "fail to keep you updated, then you are given permission to apply to the court for that specific order." But then, he also "stated that it seemed that they had your mother's best interests in mind"[90] because they had not asked for any recompense for everything they had done. What he didn't know of course was they had already syphoned $20,000 from her bank accounts, and that their plan was to get their big payoff in the long end when they probated their still secret will, something that was now on the horizon.

In any event, these truly caring women, as they were perceived to be by the judge, who it seems did not have a very good insight into human behavior considering his position in adjudicating the issues of people's lives, should have at least let us know what was going on. We were her family. But, that is not what they did. They did the reverse, preventing us from talking to her or finding out the reality of her condition. My children and I were not allowed even the soupcon of solace that would have come with finding out what her prognosis was. Because the hospital continued to deny she was there, I knew that going to Victoria at this point would be futile. They would not let any of us see her. She was basically a hostage.

After all the things they had done to our family, this still seemed like a new low. It was however a true testament to what kind of these women really were, as if I had any doubt by this point. They were cruel and vindictive and were punishing me for interfering with their plans. I had fought back. What should have been an easy plan to defraud a sick old woman and turned into a battle.

Later that afternoon, I called her doctor, Dr. Houghton who had been so kind to us over the preceding months. He did talk to me. He confirmed her whereabouts and told me she had a blockage in her bowel and that it might be necessary, if it did not clear, to operate. The next question I asked him was one that we both knew the answer to.

"Would she survive such a major operation?"

At the other end of the phone there was silence. Then he spoke. "She's very weak. It would be unlikely." I thanked him for being so candid and for having the guts to talk to me, in spite of the looming presence of the terrible twosome.

The following day, I received this email from Horton.

"Glynnis,

As committees of person, Mrs. Brewer and I make all decisions regarding your mother's care and medical treatment. You are not to contact the hospital as they have been instructed to keep all of your mother's medical information private and confidential. Those are your mother's express wishes.

I will be contacting Dr. Houghton on Monday to ascertain what information he gave you. As your mother's doctor, he has no authority to instruct the Royal Jubilee Hospital, or anyone else for that matter, to give out personal and confidential medical information about your mother. He was advised of that when I provided him with the Committee Order as well as your mother's express wishes in April 2011. If he has breached his duty of confidentiality to his patient I will be taking this further.

If you continue to embarrass your mother, Mrs. Brewer and me, I will not provide you with any further information."

Needless to say, it was a long time before I had any more conversations with Dr. Houghton. But, about eighteen months later he called me out of the blue. He told me he was very sorry about what had happened and that he had been prepared to testify against these women in court for what they had done. He also asked if it had cost me a lot financially. When I told him how much he reiterated his comment. "I am so very sorry."

I knew from reading the hospital notes that at this point my mother was in no position, mentally or physically to make "her express wishes" known to anyone. This was just one more lie, more words they were putting in her mouth to bolster their control over her.

On May 28th, 2011, the day my mother was admitted to the ward, the notes read "patient not oriented to place and time. Patient sleepy, waking only to loud vocal prompting. Patient unable to provide any verbal response." Obviously she was not able to "express her wishes" since she could provide no verbal response. They gave her morphine for the pain and when she pulled out her NG tube – a tube inserted through the nose and designed to remove air and fluids from the stomach or deliver food or medicine - they put her in restraints.

According to the nurse's notes, the two women had told the staff they were concerned about "patient's daughter, "Glynnis" and granddaughters "Sabrina and Arabella", stating that there was a history of "elder abuse"". I imagine this was in case we decided to show up. The hospital never checked to see if there really was a history of abuse or what the history was. They could have asked for a copy of the judge's decision about guardianship handed down in the previous month. There is no mention of elder abuse in it. But they didn't. They did not have the compassion to call me – even though my number was in her file and my legitimate will and POA attached to it. They were remiss in their duty to their patient and their humanity is also in question. They believed the two women, who had no family connection with my mother, over her own flesh and blood. To them she was just a bed number. As a result they hurt our family even more.

At noon on the same day, Dr. Houghton wrote in his notes that he had talked with both Brewer "who along with Horton has POA." (Brewer never had a POA and Horton's was dubious at best since it was signed after my mother was diagnosed as extremely cognitively impaired. What they had was guardianship of person and they had only had that for the past month even though they had been making decisions for her for almost a year. This mistake appears throughout the doctor's and nurse's notes.) One would hope that any facility charged with caring for people, St. Mary's and RJH included, would at least have the wherewithal to check and see if they were being given accurate information before they acted.

Dr. Houghton continued his notes in his own handwriting. "Mrs. Brewer says she thinks Mrs. Walker would want full intervention. I have explained that with her age, frailty and possible bowel obstruction that she may well decline and that full code and CPR etc. would not seem to be the kind thing to do. Mrs. Brewer wants to discuss this with Mrs. Horton."

In the hospital notes from April/May 2010, my mother has a DNR (do not resuscitate order) in her file. We had discussed this at the time and I

189

had explained to her what it meant. She agreed that a DNR was what she wanted and it is in the hospital records. In August of 2010 that DNR was changed to a request for Full Code by Brewer even though, in the nurse's notes from that time my mother is quoted as saying she does not want to be resuscitated if she codes. Even though the neighbor, whose daughter is a nurse and so she would have known what full code meant, had no legal right to represent my mother or make decisions for her since the guardianship hearing was still many months down the road, she made sure that my mother would suffer if she got to point where resuscitation became a possibility. But still she played the "caring friend" and spoke for my mother implying that a kind of intimacy existed between them when it most certainly did not and never had.

It may seem to those who have little experience with hospital lingo and are familiar with hospitals only from what they see on television that the neighbor requested a change of order from DNR to full code because she wanted to appear to be concerned about saving my mother's life at any cost, thereby boosting her image is a caring friend. And too, the lawyer, who was formerly a nurse, would also have known that an order for full code was basically a death sentence for someone of my mother's age and frailty. But the request was acted upon and the order changed. This begs the question, are medical staff ethically bound to do what is best for the patient or do they just do as they are told to by "caring friends". If so we are all at risk.

In people over 70 the chances of coming back after resuscitation are less than 15%. This does not mean "back to normal". This just means "no longer being technically dead". My mother was closing in on her 88th birthday. Even in the presence of medical personnel, only about 20% of resuscitation survivors of any age live long enough to be discharged from the hospital.

As people age, the bones become more brittle and my mother already had severe osteoporosis. During chest compressions, there is about

100-125lbs of force applied to get the heart started. The result of such force would have caused her ribs to fracture. This would then have caused a stabbing pain with her every breath. Full code meant that there was an 80% chance that my mother would have spent the rest of her short life in the hospital in incredible pain.[91] And both of the women would have known that. They also knew that by torturing her, they were torturing me. It was punishment for my interference with their plans.

Then there is intubation in which a tube is forced down the throat and into the lungs to facilitate breathing. This often results in damaged vocal cords, permanent difficulty in swallowing, broken teeth and more pain. [92]

But then, I already knew, the neighbor had a cruel streak. The previous year she had gone to the dentist with my mother for her to be measured for new dentures. She had lost her old ones on her first visit to RJH. My mother hated the dentist and especially the taking of the impression where they put the compound into the patient's mouth. It made her feel like she was suffocating. She panicked and tried to make the dentist stop by pushing him away, but the neighbor intervened, holding her arms down on the chair while panic-stricken, she struggled to get free.

Later that night, the nurse on duty notes that "patient has become increasingly more agitated and has managed to loosen her restraints." Alzheimer's or not my, mother always hated to be restrained. Even my father, who was six foot three to her almost five feet, had trouble hugging her. She would push him away and say, "I can't breathe! I can't breathe." And he would hold her tighter because he thought it was funny. Having her wrists tied to the bed must have been horrific for her.

The following morning, May 29th, the on duty nurse notes, "patient pleasantly confused stating "is this a dream? Where is my husband? I have to let the dog out". She was still confused as to time and place. When asked her age, she told the nurse she was 47.

As the day wore on, she became more agitated again. The term sun downing appears in the notes. She tried to crawl out of bed yelling loudly "you're burning my dog!! You're killing me! Help. Help me now." This time it took two nurses to get her back into bed and put the restraints back on.

On May 30th, the nurse notes that they had to call security because my mother was attempting to hit the nursing staff. They placed her back in restraints. The nurse notes she is still not oriented to time and place.

On the same day this was happening, I got an email from Horton.

"Your Mom is doing OK. She has a partial bowel obstruction due to impacted stool, as well as a urine infection. The Doctors are hoping the bowel will begin moving again without the need for surgery. The hospital is hoping to discharge her back to Mount St. Mary's in the next few days. She has been quite confused due to the urine infection but was a lot better yesterday."

I found this email quite confusing. The lawyer always told everyone that before becoming a lawyer she had been a nurse. It says so on her website. This means that all along she should have understood that my mother's deteriorating mental condition was only going to get worse. And yet for months she had been protesting that she was getting better.

The on call doctor notes that my mother has dementia and delirium and that she is "estranged from her daughter" and that her POA was in this morning. The house doctor on May 31st again notes the history of elder abuse. He says that "caregivers want full medical support and would not rule out surgical intervention." So as early as May 31st, five days after she was taken to RJH, the two women were discussing life threatening surgery, even before the blockage had a chance to correct itself and Horton was still telling me she would be back in St. Mary's in a few days! They knew full well that surgical intervention would be the beginning of the end for her.

By the afternoon of May 30th, my mother was continuing to refuse food and would not take the pills they wanted her to take because she said she felt sick. At 6pm, the neighbor appeared and asked what the doctors were doing for my mother. She said she was concerned that she was not eating. The nurse explained that my mother stated several times that she felt sick. "Patient is refusing to eat or take pills." The nurse told her that my mother's bowl needed to rest; "that her diet should be increased slowly."

But the neighbor was adamant that my mother would eat if food was put in front of her. The nurse noted that "patient has refused all food today". By 7:20 that evening when the nurse checked on her again, my mother was vomiting. Apparently Brewer, her cruel streak showing once again, had been force feeding her. The nurse notes "told Joan that patient needs time to rest and to stop pushing food in her". The nurse called the house resident. My mother continued to vomit for the rest of the evening.

The next day – May 31st – the lawyer called the hospital and asked what the plans were for my mother. She "expressed anger" and requested a consult with the doctor. She "states she is not impressed with information being given to friends of patient and not to her." In other words the lawyer felt left out of the loop. In typical sociopathic fashion, she was angry at the slight. Later that evening, the nurse's notes state, "Dr. spoke to Joan and Jackie and new orders were received."

On June 1, my mother pulled out her IV again. She was found standing beside the window, naked. According to the notes she remained confused.

That evening the neighbor came to see her again. She told the nurse that she wanted my mother to have surgery. The nurse explained that that decision was not up to the nursing staff and that in any event my mother "needed to be well enough to make it through surgery". The bowel obstruction was the perfect opportunity for the two women to advocate for something that would end in her demise.

At this point the nurses had been giving her Dilaudid – a very potent analgesic drug derived from morphine, though her IV. It is a drug given for severe pain.

On June 2nd the house doctor noted she again pulled her IV out and "caregivers are not comfortable with palliative approach." Of course they weren't. "Palliative care is specialized medical care for people with serious illnesses. It focuses on providing patients with relief from the symptoms, pain, and stress of a serious illness—whatever the diagnosis. The goal is to improve quality of life for both the patient and the family."[93] A palliative approach might mean that she could live a little longer without being in pain, or maybe even get over the bowel obstruction and go back to St. Mary's, foiling their plans for their secret will and ultimately costing them money since her bank account was now empty.

Later that evening, Dr. Cunningham tried to call Horton, but only got her voicemail. He decided to try and contact her in the morning.

On June 3rd at Dr. Cunningham's request, the nurse "rang contact person. She stated she would be right in." The doctor's notes say "patient will decondition if she has surgery and will have decreased level of function after surgery. Dr. Cunningham's notes on June 3rd say "the patient's level of function will deteriorate in all probability and she will never have the level of function/mobility/cognition that she had prior. Want to discuss this…"

In spite of his warning, and that of several other doctors, about the probable outcome of surgery, that evening at 6:35, Horton and Brewer signed the consent for surgery, including a possible bowel resection.

On June 4th Dr. Glen's notes from the previous evening say "reviewed with Jackie and Joan yesterday. They have been well counseled as to reservations. Jackie will arrange a 24 hour caregiver if required." Again they were spinning a web of lies. There was no money left for a 24 hour caregiver and they knew it, but they told the doctor differently because they wanted to make sure she had the operation. The doctor may have counselled them to his reservations about surgery which of course only increased their intention for her to have it.

On June 4th at 12:44, Dr. Orrom's nicely typed notes reveal the entire pre-surgery scenario.

"Dr. Cunningham met with her two guardians who have power of attorney. After considerable debate (what were they debating about, what the ultimate outcome of surgery was likely to be?), it was decided that they did want her to have surgery. I had further discussions with Dr. David Glen and the instructions (from the women) were very clear that she undergo surgery.....She is booked for OR today and hopefully we will get this done within the next 24 hours. There was no one to talk to with respect to the procedure. (So the two women didn't even bother show up for the pre surgical consult.) My feeling is it is unlikely that she will get back to her premorbid quality of life and these may be the initial steps in her decline to the point where she will not have good quality."

So Horton and Brewer wanted her to have surgery in spite of the doctors' reservations about the outcome.

On the same day that doctors were doubting the advisability of surgery, I got this email from Horton:

"Your Mom's condition has not improved and the bowel obstruction has not resolved.

We made the decision today for her to have surgery. It will be done sometime this weekend. I do not know what the outcome will be, but the alternative was a death sentence. We talked to your Mom and she wanted to go ahead with the surgery, despite being very weak. She is comfortable and not in too much pain."

What the lawyer was telling me was my mother wanted the surgery. This is not true since she had no idea what was going on. What she really wanted me to know was that my mother was in pain. This was confirmed later by the hospital notes. She was in a lot of pain, hence the amount of pain killers they were giving her.

The surgery was a death sentence and both women knew it. At least five doctors had warned them of the likely outcome. I still fail to understand how a lawyer and a neighbor were allowed to consent to a surgery that several doctors felt was a bad idea, and that the hospital went along with the wishes of these women against the advice of their own staff! The idea that my mother was able to give her own consent for the surgery is absolutely ludicrous given her physical and mental state, as is clear from the hospital notes.

On June 5th the nurse's notes reveal that my mother was back from surgery, "patient demented pre-op, remains very confused now. Patient in restraints." So even though she had just had major surgery they tied her to the bed once more. If someone did that to an animal, they would be arrested.

⟵⟶

Email from Horton June 6th.

"Your Mom had the surgery on Saturday. It was not as serious as we had thought, although she had some small bowel resected. She is doing fairly well and is recovering. I went in to see her on the way to work this morning and the nurses will be getting her up today."

More lies.

The nurse's notes tell a different story. "Overheard a voice coming from patient's room. Upon entering found NG tube had been removed from patient's nose and patient clutching tube. Assessed patient for bleeding, washed her hands and changed top linens." Later they put my mother in hand and leg restraints and put a bed alarm on. The notes relate that she remained confused and delirious, "remains distracted and is unable to use her walker".

Then the notes reveal that there was some redness around the operation site and an open sore on her coccyx. Infection!

On June 9th the nurse contacted Dr. Orrom and he tried to contact Horton, but could not, "geriatric doctor later called POA and it was decided that there would be no further surgery." They didn't need to do anything else to bring about her death. All they had to do now was wait.

According to the lab, at that point, my mother had tested positive for CDiff, a bacterium that causes excruciatingly painful swelling of the intestines and preys on people in hospitals, nursing homes and other medical facilities. As one CDiff survivor put it, "No one deserves to die so horribly."[94] CDiff causes 30,000 deaths a year in the U.S according to USA Today. [95]

Late on the evening of June 11, the on call doctor was called for pain management. Between the bowel resectioning and the C-Diff she must have been in terrible agony. On June 13th, the nurse notes, "Guardians requested no surgical intervention". Several times that night and on into the early morning hours of June 14th, the house doctor was called by the nurse who notified Horton. The nurse notes that my mother's skin is "cool to the touch" and that she is not verbally communicating. Her breathing is shallow. A call is put into the hospitalist. He speaks with Brewer by phone. They agree to talk the following day.

At 6 a.m. my mother was transferred to an air bed. She cried out in pain and began thrashing and moaning. Her breathing was labored. The nurse called the on call doctor but she was not in yet. When she came in, she called the POA and informed her of my mother's deteriorating condition. Later both POA's were called by the nurse.

At 3:30 pm on June 15th the Privacy ban was apparently lifted. No one bothered to call and tell us of course. We were just the family who loved her. Horton told the nurse that "her daughter might be coming from Chicago". Meanwhile, late that afternoon, the neighbor hightailed it over to the Public Guardian's office on Broad Street clutching a copy of the September 15th will. This information I got from the PG herself.

Late on the afternoon of June 15th, Horton sent an email to Arabella.

"Hello Arabella

I just got back from the hospital. Your grandmother is very poorly and is unresponsive now. She is in the Jubilee hospital. I hope your mom can get there before it is too late."

Horton never bothered to mention that the privacy ban had been lifted, either.

On June 16th the nurse wrote, "continued deterioration overnight. Small seizures, pursed lip breathing, in obvious discomfort. Have advised both guardians by phone. Will change to purely palliative measures and expect she will likely pass soon."

On June 16th Horton sent another email to Arabella.

"Hello Arabella

I was in to see your grandmother last night as well as early this morning. She is pretty well the same as she was yesterday, still very poorly. She is having pain medication on a regular basis and the nurses are taking very good care of her. Did your Mom make it to Vancouver last night??"

If she went to see my mother on the morning of June 16th why did she not know they had switched to palliative care as the nurse says in her notes? Why did the nurse say she had contacted both guardians by phone, if the lawyer had been in to see my mother that morning? How did she expect me to get a flight late on Wednesday night when she had only just told us of the severity of the situation late Wednesday afternoon? Why would she ask if I had made it to Vancouver the previous evening when my mother was in hospital in Victoria?

The answer to the last two questions was simple. She wanted to know if I was in the neighborhood because on the afternoon of June 15th, Brewer, sure that my mother was going to die soon went to the PG with her homemade will – the one I was never supposed to find out about.

The answer to the first two questions was also simple. They did not know what was going on with my mother because they were not there. The last few communications from staff to them in the days before my mother died were by telephone. They are not mentioned as visiting her in the hospital notes.

On June 17th, at 10.30 am my mother was pronounced dead. The official cause of her death was small-bowel obstruction, (SBO). The leading cause of SBO in industrialized countries is postoperative adhesions (60%). Adhesions or scar tissue form as a natural part of the body's healing process after surgery. The term "adhesion" is applied when the scar extends from within one tissue across to another and can begin forming within hours after surgery. My mother lived for almost two weeks after the surgery. Long enough for adhesions to form. The secondary cause of death was C-diff. In other words, the most likely cause of her death was, the operation.

The nurse notes that her pupils were fixed and dilated and there was no heart beat, "family at beside. Funeral arrangements have been made at Royal Oak. Patient washed and shroud put around body. Family notified that they need to call funeral home and co-ordinate pick up."

We were never notified by the hospital of my mother's demise. I did not make arrangements for her at Royal Oak. We were most definitely not at her bedside. Which of course begs the question, who was there and why, and why did the nurse think they were her family? Was hospital security that lax that anybody could walk in and sit beside a dying patient?

This is last email we received from Horton, sent on Saturday, June 18th.

"Hello Glynnis and Arabella

I was not in the office yesterday to email you, but I want to express my sincere condolences for your loss.

I also wanted to let you know that your Mom (and grandmother) passed away peacefully at around 10:20 Saturday morning. She had been determined to get better, but it was not meant to be. I was with her all night and never left her side."

If that was the case she would have known that my mother died on Friday morning not on Saturday morning.

My mother's death was not peaceful. Her last two weeks of life were torturous.

200

In the end because of these two women, my mother died, without her family or her tormentors at her bedside, on Friday, June 17th, 2011, one year to the day after these women took over her life.

We arrived in Victoria on Saturday afternoon. On Monday morning I went straight to the Public Guardian's office. She would not return my calls and so I decided to sit outside her office until I got to talk to her. I needed to know how to proceed from here on. Should I make funeral arrangements etc.

Finally my tenacity paid off. About half way through the morning she granted me five minutes of her time. She answered my questions briefly and then showed me the door. As I was leaving she looked up from her desk and said, "you know there is another will."

I had always suspected it, but now I had confirmation. The next question was where was it and where was my original will?

Brewer wrote an obituary which was submitted to the newspaper the following Monday morning. She thanked the staff at VGH (Victoria General Hospital) for their wonderful care in my mother's last days. My mother died at RJH. They got the day wrong and the hospital wrong because they weren't there or because they didn't care enough to get it right. Brewer said a lot of good things about herself and Horton, but very little about my mother because, even though they were supposedly such "good friends", they didn't know much about the details of her life, not even where she was born. Even though there was no longer any necessity, they just couldn't stop lying and fabricating and boasting.

On the day after her birthday, July 1st, I had the newspaper print the obituary I wrote. It was appropriately, all about her, her accomplishments, and her life. The photo I used was one from when she was young, lovely, dancing at a ballroom. She was smiling. Her whole life lay before her. It is the way she would have wanted to be remembered.

PART THREE

Chapter Eighteen

IMAGINARY FRIENDS

"The noblest pleasure is the joy of understanding."
– Leonardo da Vinci

As I write this, it is now January of 2013. My mother has been dead for eighteen months. My dining room table is covered with files. My desk is bursting at the seams. Papers are starting to creep onto the island in the kitchen. I have collected every piece of information about my mother, from hospital records, to bank statements, to credit card receipts to the bills that were unpaid. I have printed every email Arabella and I ever received from or sent to the women who stole my mother. I do this not do this just because I am obsessed with seeking justice for her, or because I am her daughter and the truth about what happened to her needs to be shared, but also because since she died, these women have switched their unwanted attentions from my mother to me and my daughters. During many thoughtful evenings, I came to the conclusion that even if this started out being about elder fraud; it turned into something of a vendetta against me and my girls for foiling their plan.

They have continued to harass me with the bogus wills, even though Horton had said in July of 2011 that she wanted nothing more to do with this case or the wills that Brewer had created. She also said she wanted no recompense for all the hours she says she spent working on my mother's behalf. But, somehow she is still involved in this case, still telling nasty lies about me, still teaming up with Brewer to get money out what's left of my mother's estate. Mills has disappeared from the scene. Her usefulness to them ended with my mother's death. They used her, reeled her into their evil plan because they didn't really want to deal with a demented old lady on a daily basis, so they let her do it. I have heard that when my mother died, Mills cried. But I also found out later from the bank manager that Mills had also emptied another one of my mother's bank accounts in March of 2011 of $2200 leaving only $9.00. So, perhaps they were simply crocodile tears, shed not for her part in the abuse of a trusting old lady, but for the loss of access to her bank accounts.

When my lawyer deposed Mills, she was scared and nervous. Brewer and Horton sat in the room, like vultures in a tree, making sure she did not get a chance to speak freely. I think she is afraid of them. She is not the only one.

After my mother died, Brewer became like a pit bull. She just would not let me go. She lawyered up – one of the most expensive lawyers on the Island – and she inveigled Horton to join her in trying to stop me from probating my legitimate will and put her own homemade will before the court. Maybe she played to Horton's greed, or maybe she played to the fact Horton was in too deep at this point to just walk away. She had done things as a lawyer that were not only unethical, but illegal. The truth could never come out. They became even more of a vicious nuisance.

I understood by then that Brewer, in particular, would not, could not let go. She had to win, and in order to do that, she had to make me lose. That's why she kept going when any other fraudster would have folded their cards and moved on to another victim who was not so much trouble. I also understood that, for her, it had never really been about the money. It was about hurting people - my mother first, and then me and my daughters. Perpetually bored with her own meaningless existence, she

204

was actually enjoying the game of destroying our lives. It was stimulating to her, and it beat the heck out of making silk flower arrangements.

In The Sociopath Next Door, Martha Stout raises the following question: "If sociopaths are so focused on their goals and so driven to win, then why do they not win all the time?" She goes on to explain that, basically, sociopaths are losers: "For they do not (win or succeed in life). Instead, most of them are obscure people, and limited to dominating their young children, or a depressed spouse, or perhaps a few employees or coworkers... Having never made much of a mark on the world, the majority are on a downward life course....... They can rob and torment us temporarily, yes, but they are, in effect, failed lives." [96]

For my part, I knew that I could not let them get away with what they had done to my mother. I owed it to her and the millions of other seniors and their families who could be victimized by people like Horton and Brewer and their ilk. I had to keep on keeping on until this was settled, no matter the personal cost to me. The idea that all the hurt they had heaped on my family would be rewarded by them getting the house my mother loved so much was untenable. I had not been able to save her, but I was determined to save her beloved house.

Over the preceding months there had been all kinds of legal maneuverings. My lawyer filed a caveat to stop them from probating their will. Then their lawyer contacted the PG and tried to force him to sell my mother's house. He was more than happy to oblige because the money from my mother's retirement savings account which had been paying some of the expenses of the house was running out, even though I was $6000 out of pocket for paying for the BC Hydro bill for the house. For some reason the PG had not been paying the account and I got an email that they were cancelling the service. I knew that, in the moist, rain forest climate of British Columbia, without any heat, mold would soon grow all over the house. The house my mother loved so much would be ruined. So I paid the bill, plus an extra $500, because, thanks to the PG, the account was now in arrears and a security deposit was required. The two women didn't care about the house of course. It could fall into ruin and that would suit their plans just fine. I would lose and they would win, because I would not have the house, just a pile of moldy rubble.

Oddly enough, I was supposedly the owner of the contents of the house. My lawyer said that the PG would put everything in storage if the house was sold. I asked him who was going to have to pay for that. "You are," he said. I told him there was no way I wanted complete strangers pawing through my mother's things. Besides which I didn't have the money for that. I had already spent tens of thousands on fighting these women. I was skint.

Sometime around the end of summer of 2012, Brewer's lawyer made an offer to my lawyer. She said she would settle for half the estate, what she would have got if the bogus will had been probated. If I agreed to that, I would get to probate my will. I told him no way, with a few expletives deleted for this book. I simply could not live with myself if I paid this woman $300,000 for killing my mother. We went back to wrangling.

I was physically and mentally exhausted by this point. I despaired of ever having an end to this nightmare, but I could not just walk away. Inside the house were precious treasures – photos, mementos of family and our life together. I had to save them.

It was about this time that a new lawyer entered my life. She told me that she felt a solid sense of outrage about what had been done to my family. Like me, she felt she had an unfailing duty in life to put things right.

She told me that all this time, "The tail had been wagging the dog". In other words, I had been put in the position of proving that I had not done anything wrong whereas they had never been forced to account for their actions against my family. She set out to correct the situation.

We had a court date for April 2013, months away at the time. We were going to have to go to court to let a judge decide which will should stand, a very expensive undertaking.

The new lawyer, a former prosecutor, began her investigation into the case by visiting my mother's neighbors. They were also Brewer's neighbors. After hiking up hill and down, knocking on doors, she discovered that they didn't have a good word to say about her. They did on the other hand speak highly of me and of my mother's feelings for me and her granddaughters.

Apparently, Brewer had not been able to turn off the tap of her rage when it came to me. Outrageous lies continued to gush forth about me and my girls, whenever she could corner one of the neighbors. To me, the need for her to keep on lying, spoke to her desperation. She could not lose. She had to win. Fortunately, they didn't believe a word. The one neighbor who, along with her husband, had taken care of my mother's dog when she first went into hospital, even volunteered to testify on my behalf in court if necessary.

Then my new lawyer went to see the lawyer who represented me in the guardianship hearing. She was more than willing to sign an affidavit attesting to the fact that the secret wills had never been divulged to the court. The following is part of her affidavit.

"I was made aware by my client that her mother, Rosalind Walker had executed a 2006, drawn by Jackie Horton and under that will Glynnis Walker would be the sole beneficiary of her mother's estate.

In preparation for the hearing of the guardianship matter I wrote to Iris Foster, counsel for Joan Brewer and Jackie Horton. I asked Ms. Foster specifically whether her clients had any knowledge of any change in Mrs. Walker's estate plans and in particular, whether Rosalind Walker had made a new will since her will dated

October 19, 2006. I was assured by Iris Foster that there had been no change to that 2006 will and thus it stood.

In reliance on that representation, during the guardianship proceedings, I advised the judge both orally and in my written argument that Glynnis Walker was sole beneficiary under her mother's last will dated in 2006. During the proceedings Ms. Foster also assured the judge that neither Joan Brewer nor Jackie Horton had any financial interest in the affairs of the Rosalind Walker.

Both Joan Brewer and Jackie Horton were present throughout the proceedings including both for my argument and that of their counsel Iris Foster.

At no time in those guardianship proceedings did Ms. Foster, Jackie Horton or Joan Brewer ever disclose to the judge the existence of any will later than the 2006 Will naming Glynnis Walker as sole beneficiary.[97] (Lawyer's own formatting)

Later, the judge specifically comments on the fact that neither Jackie Horton nor Joan Brewer were seeking any reimbursement for their services in assisting the Mrs. Walker, that they had simply stepped forward to help and that Glynnis Walker was needlessly suspicious of their motives in helping her mother.

So, Horton and Brewer and possibly even their own lawyer kept information from the court pertaining to the existence of the 2010 wills. This affidavit was an important piece of evidence, especially since it was given by a lawyer. "As officers of the court, lawyers have an absolute ethical duty to tell judges the truth, including avoiding dishonesty or evasion....."[98] Although, it would seem, that not all lawyers follow that duty. Some or all of these women on the opposing side were obviously guilty of perjury.

At Christmas of 2012. Arabella came home from Los Angeles where she had been working for HBO. It was lovely having her back. I missed her a lot. I was missing a lot of people these days. My little family had now shrunk down to two. Sabrina had stayed home with me and was working in a restaurant in the small town where we live. I know she did this because she felt that someone needed to look after me. I was a bit of an emotional wreck after the last three years. But I also know that, after what happened to their grandmother, both my daughters were afraid that something similar might happen to me.

One day between Christmas and New Year's, Arabella decided she wanted to get her hair done by her old hairdresser. She made an appointment and we went together to have some mother/daughter bonding time. I sat and watched while the hairdresser worked on her. When her head was a mass of tinfoil strips, we had to wait for the color to take. We started to talk about "the case" as we now referred to it. I told her that, Brewer, was still insisting, as she had been insisting throughout this ordeal, that she and my mother were long term, close, friends and that's why my mother had changed her will to make Brewer and her husband her major beneficiaries. We both knew that that was simply not true. But how did we prove it?

Suddenly, Arabella came up with an idea, an idea that was the hinge on which the rest of the case would turn. "Why not get hold of her hairdresser? Nanny went to her every week for twenty-five years. Women always tell their hairdressers everything."

It was simply a brilliant idea. I wish I had thought of it. So I called my lawyer and gave her the name and phone number of my mother's hairdresser. I had this number quite by accident. I had taken it from my mother's telephone book when she was first in the hospital, thinking that maybe Uta would come and do her hair for her. I knew it would make her feel better. But, the hairdresser was away on a cross country biking tour, so I found someone else to do it.

What the hairdresser said in her affidavit confirmed everything I had been saying all along. My mother had never considered Joan Brewer and Jackie Horton as friends, and especially not close friends.

In her sworn affidavit, the hair dresser said the following:

"For about twenty years, Rosalind Violet Walker had a weekly appointment with me every Thursday morning at 9 AM. As with many of my long-term clients, she and I often chatted about personal matters and she shared with me many details about her life and her relationships. I knew from her, that she and her husband, Bramwell had only one child, their daughter Glynnis who was apparently married with children and living in the United States.

The last time that I saw her was when she came for her usual weekly appointment sometime in the spring of 2010 after she apparently had been briefly hospitalized. At that time, she seemed mentally competent and her usual self so far as I could tell. (That was true. The changes in her mental state had been so subtle that it would have been easy to miss them until she started having the ischemic strokes after she went into RJH in April of 2010.*)*

The following week, I was very surprised when she did not show up as it was most out of character for her. I phoned her to find out what had happened but did not connect.

A couple of weeks later I received a phone call from a woman, saying she was Mrs. Walker's neighbor, Joan Brewer, (Brewer must have found Uta's number in my mother's phone book, just like she did the pin numbers for the Visa and ATM cards because they did not know each other and had never met.) *She told me that Mrs. Walker was in the Royal Jubilee Hospital ("RJH").*

Within a couple of weeks, I went to RJH to visit her but left without seeing her after being told by a nurse that she was not accepting visitors that day. A couple of months later, I was contacted again by this Joan Brewer. She said she wished to make an appointment for Mrs. Walker for a permanent wave and she told me that she was now in Mount St. Mary's care home. For some reason she wanted the appointment on a Wednesday and I agreed to change my regular day to accommodate her.

Soon after, however, Joan Brewer phoned back to cancel, telling me that Mrs. Walker would instead have her hair done by a stylist at Mount St. Mary's (as I had arranged previously when I had signed all the papers for her admission). *I was disappointed as I would have liked to see her.*

Thus I never had the chance to compare any changes in her mental state over the months since I had last seen her. (It would have been unwise for Horton and Brewer to let someone see her who could have noted the deterioration in my mother's mental state when, at this point, they were still insisting she was getting better and should be able to go home.)

For over twenty years, I had followed Glynnis Walker's life through her mother. In all the time I knew her she always spoke lovingly of her daughter Glynnis and with great pride at Glynnis' many accomplishments. I knew Glynnis to be both a successful author and a radio talk show host in addition to raising a family. In all the time I knew her, I never heard her complain about Glynnis nor say even a single, solitary negative thing about Glynnis.

From our conversations over the years, I understood from her that she was frequently in contact with Glynnis by telephone and that Glynnis phoned her very regularly. She often expressed regret that she could not see Glynnis more often and I suggested she fly down to visit Glynnis, but she told me that she did not like to travel and she did not like to be in someone else's house—even her daughter's home.

In all the years she was my client, she never paid by cheque but always paid with cash. (My mother did know how to write a check until I showed her after my father died. Even then she still preferred to pay with cash. This made the made the check writing spree that took place after Brewer and Horton got hold of her even more out of character.) *I knew over the years that Bramwell, Mrs. Walker's husband, was apparently somewhat controlling of her. For example, he always insisted on driving her to her appointments.*

According to what she told me, Bramwell definitely controlled the family finances.

When Bramwell died, she seemed lost as to how to proceed and appeared to rely greatly on Glynnis, who came up to help her organize her finances and her life. I always had the impression from my discussions with her that she continued to rely greatly on her daughter Glynnis, even though she was far away. She spoke of Glynnis handling all of her financial affairs after Bramwell died.

I knew also from her, that Glynnis brought her a little Yorkshire terrier who was much loved and was great company to her. She told me she used to talk to the dog. (Brewer and Horton lied about the dog and said that she was acquired from a pet store which would have been odd since the dog was five when I got her. I sent my lawyer a document from the Illinois Department of Agriculture which showed that I had gotten the dog a rabies shot in October 2006 in Illinois, so I could take her into Canada.)

I knew from my discussions with Mrs. Walker that she was a very private person who seemed to spend a lot of time alone. Apart from family, she only spoke of one person as a friend—someone whom she met for coffee at Broadmead Shopping Centre. (This was a lady who I did not know, but I knew she used to go for coffee with my mother about once a week.)

Mrs. Walker did speak of her neighbor Joan Brewer, but she spoke of Joan Brewer always as a neighbor and never as a friend. Never once did she describe or mention Joan as being her friend. She talked about getting rides with Joan Brewer for example, to Costco or to Sears, but nothing beyond that.

Mrs. Walker never spoke of socializing with Joan Brewer and repeatedly expressed her lack of interest in doing so. (Brewer always maintained that my mother and my father were frequent guests at her home, but when asked by my lawyer to provide proof of this in the way of photographs she could not come up with more than half a dozen of my mother, all taken in the two years before her death, and none of my father. She did manage to provide two photos of very fancy table settings however.)

I never ever heard of Mrs. Walker speak of Joan Brewer with fondness and affection nor as a friend. Rather, she would complain about Joan Brewer, particularly after Bramwell's death, telling me that she was always inviting her over or inviting her out and that she did not want to go. She told me when speaking of these frequent invitations "I'm not interested."

She did mention one night that she apparently spent in the Brewer household during a power outage in the neighborhood, saying that the next morning she could hardly wait to leave the Brewer home. (I remember my mother telling me about that night. She called me first thing the next morning when she got back to her house. She said she had wanted desperately to go home, but the Brewers had made her stay.)

Mrs. Walker, mentioned with disapproval the fact that Joan had got a dog—saying words to the effect that why did Joan want a dog when she was hardly ever home and the dog was hollowing so much the neighbors had to call animal control.

So finally the truth of my mother's relationship with these women was revealed. Unfortunately it was too late.

Chapter Nineteen

TRUTH AND CONSEQUENCES

*Three things cannot be long hidden: the sun, the moon,
and the truth. - Buddha*

It is difficult to convey to anyone who has not experienced it the frustration of knowing what is true and despite extraordinary efforts being unable to convince the powers that be that veracity was on our side. I can only liken it to the feeling of knowing one is stuck in a terrifying nightmare and not being able to wake up no matter how hard they try.

So we hired an expert witness to review all the files of the case and give her unbiased opinion to the court.

Our expert witness was a licensed physician and one of the few geriatric psychiatrists in Canada who had completed an accredited postgraduate training fellowship program in the subspecialty of geriatric psychiatry. She had years of experience in the assessment (and treatment) of dementia, personal and financial competency assessments, testamentary capacity, elder abuse, and nursing home care. After hearing our story, she agreed to look at the pile of binders that my lawyer had compiled on our case.

We were particularly interested in her views on the following points:

a) Whether the my mother had testamentary capacity at the time that Brewer's homemade will was signed in September, 2010;

b) Whether there was evidence to suggest the my mother was vulnerable to undue influence at any significant time leading up to the signing of Brewer's impugned will;

c) Whether there was evidence to suggest that, in practical terms, my mother could have returned home at any time after her discharge from hospital and transfer to St. Mary's on June 2, 2010. She was also asked to opine on the potential risks to my mother from living in her home setting versus an institutional setting;

d) Whether there was any evidence to suggest that my mother's cognitive capacity improved in any significant manner from June 2, 2010 until the signing of the impugned will in September;

e) Whether there was any evidence from the medical records and documents to indicate that my mother was inappropriately treated by me in the months from March 2010 up to the signing of the impugned will on September 15, 2010 (including directions as to her care, housing, and medical treatment).

f) She was also asked to address points or concerns about Dr. Jenkins' report (dated October 23, 2010).

After reviewing all the hospital notes both from St. Mary's and RJH plus the copious evidence I had given my lawyer, she wrote a seventy page report which was eventually cut down to twenty-five pages since judges do not like long documents. (Dr. Culo's entire report is in the Appendix.)

Her opinion was that the medical and documentary evidence over-whelmingly suggested that my mother did not have testamentary capac-ity in September, 2010 due to advanced dementia (mixed Alzheimer's and vascular type). It appeared that my mother suffered some small strokes in the spring of 2010 due to atrial fibrillation (irregular, rapid heart rhythm). These small strokes led to a precipitous and rapid de-cline in my mother's cognitive function.

I did not know about these strokes until I read her report in the middle of January 2013. But it explained a lot. We had seen an overnight change in my mother when she first entered RJH in March of 2010. She had become delusional and paranoid between the time we left her on the first evening and the time we got back the next morning. If the staff had said anything about her odd behaviors to me, I would never have let her be discharged. It was dangerous for her to go home, even more so since Brewer was already baiting her trap. But nobody at the hospital said anything about her behaviors being anything more than the result of a case of anemia.

In her report, the geriatric psychiatrist said that she did not believe that my mother understood the relevance of signing a new will and did not appreciate the consequences of disinheriting her family. She also noted that my mother suffered from paranoid delusions involving me – planted by Brewer and Horton - and that these delusions affected her decision-making with regards to the disposition of her assets.

Her review of the facts indicated that my mother had grossly impaired judgment. She had very poor awareness of her assets, care needs, medi-cal problems, and personal and financial situation around the time of the signing of the Brewer wills. Her memory deficits were severe and she had poor insight.

It seems that my mother also exhibited behavioral and psychologi-cal symptoms of dementia such as fearfulness, confabulation, crying, anxiety, sleep disorder, change in personality and social skills, paranoia, and hallucinations, which are common in individuals with dementia, and usually become more prominent as the disease progresses.

My mother had always wanted to return to her home, but I had known that it would have been not only financially impossible but also not in her best interests because of her physical and mental state since May of 2010 which is why I accepted the doctor's recommendation that she go into care. The psychiatrist agreed, saying that my mother likely held a grudge against me for placing and keeping her in the nursing home. This is a common problem seen frequently in people with Alzheimer's.

The psychiatrist read the medical notes. It was clear that it would not have been safe or practical for my mother to return home. She had advanced dementia, was physically frail, and had several acute medical problems that required frequent assessment and laboratory monitoring. She had been hospitalized three times; required constant nursing support; was deemed to be a high fall risk and was also a high elopement risk; was becoming more disoriented and confused; was getting up in the middle of night, and could easily have wandered outside if she were in her own home. Wandering almost always precludes a person with dementia from living in his/her home. (Indeed the hospital notes related several incidences of her wandering at night in the hospital where she had a least one serious fall.)

In spite of this, or maybe because of it, Horton and Brewer continued to support my mother's wish to return to her home, and were actively pursuing this goal. They told her that I was the one interfering with that plan, which fueled her anger towards me.

The psychiatrist then addressed the issue of undue influence. She said that my mother was vulnerable to undue influence (or the subversion of her will) by the people she became dependent on in the last stages of her life - Horton, Brewer and Mills. Individuals with my mother's degree of cognitive impairment require only very subtle influence to be "unduly influenced" due to this increased vulnerability. Her self-appointed care givers had the potential to exert great power and control over her because of her dementia.

The doctor also noted that the circumstances of the execution of the new or 'home made wills' and their contents should have aroused suspicion of undue influence. Unnatural provisions; radical changes in the beneficiaries and pattern of distribution; persons of influence possible involvement in the procurement of the changes; and contents not in accordance with previous wishes are signs of the presence of undue influence.

The other obvious piece of information that relates to this specific task of testamentary capacity is that my mother did not account for the disposition of her entire estate in the 2010 wills. She accounted only for $600,000 and this specifically from "the sale of her house".

The doctor also thought it highly unusual that my mother included Mr. Brewer as a beneficiary ($100,000) when it appeared that he played a limited role in her life, if any. Mr. Brewer is not mentioned anywhere in the medical records, nor was there any other evidence that he was close to my mother or father.

The report also identified numerous "risk factors" or "red flags" for vulnerability, elder abuse, and undue influence that anyone with a senior at potential risk of Alzheimer's needs to know.

- Diagnosis of **dementia** (i.e., "cognitive vulnerability" due to poor decision making, insight, and judgment). Appraisal of others may be tainted by dementia, even in the early phases. People with dementia may change their attitudes towards significant others during the course of their illness. This change may be triggered or fed by the disease, as well as by natural frictions and events that occur normally in families.

- Presence of **paranoia**. Paranoid ideation can poison affections, and new alliances can be formed based on the exploitation of these altered affections. When the patient suffers from paranoia, his/her suspiciousness of potential benefactors may be fuelled by an influencer.

- Loneliness, social **isolation**, and sequestration (i.e., "emotional vulnerability"): the Deceased's main contacts in the last year of her life became Ms. Horton, Ms. Brewer and Ms. Mills. Her daughter who lived at a distance was essentially warned to keep away from her.

- Past history of **emotional abuse** and **dependence** on others. It is believed that Mrs. Walker sustained emotional abuse at the hands of her mother and husband, that her husband was controlling, and that she was highly reliant on others for assistance with her day-to-day affairs.

- Recent **nursing home placement** (i.e., this move away from the Deceased's "normal environment" was an additional stressor).

- Recent **medical illnesses or hospitalization.**

- **Physical, emotional, and mental dependence** on others.

- **"Family conflict"**/estrangement from daughter who was previously favored (prior to the onset of dementia). Creation of new "alliances" with individuals previously unknown or "on the periphery".

- Relationship of **informal care giving** (leading to new found faith or gratitude on the part of the vulnerable individual).

- **Conflict** between family and informal care givers/new friends. This conflict forces the vulnerable elder to have to "choose sides".

- A **"confidential" or "special" relationship** existed between the Deceased, Ms. Horton, Ms. Brewer, and Ms. Mills. Their frequent contact with the Deceased likely led to their having positions of influence and possible **control** over the testamentary act. The facts in the records indicate that their contact with the Deceased significantly increased once Mrs. Walker became infirm, disabled, and unable to make her own decisions.

- Presence of a **"helpful" neighbor"** and/or friend, "new on the scene" since the Deceased became infirm and in need of assistance.

- Presence of a **trusted professional person**: example, lawyer.

- Possibility of **collusion** between new care givers/friends who are in support of Mrs. Walker's unrealistic desire to return home (as opposed to her daughter who followed medical advice to have Mrs. Walker placed in a care facility).

- Deficits in hearing, mobility, and communication; **frailty.**

- **Submissive personality** type

- **Events occurring in haste**. The daughter's POA was revoked and reassigned to Ms. Horton, a health care representation agreement was obtained, guardianship of person was obtained, and Mrs. Walker's will was purportedly changed. All of these events occurred in less than one year.

- Apparent **involvement by the ultimate beneficiary or benefi-ciaries in the legal transactions.**

- Female gender.

- Advanced age.

- Widowed status.[99]

The psychiatrist also had some reservations about Dr. Jenkins' report, as had I. The October 23, 2010 report was addressed to Iris Foster, Barrister and Solicitor for Ms. Horton for the purpose of evaluating Mrs. Walker's "ability to have input into decisions involving who should be her surrogate decision-maker" and "who would best represent her wishes for care if she fails to meet the criteria for full competency". (In other words, Horton and Brewer needed my mother to say that she wanted them to be her caregivers and make decisions for her so the judge would make his decision in their favor.)

Dr. Jenkins' opinion was formed on the basis of one interview on October 23, 2010. She indicated that she reviewed "supplemental" information but it is not clear from the content of the report what specific aspects of the medical record were reviewed.

Contrary to customary process for these assessments, Dr. Jenkins allowed Joan Brewer to remain present for much of the interview to protect Mrs. Walker from undue distress. Based on the literature this decision affected the validity of Dr. Jenkins' assessment and opinion. This is not the usual practice and is not recommended. The doctor agreed that Brewer's presence likely influenced my mother's answers.

Dr. Jenkins had pointed out that she could not be certain whether my mother actually remembered these events or had merely been told about them, especially since she had no recollection of either the original 2006

POA or will or the more recent 2010 POA or wills; could not recall the circumstances leading up to her admission to Mount St. Mary's; could not recall how she knew Brewer and could not remember Horton's name at all and had no recollection of either hospitalization.

Dr. Jenkins opined that it was in my mother's best interest to have Brewer and Horton serve as her substitute decision makers, in part because my medical direction in the past had not been appropriate. There is no evidence in the medical records to support this. I had simply acted in accordance with the physician's recommendations.

Unfortunately, Dr. Jenkins' assessment, even though it did not have the necessary information and expertise to provide a medicolegal opinion of competence in this case was central to the judge's decision to turn my mother over to Horton and Brewer.

By now we had a very strong case. Everything that Horton and Brewer had said and done was now suspect. They were not my mother's friends, did not have her best interests at heart – in fact quite the opposite, used undue influence on her to get her to sign a POA and a couple of wills, an action she did not understand, turned her love for me and my girls into hatred, and ended her life in a most painful and egregious fashion, ruined my health and my daughters' trust in just about everybody. Horton and Brewer had left a long line of pain in their wake, damaged my family beyond repair and took away the mother that I loved. I couldn't wait to get into court!

But towards the end of January, my lawyer informed me that there was a possibility that we had hit a snag. She had asked for Horton and Brewer for documents. She wanted all the emails between the two of them, all their phone records, all the photographs of them with my mother and perhaps worst of all for them, their tax returns! I knew that Brewer's husband would not be happy about that, and they would have trouble coming up with the other documents because many of them simply did not exist. They countered by demanding a gag order so that I would never be able discuss this case. I was almost finished the book at this point. I told my lawyer that was absolutely not an option. If for no other reason than I felt obligated to warn the rest of the world about situations like this so other people didn't end up like my mother.

The following day she told their lawyer that the gag order was off the table. Their lawyer said he could ask the court for more time to make their documents available. It could be another year!

Another year! Another year of paying the bills for the house; paying lawyers; putting my grief on hold. I wanted justice for what they had done to us. I wanted some kind of recognition for the havoc they had wreaked on our lives. In my head a single phrase kept repeating itself. "Justice delayed is justice denied."

But more than anything, I wanted it to be over!

Chapter Twenty

"PLEASE, I JUST WANT TO GO HOME"

"Turn your wounds into wisdom." – *Oprah Winfrey*

Three years after our story began, on May 15, 2013; my legitimate will was finally probated. I immediately had the locks changed on the doors. When I arrived at my mother's house, now my house, a couple of weeks later, I held the brand new key in my hand.

I was apprehensive. What would I find inside? The real estate agent, who I had hired to sell the house, had already been inside with her daughter. Her daughter, who did not know our story, made her mother promise never to be alone in the house. She said she felt something very bad had happened there. She was right.

My hand trembled and I hesitated over the shiny new lock on the front door. How many times had I thought this day would never come? How often had I just wanted to stop fighting for what was right and get on with my life? How many sleepless nights had I a lain awake trying to figure out what to do next?

The key did not turn. For a moment I wondered if Joan Brewer had had the locks changed yet again. She had already told the gardener I had hired that she owned the house. She then started to tell him what she wanted done with the yard. He phoned me and I told him that if she set foot on the property again he should call the police and I would have her charged with trespassing.

I tried the key again, pushing and turning at the same time and this time the stiff new lock gave way. Gingerly, I opened the front door and went inside.

In the fading light of day, the house was gloomy and silent. In fact, the absolute want of any sound was unnerving. It was like being in a tomb.

Even though the blinds were all closed, here and there slivers of dust-speckled sunlight streaked across the dimness. As I moved from room to room, I noted what was missing and what remained. Things had been moved around. My mother's favorite photo of me that sat on a table next to the living room couch was lying on the floor. The glass was shattered. I doubted that was by accident.

The silence was consuming. I had been hoping for was some sign of my mother's presence. I was sure that somehow the essence of her would have found its way back to her beloved house – that somehow I would be able to feel her. But, I had no sense of her being there at all. There was just the musty smell of a house where lives had once been lived and memories made and lost.

I went into the kitchen. There were now two tea pots in the counter instead of one. I had already noticed that there was a new set of bedding in the guest bedroom. Somebody had been availing themselves of the use of the house. A brown purse lay on the kitchen counter. I recognized it as the one that had been bought on her Sears account. It was empty except for a large set of keys – not my mother's. There was no sign of her wallet. There was also a plastic bag from St. Mary's containing a pair of sneakers, a pair of brown pants and a beige sweater. The last things she had worn? How did they end up in her kitchen? I don't know. Perhaps the Public Guardian had placed them there. They were after all a part of her estate. Perhaps the women who had taken over her life had put them there. It did not matter now.

Then I went into the garage. All the gardening tools were gone. Their empty boxes a testament to the fact that they had ever been there. Brewer had struck again. The photographs and the girls' drawings from when they were children, which comprised the contents of the blue storage containers that I had stored there many years ago, were strewn about. Copies of my books were tossed here and there on the floor. Incongruously, my framed Ph.D. had been placed in the den.

My mother's car was parked, as usual on the left side of the garage. I was a little surprised it was still there. I noticed that the automatic garage door openers had been detached from their power source, the plugs hung impotently from the box on the ceiling. Wire coat hangers were jammed into the garage door tracks. Somebody didn't want that car going anywhere – yet.

I noticed that the car looked too clean. It fact it gleamed. I opened the door and looked in. Clean as a whistle inside too - much cleaner than when I had last driven it three years before. I took the car keys out of my purse. I had kept them just in case my mother had ever come back to the house and tried to drive the car. It was the only set. Or so I thought.

I slid into the driver's seat and put the key in the ignition. Nothing happened. Probably a dead battery. The car had been sitting idle so long. So I got out and went around to the front of the car and popped the hood. Everything looked in order. In fact the engine was pristine. I poked around, not really knowing what I was looking for. I got back into the car and tried the ignition again. Nothing. For some reason I decided to look in the glove box. Although the insurance and registration were missing, there was a short black cord inside. I had seen enough "girl- gets- abducted when- the- bad- guy- disables- her- car movies" to know what it was.

The distributor cap! Someone was making sure that I would not be able to drive the car if I suddenly showed up. But we writers are resourceful lot. The half of our life that is not spent writing is spent doing research. We are an ever growing repository of unrelated but sometimes useful information. I got out of the car again and put the distributor cap back on. This time when I turned the key in the ignition, the car started!

Then I walked around the back of the car. What I saw stopped me in my tracks. An Alberta license plate had been substituted for the British Columbia plate that had been there the last time I had driven the car. My mother had never been to Alberta. The registration stickers were for the year 2010 to 2011. My mother had been in St. Mary's during that time and was totally incapable of driving. So somebody had been driving the oh- so-clean car.

I phoned the Saanich police and asked the dispatcher if she could run the plates and tell me to whom they belonged.

She came back in a couple of minutes.

"Do you have any idea who owns the plates?" she asked.

I told her I had a pretty good idea and that it was my mother's next door neighbor, Joan Brewer or her husband or their used car company, Northpark Motors.

"Why would you say that?" she asked.

"Well, she and her husband have a used car dealership in Edmonton and they live next door to my mother." I didn't go on about the rest of it. What was the point?

She confirmed the information. I told her that I had checked earlier that day and the car was still registered in my mother's name so they had not changed the ownership – just the plates. A police constable was dispatched to take my statement.

Later, when he spoke to the Brewers, they told him that they had put the plates on a car that wasn't theirs, parked in a garage that wasn't theirs, so they "could drive it around the block and see if it still worked." This meant that they must have been the ones to remove the distributor cap and disable the automatic garage door opener.

If they had no interest in the car why then did they take off the distributor cap and hide it in the glove box? I asked the constable. Why was the car specifically mentioned in the will that Joan Brewer had handwritten as something that should go to her husband when my mother passed away?

The constable told me that the Brewers had sworn they had no interest in the car. Case closed.

I shook my head in further disbelief at the overwhelming incompetence of a justice system that just refused to protect the vulnerable elderly and went back into the house.

<hr />

I have never been one for poking around in other people's things and certainly I had always respected my mother's privacy. This meant I had no idea what treasures I had inherited. But they were legion.

I found the box that held every piece of paper my mother had ever gathered about me. Report cards, essays, newspaper columns I had written, reviews about my books, tapes of my radio show. She had kept everything about me. It was a gift of the past from her to me, the only record of parts of my life that I did not have the wherewithal to keep. I had no idea she been keeping mementos of me all these years. It was the thing a mother would do for a beloved child. It brought me to tears. In spite of all Horton and Brewer's efforts to poison her against me and to lie to everyone they could about how my mother hated me, she had loved me after all. Finding that memory box made all the suffering and anguish of the last three years begin to recede. She did love me. Even if the three women had, in the last year of her life, taught her not too.

I also found copious boxes of slides and home movies my father had taken during my childhood. It was apparent he loved us, and especially my mother, very much. Whatever had happened because of the evil machinations of these three women, there on the celluloid was the true story of my family.

Then, tucked away in the top of a closet that was blocked by a dresser which had not been moved in decades, I found all the love letters that my father had written to my mother during World War Two. Later, when Arabella arrived and we sat down to read them it gave us a glimpse into the young lives of my parents as newlyweds before I was born, before they grew old and frail, before he died and she became a victim of greed and cruelty. Reading those letters I understood more than ever that it is so important to remember that every victim of elder fraud deserves to be treated with respect. The crimes committed against the fragile elderly are still crimes even if they can't testify, can't remember what happened, or have died. They were not always just old men and women, disposable people who were easy pickings for fraudsters, dismissable by a society that only pays lip service to elder fraud and does not make it one of its priorities. Once, these people were young and vital and in love, giving up their youth to fight a war that spared following generations an uncertain fate. Crimes committed against the elderly are just as diabolical as those committed against vulnerable children and deserve to be prosecuted to the fullest extent of the law, not ignored by it.

The treasures I found in my mother's house would have been lost to us forever if we had not fought back against the evil these women had perpetrated on our family. They had been motivated only by dollar signs and cruelty. But we had been motivated by love of family and an enduring need to keep our family memories intact. If we had not persevered, all these treasures would have ended up in the nearest dump.

The day before I left for Victoria to take possession of my mother's house, the mortuary where my mother's ashes were interred had called me and said they were looking for volunteers to pick up the ashes of their loved ones since their storage had become impossibly overcrowded due to the especially large senior population on the Island (locals call Vancouver Island the home of the "newly wed and nearly dead"). Would I consider coming to get my mother's ashes?

Of course I would, I told them. In fact I had already planned on it. I had been thinking for a while of some way of bringing my mother back to her beloved house and now fate had handed me the perfect opportunity.

Brewer and Horton had insisted doctors give my mother multiple cognitive ability tests to prove she was improving cognitively so they would be able to get the court to agree that her intention to change her will in favor of them was a valid one. This would mean that the will Tuner had written would stand and my will would be cast aside. On one of these tests my mother had been asked to draw the face of a clock. She could not manage it. Instead, in her trembling handwriting, she had written at the bottom of the page a plea for her salvation. "Please, I just want to go home," she had begged. I got a lump in my throat when I read that in the hospital notes. I wanted desperately to make that request come true.

So the next afternoon, I got into her car and drove over to the mortuary. The ashes were waiting for me. A very nicely dressed young man in a dark suit and crisp white shirt, who was, I thought, overly cheerful considering where he worked, handed me a form to fill out and then when

I had finished, he passed me the ashes. They were in a brown container, with her name taped to the outside.

It felt a little odd carrying my mother in what amounted to a coffee can, but as I walked out to the car I addressed the container. "Come on Mum, we're going for a little ride in your car. I'm going to take you home." They were words I had been holding inside for three years and they needed to be spoken, even if only to a can full of ashes.

When we got back to the house, I noticed that Mrs. Brewer was peering nosily through her front blinds. I ignored her. She continued to do that every time I was at the house. Sometimes if I was doing yard work she would park at the end of the driveway and just stare at me. Once she did a U-turn and chased me up the hill as I was coming back from the grocery store. She was creepy all right. But I was not afraid of her anymore. In fact she seemed quite a pathetic figure now.

Inside, I placed my mother's ashes on the pot-bellied stove in the family room next to my father's ashes and all of their dogs. I knew she would like that.

It was time for a cup of tea. I made the tea and sat down at the dining room table to address the pile of mail that had been waiting for me. It was a lovely, sunny June day and I had the door to the patio open to let in the summer breeze that blew straight off the ocean and through the huge pine trees behind her house. The tang of sea brine mixed with the scent of pine swept away the musty smell in the house. Aside from the whispering of the summer wind, it was peacefully quiet.

Making an inroad into the pile of mail, I finished the tea. My mum and dad were both still getting mail, years after they had departed this reality. Some of it would have to be dealt with. Mostly it was junk mail and charities asking for money. Little did they know my parents had already donated heavily to the Horton/Brewer/Mills charity. I sat back and stared out the door.

There on the patio was a huge black and white cat with big green eyes. She was just sitting there staring at me intently as cats tend to do. We locked gazes. My mother had had such a cat from the time she was a little girl until after I was born. The previous evening, I had found a picture of her as a young teenager holding her precious cat in her arms. His name had been Whisky. I remembered her telling me that she had kept that cat safe throughout the war, taking it down into the Anderson shelter at the bottom of her parent's garden when the Germans made their nightly bombing raids on London. My gaze wondered over to the fireplace where the ashes of my family sat. Then back to the patio. The cat was gone.

Still, the atmosphere of the house seemed to have changed. Probably the fresh air, I thought. The house had after all been closed up for a long time. I went back to the mail.

About a half an hour later, Arabella phoned me from Los Angeles. She told me that the strangest thing had just happened. She had come downstairs to go to work and there had been a huge black and white cat with big green eyes sitting on her car. I told her the story of her nanny's cat. Neither one of us ever saw the black and white cat again, but we both had a feeling that my mother was telling us she was glad to be home.

A few days later, Arabella arrived to help me with a garage sale. My mother had collected a lot of things over the years and although it was difficult to see her little possessions going out the door in the hands of strangers, we could not keep everything.

Exhausted at the end of a long, emotionally draining day, we sat down when everyone was gone, talking about my mother, sharing stories and memories, until gradually we lapsed into silence. Each of us was dealing with our own feelings. It was not easy for either of us to dismantle my parent's house. But it had to be done.

After a while, Arabella decided we needed a pizza and so she went off down the hill in her nanny's car to the local Italian restaurant to get one. I decided since the evening had turned chilly, as it often does in the Pacific Northwest even in June, I would make a fire. It would be cheerful and there was plenty of wood.

We had sold most of the lamps in the garage sale, but there was still enough twilight to see for the moment. Soon a blazing fire was flickering and dancing, holding the shadows at bay for the moment. Arabella returned with the pizza. We both realized we were famished and demolished it forthwith and then settled back to retell our favorite stories about my mother and enjoy the warmth of the fire in the gathering dusk.

But, it wasn't long before we both began to detect a strange odor.

"Is that the wood burning?" Arabella asked me.

"I don't know. Better turn on the overhead light in the kitchen so we can see what's going on." I thought that maybe there was something wrong with the stove and that even though the glass doors were closed somehow the smoke was blowing back into the house.

Arabella turned on the light. Both the family room and kitchen appeared to be full of smoke.

"Let's open the doors and windows and get some air in here." I cried. But, even with the draft from outside, the "smoke" hung in the air.

Then we looked on top of the stove. Four little urns stood silently in a row. The fifth one had melted. Airborne by the heat of the fire, Mum's ashes hung in the air, covered all the surfaces, settled into the folds of the drapes, dusted the carpet and clung to us. They were in the air we were breathing!

We grabbed the little dustpan and brush and swept up the remaining ashes from the top of the fireplace before they too went airborne.

"What do we do with them now?" Arabella asked the obvious question.

"We sold most of the containers in the garage sale." I said looking around. "What are we going to do with them?" Then I spotted the perfect choice. Her teapot!

And so we poured Mum's remaining ashes into her teapot and put the lid on. She was home in more ways than we could ever have imagined. Her very essence was now a part of the house she loved.

We put the teapot on the dining room table with the rest of the little containers which had been removed from the top of the stove, just in case. And then, for some reason we both started to laugh. We had not laughed in a long, long time. We laughed out the pain and anguish and the loss. We laughed because we had forgotten how to laugh. We laughed because we needed to find humor in a world that had been so darkly sinister for so long and we needed to come back from the horrible place where three evil women had taken us. We laughed not because we had gotten true justice – the legal system is not currently constructed to meet out justice for elder fraud. But we had gotten what was more important – our memories and the knowledge that my mother loved us very much until the end.... and beyond. We laughed because finally we had won and they had lost because we had never given up. We now owned her house as she intended, including all its precious contents. We laughed because in the end, in spite of the horrendous thing that these women had done to our family, Joy finally got to go home.

Four years to the day after we last saw my mother, I sold her house. It was time to move on. In October of 2014, the RCMP opened a file on the case.

Author's Invitation

The author invites you to share your stories of elder abuse and fraud because it will be theraputic for you and help others to avoid this terrible crime.

Please email **stealingofjoy@gmail.com.**

About the Author,

Dr. Glynnis Walker Anderson is the best-selling author of eight books. She has also been a radio talk show host for fifteen years. She lives in Chicago.

Appendix 1 -

Dr. Culo's report
Medical Opinion
Re: Estate of Mrs. Rosalind Walker ("The Deceased")
Date of Birth July 1, 1923
Deceased June 17, 2011

Qualifications and Expertise

1. I, Dr. Sandi Ann Culo of Victoria, BC am a licensed physician in the province of British Columbia and am a member in good standing of the College of Physicians and Surgeons of British Columbia.

2. I hereby acknowledge that in accordance with Rule 11-2 of the Supreme Court Civil Rules, I am aware of my duty to assist the court and not be an advocate for any party. I have prepared my report in conformity with that duty, and if called on to give oral or written testimony, I will do so in conformity with that duty.

3. I am currently employed by the Vancouver Island Health Authority, Northern Health, the University of British Columbia, and the University of Victoria.

4. I am a fully qualified subspecialist in geriatric psychiatry. <u>I have attached my curriculum vitae</u> which identifies my education, employment history, and special skills.

5. I am one of the few geriatric psychiatrists in Canada who completed an <u>accredited training fellowship </u>program in the subspecialty of geriatric psychiatry. Many "geriatric psychiatrists" have not completed specialized postgraduate programs through an accredited university (none are presently available in Canada).

6. I have considerable expertise in the assessment (and treatment) of dementia, personal and financial competency assessments, testamentary capacity, elder abuse, and nursing home care.

7. I have worked in all areas of geriatric psychiatry practice in several different academic centers.

8. I have published articles on the treatment of dementia and the evaluation of vulnerable older adults.

9. I am involved in teaching students, physicians, and police, and frequently provide educational sessions on dementia, elder abuse, and complex competency assessments.

10. I have worked closely with the office of the Public Guardian and Trustee of British Columbia ("PGT"), the police, and the legal system to assist with cases involving elders who have dementia (or other mental illnesses) and have been victimized, often financially.

11. I have considerable experience in both contemporaneous and retrospective testamentary capacity assessments. I have also been called upon to provide opinions regarding vulnerability to undue influence.

12. One of my academic mentors was Dr. Kenneth Shulman from the University of Toronto. Dr. Shulman has published extensively on Testamentary Capacity and Undue Influence, and also led the 2009 International Psychogeriatric Association's Task Force on Testamentary Capacity and Undue Influence.

13. I have provided consultation services to at least 50 nursing home facilities across Canada. I presently provide outreach services to several seniors' care facilities in Victoria. Most of these consultations involve assessment and treatment of patients with dementia who also have complex medical problems and physical disabilities. I work closely with

nurses, social workers, occupational therapists, care aides, dieticians, pharmacists, and family doctors

14. I worked as an occupational therapist for five years. During this time, I developed expertise in cognitive testing, evaluation of financial and personal competency, functional testing, and determination of whether discharge home was feasible for individuals with various disabilities.

Opinion Request

15. I have been asked by Judith Milliken, QC to provide a medical opinion as to:

g) Whether the Deceased had <u>testamentary capacity</u> at the time the purported will was signed (on or about September 15, 2010);

h) Whether there is evidence to suggest the Deceased was <u>vulnerable to undue influence</u> at any significant time leading up to the signing of the impugned will;

i) Whether there is evidence to suggest that, in practical terms, <u>the Deceased could have returned home</u> at any time after her discharge from hospital on June 2, 2010. I have also been asked to present an opinion regarding potential risks to the Deceased, living in her home setting versus an institutional setting;

j) Whether there is any evidence to suggest that the Deceased's <u>cognitive capacity improved</u> in any significant manner from June 2, 2010 until the signing of the impugned will;

k) Whether there is any evidence from the medical records and documents to indicate that <u>Joyce Walker was inappropriately treated by her daughter Glynnis</u> in the months from March

2010 up to the signing of the impugned will on September 15, 2010 (including directions as to her mother's care, housing, and medical treatment). I have been asked to address specific points or concerns raised in Dr. Catherine Jenkins' report (dated October 23, 2010).

16. I am the person primarily responsible for the contents of this document.

Documents Reviewed

17. I reviewed two binders containing medical records from the Royal Jubilee Hospital (Document "1A") and Mount St Mary Hospital (Document "1B"). I also received documents "#2-25" as outlined in the letters I received on December 23, 2012, December 31, 2012, and January 11, 2013. I will refer to these documents henceforth as "the medical record" or else specifically by name and date.

Opinion

18. The medical and documentary evidence overwhelmingly suggests that Mrs. Walker did not have testamentary capacity on September 15, 2010 due to advanced dementia (mixed Alzheimer's and vascular type).

Basis for Opinion

19. My opinion in this case is based on several factors. Firstly, I have assessed thousands of elderly patients over the past 20 years in my role as a health care professional. The majority of these patients suffered from dementia, many were vulnerable, and a significant number were incapable and in need of care and protection.

20. Secondly, a vast literature has accumulated in the medical press on the clinical assessment of testamentary capacity, undue influence, and

the risk factors for elder abuse (including my own 2011 article "Risk assessment and intervention for vulnerable older adults").

21. I am very familiar with the existing literature. My previous professors and mentors have written many of the pivotal articles in the medical press (ex, Dr. Kenneth Shulman and Dr. Carole Cohen). I frequently present at meetings, rounds, and conferences on these issues, and also attend conferences to apprise myself of new material and research.

22. After careful review and consideration of the available facts, it is my opinion that Mrs. Walker **did not have testamentary capacity** at the time her purported will was executed on or about September 15, 2010.

23. Mrs. Walker suffered from moderate to severe dementia, probably due to a combination of Alzheimer's disease and cerebrovascular disease ("vascular dementia"). It appears that Mrs. Walker suffered some small strokes in the spring of 2010 due to atrial fibrillation (irregular, rapid heart rhythm). These small strokes led to a precipitous decline in the Deceased's cognitive function.

24. I do not believe that The Deceased had the task-specific capacity to execute her will. She did not understand the relevance of the task at hand, and did not appreciate the consequences of her actions. I believe that there were also situation-specific factors present that undermined her capacity.

25. I further opine that the Deceased suffered from paranoid delusions involving her only daughter. These delusions affected her decision-making with regards to the disposition of her assets.

26. Mrs. Walker had severe short and long-term memory impairment, was disoriented to time, had significant deficits in her executive cognitive functions (ie, planning, organizing, problem-solving, abstraction, judgment, insight), had difficulties with recalling names and finding

words, had visuospatial deficits, problems with calculations, and difficulty following basic directions.

27. These cognitive deficits and abnormalities rendered the Deceased incapable of executing the testamentary act on or about September 15, 2010.

28. Medical evaluations and cognitive screening tests performed by physicians around this time strongly support that the Deceased would not have had testamentary capacity at the time the purported will was signed.

29. According to the clinical information, the Deceased did not have a medical examination to assess her testamentary capacity. A contemporaneous assessment of testamentary capacity would have been very helpful, although it is very unlikely that the outcome would change my opinion.

30. My retrospective review of the facts indicates that the Deceased had grossly impaired judgment. She had very poor awareness of her assets, care needs, medical problems, and personal and financial situation around this time. Her memory deficits were severe and she had poor insight.

31. Physicians consistently stated in the medical records that the Deceased was unable to make her own personal and financial decisions.

32. The facts also strongly indicate that the Deceased's previously held relationships, preferences, beliefs, and values were significantly altered by dementia.

33. Mrs. Walker was first diagnosed with dementia in the spring of 2010, although she was likely experiencing subtle signs prior to that time. The information in the medical records supports that there was significant

progression of her dementia, particularly after she sustained several small strokes around April 2010. Further, her 3MS score (a cognitive screening tool used to assess dementia) dropped from 69/100 to 47/100 in a few short months (July-October 2010). I will address the significance of these scores later. In addition, the nursing notes reported increasingly frequent periods of confusion, disorientation, paranoia, and hallucinations.

34. The Deceased exhibited behavioral and psychological symptoms of dementia such as fearfulness, confabulation, crying, anxiety, sleep disorder, change in personality and social skills, paranoia, and hallucinations. These symptoms are very common in individuals with dementia, and usually become more prominent as the disease progresses.

35. Some of these behavioral symptoms were evident in March 2010 but they became much more pronounced over time. I believe that the Deceased developed overvalued ideas and distorted perceptions about her daughter in June 2010. These misperceptions later became frank paranoid delusions.

36. The Deceased believed that her daughter stole from her and abandoned her duty to the Deceased in her "time of need". The evidence does not support these claims. The Deceased also believed that Glynnis "turned the doctors against her" which she felt resulted in her placement in the nursing home (Mount St Mary), and the loss of her dog.

37. The Deceased wanted to return to her home and likely held a grudge against her daughter for placing and keeping her in the nursing home. We see this very commonly in clinical practice. However, it was the Deceased's physicians who insisted she move to the nursing home for medical, cognitive, and safety reasons. The Deceased mistakenly blamed her daughter, although her daughter was merely following the doctors' recommendations. In fact, Glynnis had offered to have the Deceased come and live with her in the USA but the care team advised against it.

38. The medical records indicate that Ms. Horton and Ms. Brewer supported the Deceased's wish to return to her home, and were actively pursuing this goal. This situation likely fueled the Deceased's anger towards Glynnis, who she felt was interfering with this plan.

39. I believe that the Deceased was clinically vulnerable to undue influence (or the subversion of her will) by the people she became dependent on in the last stages of her life (her "time of need"). The medical literature suggests that individuals with Mrs. Walker's degree of cognitive impairment may require only very subtle influence to be "unduly influenced" due to increased vulnerability (Shulman's 'threshold concept').

40. In reviewing Mrs. Walker's situation, I identified numerous "risk factors" or "red flags" for vulnerability, elder abuse, and undue influence that are well cited in the literature:

- Diagnosis of **dementia** (ie, "cognitive vulnerability" due to poor decision making, insight, and judgment). Appraisal of others may be tainted by dementia, even in the early phases. People with dementia may change their attitudes towards significant others during the course of their illness. This change may be triggered or fed by the disease, as well as by natural frictions and events that occur normally in families.

- Presence of **paranoia**. Paranoid ideation can poison affections, and new alliances can be formed based on the exploitation of these altered affections. When the testator suffers from paranoia, his/her suspiciousness of potential benefactors may be fuelled by an influencer.

- Loneliness, social **isolation**, and sequestration (ie, "emotional vulnerability"): the Deceased's main contacts in the last year of her life became Ms. Horton, Ms. Brewer and Ms. Tarrant.

Her daughter lived at a distance, had health issues, and was instructed, essentially warned, to keep away from the Deceased.

- Past history of **emotional abuse** and **dependence** on others. It is believed that Mrs. Walker sustained emotional abuse at the hands of her mother and husband, that her husband was controlling, and that she was highly reliant on others for assistance with her day-to-day affairs.

- Recent **nursing home placement** (ie, this move away from the Deceased's "normal environment" was an additional stressor).

- Recent **medical illnesses or hospitalization.**

- **Physical, emotional, and mental dependence** on others.

- **"Family conflict"**/estrangement from daughter who was previously favored (prior to the onset of dementia). Creation of new "alliances" with individuals previously unknown or "on the periphery".

- Relationship of **informal care giving** (leading to new found faith or gratitude on the part of the vulnerable individual).

- **Conflict** between family and informal care givers/new friends. This conflict forces the vulnerable elder to have to "choose sides".

- A **"confidential" or "special" relationship** existed between the Deceased, Ms. Horton, Ms. Brewer, and Ms. Tarrant. Their frequent contact with the Deceased likely led to their having positions of influence and possible control over the testamentary act. The facts in the records indicate that their contact with the Deceased significantly increased once Mrs. Walker became infirm, disabled, and unable to make her own decisions.

- Presence of a **"helpful" neighbor"** and/or friend, "new on the scene" since the Deceased became infirm and in need of assistance.

- Presence of a **trusted professional person**: example, lawyer.

- Possibility of **collusion** between new care givers/friends who are in support of Mrs. Walker's unrealistic desire to return home (as opposed to her daughter who followed medical advice to have Mrs. Walker placed in a care facility).

- Deficits in hearing, mobility, and communication; **frailty**.

- **Submissive personality** type

- **Events occurring in haste**. The daughter's POA was revoked and reassigned to Ms. Horton, a health care representation agreement was obtained, committeeship of person and finance were obtained, and Mrs. Walker's will was purportedly changed. All of these events occurred in less than one year.

- Apparent **involvement by the ultimate beneficiary or beneficiaries in the legal transactions.**

- Female gender.

- Advanced age.

- Widowed status.

41. In Mrs. Walker's case, the "compounding effect of multiple morbidities" can be appreciated. Social, relationship, physical, psychological,

cognitive, and environmental risk factors are all present. In such cases, suspicion of undue influence is even greater, particularly since dementia was present.

42. In addition, the circumstances of the execution of the new or 'home made will' and its contents should arouse the suspicion of undue influence in this case. For example, unnatural provisions, radical changes in the beneficiaries and pattern of distribution, persons of influence possible involvement in the procurement of the changes, and contents not in accordance with previous wishes. I can comment on these further if required by the Court. Again, these suspicious circumstances are well-outlined in the medical literature.

43. Based on information from the medical records, it would not have been safe or practical for the Deceased to return home. Mrs. Walker had advanced dementia, was physically frail, and had several acute medical problems that required frequent assessment and laboratory monitoring. She was hospitalized three times. She required nursing support. The Deceased was deemed to be a high fall risk and was also an elopement risk. The Deceased was becoming more disoriented and confused. She was getting up in the middle of night, and could easily have wandered outside if she were in her own home. Wandering almost always precludes a person with dementia from living in his/her home.

44. The Deceased also experienced paranoia and hallucinations. The Deceased continued to require 24-hour nursing care and supervision. It would have been very costly and complicated to arrange for care at home. In addition, without the sale of her home, the Deceased's income could not have supported 24-hour care.

45. There is limited, if any, information in the medical record to suggest any sustained improvement in the Deceased's cognition or function from June 2010 to the signing of the impugned will in September 2010. In fact, she continued to decline which is consistent with Mrs. Walker's

diagnosis of progressive dementia. Typically, clinicians expect deterioration in function, behavior, and cognition over time. Her medical records suggest that Mrs. Walker's cognition, behavior and day-to-day function worsened after June 2010. I will elaborate further on this.

46. <u>There is a lack of clinical evidence to suggest that Glynnis treated her mother inappropriately, or made poor decisions regarding the Deceased's hospitalizations, medical care, or housing</u>. On the contrary, the information in the medical records consistently showed that Glynnis cared about her mother's future, was involved in her medical decisions and care meetings, and followed the advice of physicians regarding the Deceased's investigations and treatment. Glynnis offered to take The Deceased home to Chicago with her after the April-June 2010 hospitalization, but the care team felt that a nursing home was the best place for Mrs. Walker due to her medical needs.

Basis of Opinion of Testamentary Capacity

47. Shulman's "threshold concept" (<u>Ref: Shulman KI, Cohen CA, Kirsh FC et al.</u>

<u>Assessment of Testamentary Capacity and Vulnerability to Undue Influence. Am J Psych. 2007 May 164(5): 722-27</u>) is a useful construct for the purposes of this case. He purported that the greater the complexity and conflict within a testator's environment, and the greater the complexity of the will itself, the higher the level of cognitive function or emotional stability necessary to be considered capable. In other words, Shulman postulated that the execution of a will, like other capacities, requires both task-specific and situation-specific capacities. He also opined that if there is a suggestion of undue influence, the legal threshold is higher, and calls for more careful probing of rationale at the time of execution of the will.

48. Re: *"Understanding the nature of the act of making a will and its consequences"*. Based on the information that I have, the Deceased suffered

from moderate to severe dementia. Her insight and judgment were poor, her short and long-term memory were affected, she did not understand complex tasks and instructions, had limited understanding of her own financial and personal circumstances, and had poor executive function (see #26). She had been deemed incapable of making her own personal and financial decisions. Based on this information, it is highly unlikely that the Deceased would be unable to understand and appreciate the testamentary act or its consequences. Although the purported will indicated that "I revoke all my other wills", it does not prove that the Deceased understood what a will was at that time.

49. Re: *"Understanding the extent of one's assets"*. Based on the clinical information, Mrs. Walker had a very poor understanding and appreciation of her financial circumstances in the months leading to the execution of the purported will. The Deceased told Dr. Arthur Prowse, geriatric psychiatrist, that her home was valued at only $100,000. She did not know her expenses or income. She could not perform simple mathematical computations. It is very unlikely that the Deceased would have known the value of her home, and been able to distribute this value among her beneficiaries at the time the purported will was signed. In addition, the Deceased did not account for the monies in her bank accounts that totaled approximately $100,000. This omission further supports that the Deceased did not know the extent of her assets.

50. Re: "Comprehending and appreciating the claims of those who might expect to benefit from the will, both those to be included and excluded". The Deceased specifically (virtually) excluded her daughter and granddaughters in the purported will and included four beneficiaries who were not mentioned in the 2006 will: Ms. Brewer, Ms. Horton, Mr. Brewer, and Ms. Tarrant. She suggested that Ms. Brewer, Ms. Horton, and Ms. Tarrant were her "true friends" as opposed to her daughter. While this potentially shows a superficial awareness of the persons who are the "natural objects of his bounty", it in no way explains the large discrepancy between the 2006 will and the purported 2010 will. There is little in the purported

document to rationalize these changes. In addition, one month after the purported will was signed, the Deceased was assessed by Dr. Jenkins who noted that the Deceased could not recall Ms. Horton's name, nor could she recall that Ms. Brewer had been her neighbor.

51. Mrs. Walker previously bequeathed her entire estate to her daughter Glynnis. She then suggested that "unfair treatment", and Glynnis' receiving "her share of money and jewelry taken from my bank account and home", accounted for the dramatic change in her wishes. The Deceased did not explain why she virtually disinherited her granddaughters in the purported will other than to say "for reasons they know".

52. It appears that Mrs. Walker only became personally close to the aforementioned individuals (her "true friends") in the last year of her life. Mr. Brewer is not mentioned anywhere in the medical records, nor was there any other evidence that he was close to Mrs. Walker. These short-term relationships, regardless of their value to the Deceased in her last surviving months, could hardly account for such a sudden alteration in her plans for distribution of her assets.

53. The other obvious piece of information that relates to this specific task of testamentary capacity is that Mrs. Walker does not account for the disposition of her entire estate in the purported 2010 will. She accounted only for $600,000. The remainder would presumably be granted to her daughter. It would seem from the document that she wished to "disinherit her daughter" and this would not happen, even if the 2010 will was a valid one.

54. It is unclear whether the Deceased had much awareness of the conflicts or tensions that existed between her family and those who would become her possible beneficiaries (if the 2010 will was indeed valid). This conflict, and also the one between the Deceased and her daughter, would be something I would have explored in detail had there been opportunity for contemporaneous testamentary capacity assessment.

55. Mrs. Walker's dementia affected her understanding and judgment with regards to her interpersonal relationships. She became angry with her daughter. I suspect she then became dependent upon and vulnerable to influence by her informal care givers. It appears that she drew false conclusions about her relationships due to both limited information and cognitive misperceptions.

56. *Re: "Understanding the impact of the distribution of the assets of the estate".* Mrs. Walker makes no mention of the potential consequences and impact on Glynnis and her granddaughters. Clearly, their omission from her purported 2010 would have significant financial consequences for her daughter and granddaughters. The only vague mention in this regard was that the Deceased allegedly felt that Glynnis had already received "her share". However, the Deceased did not identify how much money Glynnis may have already taken or received, or how valuable the alleged jewelry was.

57. I will again mention that it seems unusual that the Deceased included Mr. David Brewer as a beneficiary ($100,000) when it appeared that he played a limited role in her life, if any. The Deceased made no mention of why Mr. Brewer was being included. In my opinion, Mr. Brewer's inclusion is a result of the Deceased's lack of understanding of her personal relationships and their value to her. The impact on the other beneficiaries of leaving Mr. Brewer such a substantial sum is not mentioned.

58. Her "true friends" stood to inherit the vast majority of the Deceased's estate, including two people (Mr. Brewer and Ms. Tarrant) who seemed to have a limited role in her daily care, decision-making, or comfort.

59. *Re: "The testator must be free of any disorder of the mind or delusions that influence the disposition of assets."* Based on the information that I have, Mrs. Walker clearly suffered from a disorder of the mind, and suffered delusions that may have influenced the distribution of her assets.

60. The Deceased clearly had moderate to severe dementia, likely of the Alzheimer's type (with contribution from cerebrovascular disease). Multiple physicians deemed her incapable of making personal or financial decisions for herself, including Dr. Houghton who had known her for at least twelve years. Two geriatric specialists deemed her incapable. Her judgment and insight were grossly impaired, and all other cognitive domains were also adversely affected by her dementia (memory, visuospatial skills, language, concentration, abstraction, problem-solving, etc). She was unable to understand or appreciate the nature and consequences of the testamentary act.

61. In addition, the Deceased suffered from paranoid delusions (and other behavioral and psychological disturbances of dementia; see #34). She became convinced that her daughter did not act in her best interest, that she poisoned the doctors against her (which led to her nursing home placement and the loss of her beloved dog), that she stole money and credit cards from her, and that she removed jewelry from her home. These beliefs were false based on the evidence, or at best, were grossly exaggerated by the Deceased. Paranoid delusions in dementia patients are almost always directed towards family members, and most commonly involve theft of personal belongings.

62. It is my opinion that the Deceased's affections towards her daughter were poisoned by her paranoid delusions. These delusions were caused by dementia. Mrs. Walker developed fixed, false beliefs about her daughter that led her to change her previously expressed wishes with regards to the disposition of her estate. The Deceased's delusions completely altered her relationship with her daughter, and encouraged her to form relationships with Ms. Brewer, Ms. Horton, and Ms. Tarrant.

Vulnerability to Potential Undue Influence or Subversion of Her Will

63. I would again like to comment on the Deceased's potential vulnerability to undue influence. As I previously stated, an individual with the

Deceased's level of cognitive impairment would not require much influence in order for her will to be subverted. She had moderate to severe dementia, had poor judgment and insight, and was also dependent and socially isolated due to the nature of her disease, her limited mobility, distance from her daughter, and the influence and control of her new friends. These individuals: a neighbor, lawyer, and casual acquaintance (it is my understanding that the Deceased met Ms. Tarrant in Ms. Tarrants's role as a cashier at Thrifty's grocery store), became highly important to and valued by the Deceased. It is not difficult to surmise how in her final days, frail, demented, and experiencing delusions, she would be vulnerable to influence that could easily affect the testamentary act.

64. As I have previously outlined, numerous red flags and risk factors for undue influence are apparent in this case (see #40). They fall under the categories of environmental, relationship, social, psychological, cognitive, and physical domains. Mrs. Walker had moderate to severe dementia, and as such, these "multiple compounding morbidities" could be powerful influences and be difficult for her to cope with.

65. **Timeline of Deceased's Cognitive Testing: April 2010-October 2011**

April 15, 2010

MMSE score 14/30
Completed by Neil Taylor, occupational therapist at RJH

June 9, 2010

MMSE 18/30

3MS score 65/100

Completed by Laurie Banasch, occupational therapist at Mount St Mary

June 22, 2010

MMSE 16/30

Completed by Dr. Arthur Prowse, geriatric psychiatrist

July 20, 2010

*MMSE 24/30

3MS 69/100

Completed by occupational therapist Laurie Banasch

*The validity of this MMSE score is highly questionable. It is inconsistent with previous and later MMSE testing, and the MMSE score also correlates very poorly to the score obtained on the 3MS test. Further, it is highly improbable that the Deceased's score could improve from 18/30 to 24/30 in one month. It is not clinically feasible in light of her dementia.

August 10, 2010

MOCA 10/30

Completed by Dr. Arthur Prowse, geriatric psychiatrist

August 20, 2010

*MMSE 24/30?

Apparently completed by Dr. Houghton in his office

A copy of this test was not available in the medical record, only a fax sent from Dr. Houghton indicating the score

*The score is inconsistent with some of the previous and later testing

<u>August 27, 2010?</u>

MMSE 22/30?

Completed by Dr. Houghton?

This test was cited in the Affidavit of Dr. Houghton (dated September 2, 2010). However, no evidence of it exists in the medical records. The deceased did not see Dr. Houghton that day per medical records. Likely error; probably meant "August 20, 2010".

(Date of 'handwritten' purported will: September 14, 2010)

<u>October 23, 2010</u>

MMSE 16/30

3MS 47/100

Partial MOCA (0/5 on tests of visuospatial and executive function)

Completed by geriatrician, Dr. Catherine Jenkins

66. <u>Mrs. Walker's cognitive testing was indicative of significant disorientation to time, short and long-term memory deficits, erroneous calculations, poor working memory, language abnormalities, visuospatial deficits, difficulty comprehending and following instructions, and poor planning and ability to abstract</u>. Her test scores and day-to-day function suggest she had **moderate to severe dementia**.

67. I cannot account for the MMSE scores obtained by Ms. Banasch in July or by Dr. Houghton in August 2010 as they are <u>very inconsistent</u>

with all other former and later performances. Copies of Dr. Houghton's tests are not present in the clinical record. In addition, Dr. Houghton's affidavit (signed 3 weeks after he allegedly performed cognitive testing) stated that Mrs. Walker was 'not mentally competent', and that she would 'likely suffer further cognitive decline'. This statement would not be consistent with someone who has MMSE scores of 22-24/30 (mild dementia). It is possible, although unlikely, that the blood transfusion the Deceased received in hospital (August 11, 2010) led to some transient improvement (due to the correction of anemia), although her scores decreased again by October 2010 when she saw Dr. Jenkins (despite a stable hemoglobin level).

68. The possibility exists that there was some "coaching" or "practice" in preparation for the testing. Copies of these tests are readily available on the Internet. Another concern with the testing is that the Deceased's scores on the July 20, 2010 3MS and MMSE do not correlate well. It is difficult to understand how the Deceased could score relatively well on one test (the MMSE) and yet perform so poorly on a similar test done on the same day (3MS).

69. Mrs. Walker was assessed by Dr. Jenkins on October 23, 2010. Mrs. Walker's score on the 3MS (47/100) was considerably worse compared to the previous 3MS completed on July 20, 2010 (69/100). <u>A drop of greater than 20 points in three months is highly significant</u>. This decrease could not be attributable to test anxiety, a change in hemoglobin level, or a "bad day". The 3MS is more sensitive to change over time compared to the MMSE. Mrs. Walker's MMSE score was 16/30; identical to the MMSE completed by Dr. Prowse on June 22, 2010.

70. Dr. Jenkins reported "global cognitive deficits", inability to direct her own care, and opined that Mrs. Walker needed guidance to make financial and personal decisions. Dr. Jenkins was not asked to comment on Mrs. Walker's testamentary capacity.

71. The contents of Dr. Jenkins report strongly imply that Mrs. Walker exhibited grossly impaired recall of her own life events (remote and recent); was very vague with respect to allegations regarding her daughter; had grossly impaired judgment and insight; and lacked appreciation for her current circumstances.

72. The evidence overwhelmingly suggests that Mrs. Walker was not competent to change her will on September 15, 2010 due to advanced dementia.

Cognitive Screening Tools

73) *MMSE (Mini Mental Status Examination)*

Reference: Folstein MF, Folstein SE, McHugh PR. "Mini-mental state". A practical method for grading the cognitive state of patients for the clinician. J Psychiatr Res. 1975 Nov; 12(3):189-98.

The MMSE is a very basic cognitive screening tool used to assess various aspects of mental function including short-term memory, orientation (to time and place), attention, calculations, reading, writing, visuospatial function, and simple language function. It is scored from 0-30.

The MMSE does not assess executive cognitive functions (ie, insight, judgment, planning, problem-solving, reasoning, abstraction, etc) which is a major limitation for its usefulness in competency assessments.

Normal executive function is essential for making day-to-day decisions. It would be ill-advised to make a determination of capacity based on this test score. Even patients with normal scores on the MMSE may be incapable of making decisions for themselves due to poor judgment, reasoning ability, or impaired problem solving.

The MMSE takes *10 minutes or less* to administer.

* Scores above 26 are *generally* indicative of mild cognitive impairment (27-28/30) or "normal" function (scores of 29-30/30)

* Scores of 21-25 are suggestive of mild dementia

* Scores of 10-20 are supportive of moderate dementia (Mrs. Walker's test scores in April, June, and October 2010 fell into this range)

* Scores below 10 indicate severe dementia

74) *3MS (Modified Mini Mental State examination)*

Reference: Teng EL, Chui HC. The Modified Mini-Mental State (3MS) exam. J Clin Psychiatry. 1987 Aug; 48(8): 314-8.

The 3MS is a 27-item questionnaire used to assess a <u>wider depth of cognitive domains</u>. In addition to the areas of function tested by the MMSE, it examines long term memory, abstraction, verbal fluency, and delayed recall. It is scored from 0-100 and takes 10-15 minutes to administer.

<u>The 3MS is clinically preferable to the MMSE</u> for several reasons. It samples a <u>broader range</u> of cognitive functions over a <u>wider range of difficulty levels</u>, it is <u>more sensitive to change</u> in cognition over time, has <u>greater reliability</u> when administered by different raters, and it better <u>predicts functional outcomes</u> (ie, whether or not the testee can do their own shopping, banking, cooking, future planning, etc.).

Studies show that <u>scores below 80</u> are highly suggestive of significant cognitive impairment (ie, dementia).

75) *MOCA (Montreal Cognitive Assessment)*

Reference: Z. S. Nasreddine, N. A. Phillips, V. Bedirian et al. The montreal cognitive assessment, MoCA: a brief screening tool for mild cognitive impairment. Journal of the American Geriatrics Society. 2005 Apr; 53(4): 695–699.

The MOCA was designed in 1996. It is scored from 0-30 and takes 10-12 minutes to administer. It is more sensitive to subtle cognitive deficits than the MMSE, and better evaluates "higher cognitive functions" such as planning, organizing, problem solving, abstraction, and working memory. As with the MMSE and 3MS, it also measures short- term (and delayed) recall, language, attention, and orientation.

The MOCA has become the preferred dementia screening tool of many geriatric specialists and neurologists. The MOCA's inclusion of cognitive tasks that evaluate executive functions makes it a very useful instrument for assessing decision making capacity.

A score of less than 26 is indicative of at least mild cognitive impairment. Normal controls have scores of 27 (on average); individuals with mild cognitive impairment average 22, and dementia patients score 16/30 on average.

Mrs. Walker scored 10/30 on this test on August 10, 2010 (ie, approximately one month before the purported will was executed). Thus, Dr. Prowse surmised that she "clearly has generalized cognitive impairment sufficient to make her incapable of managing her financial affairs. Lack of insight and grossly impaired judgment".

Important Considerations in the Use and Interpretation of These Tools

76. Cognitive testing alone is insufficient to assess an individual's mental state or competence. The literature is very clear and consistent on this matter. Test scores should not be used in isolation to determine

a diagnosis, or determine competency. Functional capacity, decision-making capacity, and evaluation of recent behaviors and actions must also be assessed. Additionally, the "triggers" for the competency assessment should be identified in the report since competency assessments are usually requested when there is some type of "risk" to the vulnerable individual (no exploration of triggers was evident in the reports of Drs. Prowse or Jenkins). Collateral information from reliable informants should be gathered.

77. Testing should be accompanied by detailed clinical examination, assessment of the individual's ability to carry out activities of daily living, assessment of possible psychiatric symptoms or illness (eg, delusions, anxiety, depression, change in personality), and the gathering of information from collateral sources regarding insight, judgment, change in previously expressed wishes and behavior, and the possibility of undue influence. Mrs. Walker's clinical records do not indicate that this type of examination was ever done. Dr. Jenkins did not attempt to speak to Mrs. Walker's daughter to gather collateral information nor did she report on the Deceased's functional level.

78. Unless the tester has had proper instruction in the administration of psychometric tests, the scores may not be reliable. For example, many testers feel empathy towards the patient and will "help" them by repeating or giving extra instructions, allowing extra time, and providing hints or clues. My experience suggests that health care providers such as nurses, occupational therapists, social workers, and even family physicians may not have the proper training in administering these tests and may not score these instruments accurately (ie, tendency to "overscore").

79. Geriatricians, geriatric psychiatrists, and neurologists have the most expertise with administering and interpreting cognitive tests.

80. Another issue is that of a possible "rehearsal effect". If these cognitive tests are done too often, patients can become familiar with the

questions and answers and therefore score higher. They may appear to be 'improving' due to higher test scores. In addition, if a patient knows he/she is going for a "test", he/she has the opportunity to practice tasks and memorize the answers (ex, date, subtracting by sevens, clock drawing). Patients can also be "coached" by friends and relatives to improve their performance. The individual will obviously have a better outcome if this is the case.

81. <u>The literature strongly supports that "executive functions" (ie, frontal lobe functions such as reasoning ability, judgment, problem-solving, abstraction, planning, concentration) are more important than other cognitive domains when examining capacity.</u> The literature also supports the construct that individuals with significant frontal lobe impairment may need only minimal influence for this to be considered undue influence. <u>It was clearly and consistently documented in the medical record that Mrs. Walker had significant deficits in executive function.</u>

82. <u>In dementia clinics, the usual standard is to repeat cognitive testing only every six months</u> to evaluate an individuals' progression (unless there is a noticeable or worrisome change in the clinical presentation). This testing is done in conjunction with clinical examination and review of information from collateral sources. The frequent, repeated cognitive testing that was done in this case is not the norm.

83. **Dementia Staging**

Various clinical tools have been developed to assist health care providers in determining the severity of a patient's dementia. These tools assess cognition, day-to-day function, and behavior.

Tools that evaluate cognition include common screening tests such as the MMSE, 3MS, and MOCA. Absolute scores on these tests (in addition to other factors) help clinicians gauge how mild or severe the impairment is. These tests were described earlier (see #73-75).

Functional assessment tools are also available (examples include the FAST, Bristol, and Barthel). These tools measure how well dementia patients manage their activities of daily living (ADLs) ie, how independent they are. As an occupational therapist, I frequently made use of such instruments to help determine whether someone could remain in the community with home supports, or whether they needed nursing home placement. Mrs. Walker did not undergo these particular assessments but the interdisciplinary team (through their assessments and interventions with Mrs. Walker from April 2010-June 2010), suggested that she required nursing home placement.

Instruments are available that measure psychological and behavioral symptoms that commonly occur in dementia patients (delusions, hallucinations, agitation, depression, sleep disruption, aggression). The NPI, BEHAVE-AD, and BRSD are examples of behavioral rating tools. These tools were not utilized in this case.

The Global Dementia Rating Scale and the Global Deterioration Scale are used to provide an overall indicator of the severity or stage of dementia (function, behavior, and cognition). Dementia patients decline in ways that are predictable, and clinicians use markers of behavior and function to help diagnose what stage of dementia the patient is in (in conjunction with cognitive testing).

84. For example, an individual with **mild dementia** will exhibit some or all of the following symptoms:

-Getting lost or disoriented while travelling

-Disorientation to time

-Poor recall of recent events (noticeable to others and evident on formal testing)

-Concentration problems

-Reduced ability to manage banking, finances, shopping: may appear "normal" to casual inspection

-Moderate difficulty handling day-to-day problems

-Needs prompting with personal care

-Loss of awareness of details of one's personal history

-Poor retention of newly learned material (ie, will not recall what was read in a book after a delay of several minutes)

-Difficulty remembering or saying names

-Word-finding difficulty

-Misplacing or losing objects

-Becoming repetitive in speech

-Mild to moderate anxiety symptoms

-Denial of cognitive problems and lack of insight regarding need for help

-Social skills usually maintained

85. vs. **Moderate** Dementia

-Severe memory loss; <u>new material is rapidly forgotten</u>

-Can no longer function safely without assistance

-<u>Unable to recall major relevant aspects of their current life</u>

-Frequently <u>disoriented to time and place</u>

-Difficulty with simple calculations

-<u>Severe impairment in handling common daily problems</u>

-Marked impairment in judgment and insight

-Social skills usually impaired

-Can usually toilet and eat independently but needs assistance with financial management, using the telephone, dressing, bathing. Only simple chores preserved.

-Requires assistance in keeping of personal effects

-No pretense of independent function at home

-Appears well enough to be taken to functions outside the family home

-Changes in balance and gait may be apparent

86. vs. **Moderate-Severe** Dementia

-<u>Forgets names</u> of family members or close friends

-<u>Personality and emotional changes occur</u>: delusional behavior (may accuse family or others of stealing or theft); hallucinations; agitation; confabulation ("making up stories"); inappropriate social skills (rudeness, sexual disinhibition)

-<u>Unaware of recent events and experiences</u>

-<u>Very limited awareness of personal history/past life</u>

-Completely disoriented to time and place

-Difficulty counting

-<u>Requires assistance for basic activities of daily living</u> (ex, feeding, toileting, hygiene)

-Often incontinent

-Require travel assistance

-<u>Day-night rhythm disturbance occurs</u> (ie, awake at night or up early; may sleep in the daytime)

-'Cognitive abulia' common: loss of willpower/motivation/proper action because the individual cannot carry a thought long enough to determine a purposeful course of action

-Loss of coordination and falls are common

87. vs. **Severe** Dementia

-All verbal abilities are lost

-Unintelligible utterances

-Incontinent of bladder and bowel

-Basic motor skills are lost: cannot walk or weight bear; cannot transfer self from wheelchair to bed

-Generalized rigidity and primitive brain reflexes are present

Cognition, Testamentary Capacity and Undue Influence

88. Testamentary capacity requires an individual to have sufficient cognitive capacity to:

1. Understand and appreciate the concept and nature of a will

2. Have knowledge of the nature and extent of one's assets

3. Have knowledge of persons who may have reasonable claims to be beneficiaries

4. Understand the impact of the distribution of the assets of the estate

5. Be able to clearly and consistently communicate wishes regarding the disposition of the estate after his/her death

89. The testator should be free of any delusions that influence the disposition of assets.

90. Even if an individual has these broad cognitive capacities, vulnerability to undue influence is more likely if the person has deficits in specific cognitive abilities.

Example 1: <u>Impaired memory</u> can lead individuals to believe that family members have not called or visited, and may cause false recollections or misinterpretations of past events. The testator may form adverse opinions about loved ones as a result. Mrs. Walker had impaired memory function.

Example 2: <u>Impaired autobiographical memory</u> may lead the testator to assume that they have known "new people" in their lives for many years. This can lead to a false relationship of trust. They may forget previous dislikes, conflicts, or mistrust. Mrs. Walker demonstrated impaired autobiographical memory.

Example 3: Impaired reasoning, judgment, and insight may render the individual suffering from dementia unable to consider the meaning, significance, or morality of another person's behavior; understand alternatives; weigh priorities; and come to a well-executed decision. The person may make erroneous, impulsive, and superficial decisions based on faulty reasoning and inability to consider options. Mrs. Walker consistently had severe deficits in these higher cognitive functions.

Example 4: Impaired working memory. This type of impairment can render the individual unable to simultaneously appraise their relationships to others in the context of past and present. He/she may be particularly vulnerable to those whom they are in frequent visual contact with, or to the beneficiary who is seated within or just outside the room when the will is drafted. Mrs. Walker's working memory was impaired.

Example 5: Cognitive deterioration frequently leads to changes in personality such as apathy or passivity. These traits may cause a person with dementia to be vulnerable to influence and the opinions of others. He/she may accept information from others without being able to weigh the truthfulness or reliability of the facts. There is evidence in the medical records to support that Mrs. Walker's personality traits were affected by dementia.

91. Based on the information in the clinical record (ex. physician consultations, nursing notes, cognitive testing, descriptions of behavior and functional abilities), **Mrs. Walker was in the moderate to severe stages of dementia at the time the 'hand written' will was drafted on September 14, 2010 (see #84-85)**. Her condition worsened over time (cognitive skills, daily function, and behavior). She was highly dependent on others, had severely impaired memory function, and developed significant psychiatric symptoms such as sleep-wake cycle problems, paranoid delusions,

and hallucinations. Her anxiety worsened. The Deceased demonstrated poor autobiographical memory, impaired working memory, changes in personality, and impaired reasoning, judgment, and insight.

92. These factors combined make it highly unlikely that the Deceased had testamentary capacity at the time of the purported will's signing on or about September 15, 2010.

93. The Deceased also became isolated from her daughter, became suspicious or paranoid regarding her daughter's actions, and changed her opinion regarding her neighbor, Ms. Brewer. Ms. Brewer went from being considered a neighbor to being a "trusted friend" in a matter of weeks or months. This change seemed very out of character for the Deceased, who was considered a very private person. The Deceased also became highly reliant on her previous lawyer, Ms. Horton, with whom she previously had infrequent contact.

94. There are no copies of the August 20, 2010 or August 27, 2010 MMSE tests on the chart. The scores are inconsistent with the other tests completed within this time frame. I question the accuracy and validity of these tests.

95. Based on my clinical expertise (and with considerable support from the medical literature), I do not believe that someone with this degree of cognitive impairment could have testamentary capacity. There was ample evidence in the medical record that Mrs. Walker was exhibiting increasing forgetfulness, confusion, confabulation, anxiety, sleep disturbance, paranoia, hallucinations, and personality changes from March 2010 until her death.

96. In all likelihood, Mrs. Walker was not making rational decisions due to cognitive impairment and psychiatric symptoms secondary to dementia. In fact, a geriatrician and a geriatric psychiatrist diagnosed Mrs. Walker with moderate dementia. Both experts felt her judgment and

insight were significantly impaired and that she needed assistance with making basic decisions. They were concerned that she could not make appropriate decisions for herself.

97. A person with moderate (or moderate to severe) dementia can still maintain social graces and speak well. To the untrained observer, he or she can appear competent. However, the level of cognitive impairment Mrs. Walker possessed rendered her incapable of making appropriate personal and financial decisions. It is highly unlikely that she had the capacity to revoke her previous (2006) POA, to assign a new POA, to understand the nomination and significance of a committee, or to revise her purported will in 2010. She was potentially vulnerable to influence, had advanced dementia, exhibited paranoid thinking, and was highly dependent on her informal care givers for social contact and decision-making.

98. From the time of her hospitalization in March 2010, Mrs. Walker became highly dependent on others, became isolated from her only child with whom she had a previous close and loving relationship, and displayed values and beliefs not in keeping with her previously expressed wishes. I believe she became an incapable, at-risk, and very vulnerable adult during this time.

Conclusions

99. Based on the clinical information, and my own experience in hundreds of elder abuse cases, competency assessments, and multiple retrospective testamentary capacity cases, the Deceased did not have testamentary capacity at the time of the execution of the purported will on September 15, 2010.

100. The Deceased suffered from moderate to severe Alzheimer's disease (combined with vascular disease). She required 24 hour nursing care and supervision due to cognitive and physical disability. She could not make simple decisions for herself.

101. The Deceased's judgment and insight were grossly impaired. Her memory and other cognitive functions were significantly affected by dementia. For example, one month after the execution of the purported will, the Deceased was unable to recall how she even knew Ms. Brewer, her neighbor of several years. She was further unable to recall Ms. Horton's name during Dr. Jenkins' assessment. These facts are particularly noteworthy because these individuals were her primary beneficiaries.

102. The Deceased was unable to make appropriate decisions for herself. She had been deemed incapable of making her own personal and financial decisions by several physicians, including two geriatric specialists.

103. Once she developed dementia, many of the Deceased's previous values, wishes, and beliefs were altered due to the disease process. She exhibited changes in personality.

104. The Deceased could not understand or appreciate the testamentary act or its consequences. She had a very poor knowledge of her assets. Her wishes regarding the disposition of her assets had changed remarkably since 2006, the time of execution of her previous will.

105. It is very likely that the Deceased suffered from paranoid delusions regarding her daughter. She believed her daughter had stolen from her, was responsible for her nursing home placement, and felt that she had abandoned her. These delusions made her distrustful of her daughter's intentions and led to the dissolution of their previous close and loving relationship. In my opinion, her paranoid delusions led the Deceased to disinherit her daughter.

106. The Deceased became highly dependent on Ms. Horton and Ms. Brewer as she became more isolated and suspicious of her daughter. Their potential influence over the Deceased increased as she became more vulnerable due to advancing dementia.

107. Based on my clinical experience, the Deceased's informal care givers had the potential to exert great power and control over her. In my opinion, it would have taken very little influence for it to be considered 'undue influence' due to the severity of the Deceased's dementia.

108. It is also my opinion that Mrs. Walker would have been unable to live at home even with 24 hour care givers. Her dementia was progressing, she was at risk of falls, she was starting to wander at night, was becoming suspicious and paranoid, and she also had several medical problems that required close monitoring. In addition, 24 hour live-in care is very costly, and Mrs. Walker had a very limited income.

109. The last issue I was asked to opine on was quality of the medical care Mrs. Walker received from March 2010 onward. Particularly, whether there was any evidence that Glynnis did not make appropriate decisions regarding the Deceased's medical investigations, treatment, or housing. Dr. Jenkins alluded to this concern in her October 23, 2010 assessment.

110. I have reviewed all of the medical records in great detail. In my clinical opinion, Glynnis was actively involved in her mother's medical decision-making, participated in care conferences, advocated for her mother's best interests, and accepted the recommendations given by physicians and other health care providers. She did not interfere with or object to any treatment or tests given to her mother.

111. The medical records indicate that the specialist physicians advised against further investigation of the hypercalcemia (high blood calcium level) because it would not change the outcome. There is no clinical evidence to suggest that any medical issues were left untreated, or that Mrs. Walker merely received comfort measures. In addition, Mrs. Walker's health was never in any grave danger despite the fact that she developed several treatable conditions while in hospital.

112. I would like to conclude by stating that this report is a somewhat hurried draft. I was engaged as a medical expert at the "final hour" to meet the Supreme Court Civil Rules time deadline. As such, I reserve the right to make revisions and edits to this document if needed.

_____

Dr. Sandi Culo, BScOT, MD, FRCPC
Geriatric Psychiatrist
Signed January 15, 2013

Endnotes Chapter One

[1] (H.R. 6197 (109*th*): Older Americans Act Amendments of 2006).

[2] (Break the Silence, Report on Elder Abuse, Illinois Department on Aging).

[3] (MetLife Study of Elder Financial Abuse, Crimes of Occasion, Desperation and Predation Against America's Elders, June 2011

[4] Elder Financial Exploitation, National Adult Protective Services Association, 2013

[5] Johnson, Kelly Dedel, August 2004, *Financial Crimes Against the Elderly*, Problem-Oriented Guides for Police Problem-Specific Guides Series No. 20, Washington, DC: U.S. Department of Justice, Office of Community Oriented Policing Services, 8.

[6] Judith Milliken, QC, letter to the Attorney General of British Columbia, MR. ATTORNEY- SHINE THE LIGHT ON UNDUE INFLUENCE & PROTECT ELDERS FROM ABUSE, 2010.)

[7] Ibid Elder Financial Exploitation

[8] Congressional Budget Office, —The Budget and Economic Outlook, Fiscal Years 2010-2020,|| January 2010, http://www.cbo.gov/ftpdocs/108xx/doc10871/01-26-Outlook.pdf

[9] 2010 MetLife Market Survey of Long-Term Care Costs.

[10] 2010 NFDA General Price List Survey.

[11] Bodies pile up at Cook County morgue; activists outraged, http://usnews.nbcnews.com/_news/2012/01/27

[12] Population Bulletin, Population Reference Bureau, February 2011.

[13] National Center for the Prevention of Elder Abuse, www.preventelderabuse.org/elderabuse/fin_abuse.htm.

[14] MetLife Study 2011

[15] Alzheimer's Association Facts and Figures, 2012

[16] Agingstats.gov, 2012

[17] MetLife Study 2011

Endnotes Chapter Two

[18] The American Elder Care Research Organization, Disturbing Statistics about Long Term Care in the US

[19] Today's Caregiver, "Long Distance Caregiving - A Growing Phenomenon", Liza Berger, Staff Writer, Caregiver.com

[20] X http://www.cdc.gov/nchs/index.htm

[21] MetLife Study 2011

[22] Broken Trust: Elders, Family, and Finances, A Study on Elder Financial Abuse Prevention, MetLife, Mature Market Institute, March 2009

[23] The MetLife Study of Elder Financial Abuse: Crimes of Occasion, Desperation, and Predation Against America's Elders, June 2011.

[24] Physicians Urged to Be Alert for Signs of Elder Financial Abuse, May 2011. Caring Right at Home, http://www.caringnews.com/pub.59/issue.1550/article.6489/

[25] One in Three People Over 70 Have Memory Impairment, Published March 17, 2008, by Duke Medicine News and Communications

[26] Women over 45 more likely to commit fraud, embezzlement June 17, 2009 | By Anne Zieger, (http://www.fiercehealthfinance.com/story/women-over-45-more-likely-commit-fraud-embezzlement/2009-06-17#ixzz2Hxo0xI2C)

[27] Broken Trust: Elders, Family, and Finances, A Study on Elder Financial Abuse Prevention, MetLife, Mature Market Institute, March 2009

[28] Broken Trust: Elders, Family, and Finances, A Study on Elder Financial Abuse Prevention, MetLife, Mature Market Institute, March 2009

Endnotes Chapter Three

[29] 25 Signs and Symptoms of Alzheimer's Disease, Is it Alzheimer's? By Kristin Koch, Health.com health/gallery/0,20416288,00.html

[30] ibid

[31] Alzheimer's Disease and Paranoia, Alzheimer's, Paranoia, and Hallucinations: What to Do
By Maria M. Meyer, Mary S. Mittelman, Cynthia Epstein, and Paula Derr, Contributing writers, Caring.com

[32] http://www.disabled-world.com/news/seniors/frail-women.php#ixzz26YMxRGRv).

[33] ibid

[34] 25 Signs and Symptoms of Alzheimer's Disease, by Kristin Koch, Health.com

[35] Mild Vitamin B12 Deficiency Associated with Accelerated Cognitive Decline, Jean Mayer USDA Human Nutrition Research Center on Aging (USDA HNRCA), Tufts Now, December 5, 2012

[36] Ibid

[37] How Dementia Tampers With Taste Buds, By Marie Suszynski Medically reviewed by Lindsey Marcellin, MD, MPH, Everydayhealth.com

[38] Ibid

Endnotes Chapter Four

[39] Elizabeth Kubler-Ross M.D., On Death and Dying, Scribner 1969.

[40] *UNPLUGGED:Reclaiming our Right to Die in America*

by William Colby, Amacom 2006

Endnotes Chapter Five

[41] 25 Signs and Symptoms of Alzheimer's Disease, Health.com

Endnotes Chapter Six

[42] http://www.alz.org/research/science/major_milestones_in_alzheimers.asp

[43] (Five-country Alzheimer's Disease Survey, Harvard School Of Public Health and Alzheimer Europe, www.alzheimer-europe.org/.../Value%20 of%20%1Fknowing-..)

[44] (Myths and misses about Alzheimer's Disease by JAMES P. RICHARDSON, MD, MPH on January 25th, 2012in CONDITIONS http://www.kevinmd.com/blog/2012/01/myths-misses-alzheimers-disease.html)

[45] (Diagnosing Alzheimer's disease sooner or later by JAMES P. RICHARDSON, MD, MPH on July 29th, 2011in CONDITIONS, http:// www.kevinmd.com/blog/2011/07/diagnosing-alzheimers-disease-sooner.html

Endnotes Chapter Seven

[46] (http://sundownerfacts.com/sundowners-syndrome/

[47] Sundowner's Syndrome and Care for Alzheimer's Patients, http:// alzheimers.aplaceformom.com/articles/sundowners-syndrome

[48] The New York Times, Rationing Health Care More Fairly, By Eduardo Porter, August 21, 2012

[49] Illinois Department of Aging Report

Endnotes Chapter eight

[50] Is Wall Street Full of Psychopaths?, James Silver, The Atlantic, March 29, 2012

[51]

[52] The Wisdom of Psychopaths: What Saints, Spies, and Serial Killers Can Teach Us About Success. Kevin Dutton, Scientific American/Farrar, Strauss, Giroux, 2012

[53] PRICHARD, J. C. (1835) A Treatise on Insanity. London: Sherwood, Gilbert and Piper

[54] Journal of Clinical Psychiatry [Volume 65:948-958]

[55] Sociopath Vs. Psychopath: There is a Difference, Jeanne Marie Kerns, Yahoo! Contributor Network, Sep 15, 2008

[56] ibid

[57] Without Conscience: The Disturbing World of the Psychopaths Among Us, Robert D. Hare PhD, Guilford Press, New York, 1999

[58] ibid

Endnotes Chapter Nine

[59] Length of Stay for Older Adults Residing in Nursing Homes at the End of Life, Anne Kelley, MSW et.al., Journal of the American Geriatrics Society, Volume 58, Issue 9, pages 1701–1706, September 2010

[60] Is it Time for a Nursing Home?, Parentgiving. com

[61] Mitchell SL. et al, A national study of the location of death for older persons with dementia. *J Am Geriatric Soc.* 2005;**53**(2):299-305.)

[62] California Advocates for Nursing Home Reform, Certified Campaign Agency of the United Way, Page Last Modified: March 14, 20 http://www.canhr.org

Endnotes Chapter Ten

[63] Folstein MF, Folstein SE, McHugh PR:"Mini-mental state": a practical method for grading the cognitive state of patients for the clinician. Journal of Psychiatric Research 12:189–198, 1975

[64] Report of Dr. Sandi A. Culo, BScOT, MD, FRCPC, Geriatric Psychiatrist, Royal Jubilee Hospital

[65] Endnotes Chapter Eleven

[66] Michael J. Tueth, M.D., Exposing Financial Exploitation of Impaired Elderly Persons, American Journal of Geriatric Psychiatry, 8:104-111, May 2000.

Endnotes Chapter Twelve

[67] http://www.duhaime.org/LegalDictionary/F/Forgery.aspx

[68] http://www.disinherited.com/article/bc-wills-variation-act-basics

Endnotes Chapter fourteen

[69] Differences Between Geriatrician & Gerontologist, by Fred Decker, Demand Media

[70] (From Dr. Jenkins report, November 13, 2010).

[71] Merck Manual for Healthcare Professionals, Evaluation of the Elderly Patient

[72] ibid

[73] Elder Abuse by Stephen L. Read, MD, September 1, 2008, Psychiatric Times. Vol. 25 No. 10

[74] ibid

[75] Dr. Jenkins's report, November 2010

[76] (Undue Influence and Financial Exploitation. Issues on Aging Vol.14 no2. www.matrixadvocare.com)

[77] Dr. Jenkins's Report, November 2010

[78] Six Types of Elder Abuse From Christine Kennard, About.com Guide updated: September 19, 2006

[79] Stress, the Brain, Aging and Alzheimer's Disease, Long term effects of stress on the brain, Published on March 10, 2010 by Howard Fillit, M.D. in Alzheimer's: Hope on the Horizon

Endnotes Chapter Sixteen

[80] www.scouting.org, Child Sexual Abuse Awareness and Prevention in America: A Timeline

[81] Reports Of Sexual Child Abuse Leap, Chicago Tribune, February 17, 1985|By John Crewdson.

[82] Lawrence Journal World, June 16, 2010.

Endnotes Chapter Seventeen

[83] www.ABA.org

[84] Women in the Federal Judiciary: Still A Long Way to Go, NWLC, January 15, 2013

[85] ELDER ABUSE: A WOMEN'S ISSUE, Mother's Day Report, 2009, OWL.org

[86] Elder abuse widespread and unreported, new report by Secretary-General, United Nations, Second World Assembly on Ageing . Madrid, Spain . 8 -12 April 2002

[87] Slate, The Fairer Sex, What do we mean when we say we need more female justices? By Dahlia Lithwick, posted Saturday, April 11, 2009,

[88] C. Guthrie, J. J. Rachlinski, & A. J. Wistrich, "Inside the Judicial Mind," *Cornell Law Review*, 86, 2001, 777-830

[89] Pnas.org, Extraneous factors in judicial decisions Shari Danziger, vol. 108 no. 17

Endnotes Chapter Eighteen

[90] Justice McCauley's decision, BC Supreme Court, April 2011

[91] http://thenurseinpurpleconverse.blogspot.com/2009/04/psa-what-full-code-really-means-for.html

[92] ibid

[93] http://www.getpalliativecare.org/whatis/

[94] http://steampunkpaleo.wordpress.com/my-c-diff-story.

[95] Far more could be done to stop the deadly bacteria C. diff, By Peter Eisler, USA TODAY

Endnotes Chapter Nineteen

[96] The Sociopath Next Door, Dr. Martha Stout, Broadway Books, 2005, page 188

[97] Affidavit of Patrice Newman, , Court File No. VIC-S-S-124-7278, Victoria Registry

[98] http://legal-dictionary.thefreedictionary.com/officer+of+the+court

[99] ibid

Made in the USA
San Bernardino, CA
26 August 2017